COLOR AND CONSCIENCE:

THE IRREPRESSIBLE CONFLICT

COLOR
AND CONSCIENCE:
THE
IRREPRESSIBLE CONFLICT

BY

BUELL G. GALLAGHER

PROFESSOR OF CHRISTIAN ETHICS
PACIFIC SCHOOL OF RELIGION

HARPER & BROTHERS PUBLISHERS
NEW YORK AND LONDON

TO

MARYEL

AND

BARBARA

Freedom's children,
with less to unlearn.

CONTENTS

CONTENTS

ix

PREFACE

THIS BOOK is not written in the accusative mood. It does not blame any section of the nation for failure to meet the problems of the races. These problems are nation-wide in scope and world-wide in import. By the same token, readers will not find in these pages a defense of their own, or of any other region.

I have endeavored to bring the tangled problems of color caste under the scrutiny of an unsentimental ethical religion. The findings show that the evasions and deceptions with which men have sought to justify their defection and to accommodate themselves to color caste are no longer tenable.

The months which difficulties of manufacture have placed between the date of the completion of the manuscript and its appearance in print have witnessed a march of world events which (particularly in the Near East and the Far East) have continued to expose the insistent pressures of color in the world scene. Ample evidence of the explosive character of race relations within the United States is likewise provided by domestic developments. Events demand an answer which *is* an answer . . . not an evasion.

That answer can be given only as men and women of integrity from both sides of the caste line set to work. There is no Master Race . . . no race by nature servile. I neither attack nor defend the white man for manifest dereliction. Nor do I attempt to excuse the non-white. I write both to Philemon and to Onesimus.

BUELL G. GALLAGHER

Berkeley, California,
February 4, 1946

CHAPTER I

DIMENSIONS

> I have no prejudice in my heart; but the white race is a superior race and the Negro race is an inferior race, and the races must be kept separate by law.
>
> —SENATOR EASTLAND OF MISSISSIPPI

THESE words, spoken on the floor of the United States Senate on June 20, 1944, are an accurate statement of the intentions and defenses of the American system of color caste. They are also a revelation of the extent to which color caste can be accepted calmly by a desensitized conscience. Behind this statement and this revelation lies the labyrinthine story which we must trace if we are to understand the tragic dimensions of the dilemmas of conscience that color caste imposes upon us.

The Senator's words are those of an adult. In the words of a four-year-old, the stark and horrendous proportions of color caste are not glossed over with sophistication: they may be seen more clearly. It was on a Sunday morning in 1938. My three-year-old daughter went as usual to Sunday school in the little interracial church in Talladega, Alabama. On entering the room, she did the normal thing: she went to the little chairs for the Primary Department in the front of the room and took the first vacant seat, beside a Negro boy of four. As though propelled from his chair by a giant unseen hand, the boy leaped to his feet, his eyes wide, fists clenched, and bronze skin suddenly ashen with terror. "Don't you sit next to me, white child! You get a rope around my neck!" Thus early had the tyranny of color caste exerted itself over the mind and emotions of the little boy; and thus early did the little girl

1

meet the fact that color caste does not permit whites the integrity of a Christian conscience.

Whether in the words of a senator, or of a terrified boy, or in the bewildered heartache of a little girl, the meaning is the same. Color caste imposes relentless demands upon us. Such is the stuff out of which the conflict in conscience is created. I propose that we look behind the smooth façade of a social system to see color caste at work.

1. THE CHARACTER OF COLOR CASTE

In recent years, the concept of caste has come to be used by American sociologists in the study of race relations. A whole school of social analysts has grown up around Professor Lloyd Warner of the University of Chicago, using the double matrix of caste and class patterns in social analysis. In the past decade, it has become common, even in nonacademic circles, to hear American race relations referred to as a caste system. Some meticulous writers prefer to say that, while it is not strictly analogous to the caste system of (for example) India, it does exhibit most of the features of a caste pattern. In any case, the phrase is one which is sufficiently accurate for our purposes here. It speaks directly and simply of one of the major phenomena of American society.

A century ago, it was men of religion who first began to use the term that social scientists now find convenient. The American Missionary Association, for example, was founded in 1846 for the avowed purpose of attacking "in all heathen lands, the sins of slave-holding, polygamy, and caste." Abolitionists were particularly fond of the term, because it conveyed both a sociological description and a moral judgment.

The definitive delineation of American caste is a more extensive task than the proportions of this book or the abilities of this writer permit.[1] Our racial caste system has its historical

[1] But see my *American Caste and the Negro College* (Columbia University Press, 1938) for a concentrated outline of the essential characteristics of the

roots in slavery, but thrusts its contemporary tentacles into
every crevice and cranny of the social structure throughout the
nation. Slavery as ownership of chattel is gone: as a caste system, it remains. Its purpose is to keep nonwhites in a position
which, in one way or another, is inferior or subordinate to
that of whites. Its devices range from lynchings and mob
violence, at one extreme, through legal enactment and extralegal manipulations of courts and police, to custom and etiquette as instruments of caste control.

On this matrix of caste-and-class as elaborated in the American scene, every individual weaves the pattern of his own race
attitudes. Unless he is able to devise some other loom (say
that of the Christian ethic) in place of the ready-made patterns of his society, the individual is unable to achieve any
appreciable degree of emancipation from the attitudinal patterns which are typical of his class and caste. Generally speaking, the attitudes of whites, ranging from friendly paternalism to hatred and hostility, tend to recognize a caste status in
which all whites are in one way or another superior to all
Negroes, who in turn must in no respect be superior to any
whites; while the reciprocal attitudes which Negroes must assume in order to survive in a caste-controlled society tend to
recognize this subordinate status.

Social stance is not so much a matter of *where* as of *how* one
stands. A white man can move from a former ground of antagonism to a new position of tolerance; but, if the new posture
is still one of superiority, the fact that he stands on new ground
does not alter the basic character of the relationship which his
attitude assumes. A Negro may climb from grinning sub-
servience to quiet dignity; but, if he must continue to observe
the caste line in his contacts with white persons, he continues
to feel the bars of the prison confining him.

The attitudes of caste become generalized into stereotypes

---

caste system which are treated with exhaustive exactness by Gunnar Myrdal
and his associates in the six volumes of the Carnegie Study of the Negro in
America (cf. n.7, Chap. V, below).

which are passed from person to person and group to group, in time actually coming to have an almost independent force and power of their own. Ideas then control action. These stereotypes operate principally by governing the beliefs and conduct of individuals, few of whom form their own beliefs about race either on the basis of their own experience or by taking account of scientific knowledge. The individual merely takes over the attitudes and stereotypes which prevail in the society into which he is born. *Race attitudes in contemporary America are formed not so much through contacts with other races as through contact with prevailing race attitudes.* The individual learns to react to the symbols of race in terms of the patterns of caste, and dynamically in terms of the caste struggle. He does not ordinarily bring these beliefs under critical analysis. He learns to accept and to use them in precisely the same manner as he learns the accent or food preferences of his parents and playmates. Through the acceptance of stereotypes, ready-made beliefs, the individual forms his racial attitudes.

In a caste system, only those beliefs which guide the conduct of the dominant caste have a determinative effect. The beliefs of the subordinated caste are important in that they reveal the meaning of caste, as symptoms reveal disease; but only the notions of the group in power can be said to have a causal relation to the social process.

It is the popular beliefs, and they only, which enter directly into the causal mechanism of interracial relations. . . . The beliefs held by white people rather than those held by Negroes are of primary importance.[2]

It is for this reason that the "Negro problem" must rightly be referred to as a white problem as well. There is a job for both races to do if caste is to be corrected.

Perhaps the simplest way to summarize the actual operation of the caste system is to describe it in terms of axioms

[2] Gunnar Myrdal, *An American Dilemma: The Negro Problem and American Democracy*, p. 110. Harpers, 1944, 2 vols.

which are demonstrated in its patterns of action and in the attitudes and beliefs expressed in its functioning:

1. Any white man is "better" than every nonwhite; therefore,
2. All contacts between whites and nonwhites must in some manner express this differential; and thus
3. The etiquette must always be observed; and consequently
4. The white man's floor is the Negro's ceiling.

These are the axioms that undergird the cogent expression of Senator Eastland at the opening of this chapter. They are seen in every meeting of two or more persons from different racial castes in American life—*unless the individuals concerned have learned to transcend the caste system*. They are demonstrated in the eating taboo, the failure to use the polite terms of address or to show the common courtesies toward nonwhites in the presence of whites. The fourth axiom summarizes the whole meaning of the patterns of segregation and discrimination: no nonwhite is to be permitted to rise above the level of the lowest white man, lest the integrity of caste be threatened.

In general, it may be said that, with variations and inconsistencies, both in intensity and in configuration, these axioms are applied to every section of the nation. The caste system is an established part of American culture, with clear legal and social definitions in the South, but with general characteristics of similarity in all parts of the nation. This is the caste system that confronts and confuses the Christian conscience. This is the social subsoil of our dilemmas.

2. COLOR IN THE WORLD SCENE

Acting and thinking as though he were a majority, the Caucasian is a minority group in the world's population. The best available estimates of population show:[3]

[3] *Survey Graphic*, Vol. XXXI, No. 11, November, 1942, p. 505.

Eastern Asiatics	600,000,000
Brown Asiatics	610,000,000
Negroes	140,000,000
Indians and Mestizoes	60,000,000
TOTAL NONWHITE	1,410,000,000
WHITE	740,000,000
World Total	2,150,000,000

The Caucasian is outnumbered in the present population of the world two to one. When the American white man speaks of the problems of minorities, he is seldom conscious that he is actually speaking about himself and his own problems. Yet, both in size and in performance, the Caucasian rates a position as the world's number one minority problem.

The Caucasian minority has a majority psychology. Either in ignorance of his minority world status or in spite of it, the Caucasian feels that he owns the world and all the lesser peoples in it. He adduces concrete evidence to support his feeling. He has thrown the girdles of commerce and trade around the globe, planted outposts of financial and political empire (with the necessary military backing) in its remotest quarters, and built the cultural outposts which, supported by power politics and a show of military and naval strength, have given him a position of dominance from which he looks down upon the subjugated peoples in much the same manner as a feudal lord was accustomed to survey his vassals from the castle tower. The Caucasian has a majority psychology.

It was not until the turning of the present century that a nonwhite people challenged the dominance of the white world in language which the whole nonwhite world understood. Czarist Russia was then thought of as a "white" power, although her great, sprawling hegemony from the Baltic to the Pacific included more than one hundred ethnic, racial, and national groups over which a comparatively small number of Russians ruled. And amongst the pigmented peoples of the world, the fact that Japan successfully challenged "white" Russia in the arena of modern warfare as the new century began is, even to this day, a burning beacon of immense significance.[4] When Japan in 1932 entered Manchuria, there was no great stir amongst the colored peoples of the world outside of China; but when Mussolini, a little later, marched into Ethiopia, the Negro press of the United States followed each development of the unevenly matched campaign with a withering fire of excoriating denunciation—a sharp contrast to its apathy over Japan's aggression on the Asiatic mainland. White aggression against a colored nation in Africa was deeply resented by colored peoples in other parts of the world, while the despoiling of one colored nation by another scarcely caused a ripple in the surface of the colored world. In the early years of World War II, before the United States became an active participant (and it became less politic to speak openly), it was not unusual to hear amongst Negro Americans and members of other racial minorities (except the Chinese Americans), expressions of approval over the way in which Japan, twisting the tail of the British lion in the Far East, was showing the white man that he did not own the earth. The Caucasian lives in a fool's paradise if he thinks that there is no resentment amongst the darker peoples, directed toward white imperialism and world domination.

This antagonism of the colored peoples toward domination by the white is seen not only in minorities within the United States, but in all quarters of the globe. One of India's most moderate and reputable spokesmen, Krishnalal Shridharani, cautiously and mildly states the essence of a bold thesis when he contrasts the attitude of Indian minorities toward the British Raj in the last century and at present:

In the beginning it was the realization that the British had come to stay which had prompted the minorities to jump on the British bandwagon. Now it was the realization that the nationalists will not allow the British to stay much longer which changed their attitude.[5]

[4] Cf. Leonard Woolf, *Imperialism and Civilization*, p. 76. Harcourt, Brace, 1928.

[5] "Minorities and the Autonomy of India" in *Group Relations and Group Antagonisms*, edited by R. H. MacIver, p. 204. Harpers, 1944.

The British know that this is the case, just as the Indians know that the British know it, and the British know that the Indians know that they know it. It is the openest secret of all open secrets. Sir John Seeley wrote:

> You see, the Mutiny was in a great measure put down by turning the races of India against each other. So long as this can be done, and so long as the population have not formed the habit of criticizing the Government, whatever it be, and of rebelling against it, the government of India from England is possible, and there is nothing miraculous about it. But, as I said, if the state of things should alter, if by any chance the population should be welded into a single nationality, then I do not say we ought to begin to fear for our domination; I say we ought to cease to hope for it.[6]

Shridharani's use of this quotation to support his argument is a masterpience of mild understatement in which he lets the white man state the case against himself. The British know that if the colored peoples of India are ever united against them, the day of the white man's empire in the Indian subcontinent is at an end.

Similar expressions of a determination to be rid of white domination could be adduced from leading thinkers and writers in every nonwhite portion of the globe—which is most of it. Such citations would serve only to swell the size of this book without adding to the weight of the argument that appears to the writer to be axiomatic in present world conditions: *the colored peoples of the world aspire to a position of freedom from white control and to acceptance in a position of equality. They will endure white domination as long as it is physically necessary to do so, and not one moment longer.* The 1.4 billion pigmented peoples of the world do not want, and will accept only under duress, the continuing domination of the .7 billion whites. The racial jitters of the whites in South Africa; the rigid governmental controls of the Portuguese in East Africa and West Africa; the unequivocal stand

[6] *The Expansion of England*, p. 270. Little, Brown. Quoted by Shridharani, *op. cit.*, p. 205.

taken by men like the late Félix Eboué (an African), governor of the principal French slice of the African continent; the unrest and intrigue in Egypt and the Near East, with the development of a solid phalanx of Pan-Arabism under the headship of King Ibn Saud; the attempt to play Arab against Jew and Christian against Muslim; the seething caldron of the Caribbean which appears in American news stories in the pleasantly reassuring proportions of a simmering teakettle; the coming of age of the populations of the Island Indies; the great question mark of the China of tomorrow; the growing importance of color in the problem of relations between the United States and Latin America—all these are an authentic part of the white man's dilemma of world dominance.

I shall return later to this dimension of color caste as it confronts the Christian conscience. The presence of color in the world scene gives to the dilemmas of domestic concern a global scope and importance that italicizes the handwriting on the wall.

3. THE DEMANDS OF CONSCIENCE

The general quandaries shared by all white men are greatly increased for that fraction of the Caucasian group which seriously intends to follow the demands of conscience. The Christian faith is color blind. Every great affirmation of Christianity cries out against distinctions drawn between people on the basis of skin pigmentation. It is not in response to the Christian conscience that we erect color bars and build racial caste systems. It is not in pursuance of the teachings of Jesus that we nurture race prejudice. It is not in the Bible, nor in the writings of the early Fathers of the Church, nor in the great creeds of Christendom, that we find support for the dogma of white supremacy.

To be sure, there are men who manage to tear a few verses of Scripture from their context, and by ignoring all the weight of Biblical and Christian teaching, to erect a fantastic edifice in which white supremacy passes an uneasy existence. But the burden of proof rests heavily upon them, to show that white supremacy and Christian brotherhood are good bedfellows. Theirs is the responsibility for demonstrating that God is white, a respecter of persons because of skin color. Our task is less ambitious. We have only to let the faith speak for itself.

The precise formulation of that faith, whether in a particular creed, or a theological system, or a churchly tradition, is a matter of real importance to Christian people, as the controversies of nineteen centuries testify. But there are wide areas of fundamental agreement in all branches of Christendom; and in these areas of ethical understanding, the Christian conscience speaks a consistent and insistent word to condemn color caste unequivocally—in the name both of justice and of brotherhood.

4. BROTHERHOOD

The idea of the universal brotherhood of all men is as profound as it is simple. We too easily assume that, because the idea is readily grasped, it is not profound; or, on an occasion when we glimpse some of the deeper meanings of the notion of brotherhood, we hastily avert our eyes lest we should be too shaken by the ethical insights of that moment. When one meets persons who are unable or unwilling to make the simple, yet profound, step from the Fatherhood of God to the brotherhood of all men, it excites not so much one's moral indignation as one's intellectual contempt. The step is such a simple one. Why ought it to be necessary to argue it?

The necessity for discussion lies in the revolutionary meaning of the idea. The demands upon personal and group conduct which the notion of brotherhood makes are fundamentally at variance with the demands made by racism. The belief in the Fatherhood of God and its necessary corollary, the brotherhood of man, is our greatest affirmative religious resource for attacking the caste system. It is a belief that is triumphantly affirmed by every branch of the Christian church. It stands at the heart of the teaching and life of Jesus. The fact that the churches have not, in their organization and action, demonstrated a high degree of faithfulness to their profession does not invalidate the faith. On the contrary, the persistence of the faith in spite of its denial in practice encourages us to hope that the tenacity of the faith will at long last awaken the churches to a realization of their false and untenable position, liberating them from bondage to racial distinctions.

Either God is the Father of all men or He is not. If we say He is not, we deny the Christian God and resort to some lesser pagan god of tribe or clan or race. That is what Hitler commanded his followers to do. That is what Jesus did not command his followers to do. If we accept the Fatherhood of God, we must accept the brotherhood of man; and if we deny the responsibility of brotherhood, then, like Cain of old, we go out from the presence of the Lord.

In some circles, this belief in brotherhood is qualified by the teaching that only persons who have gone through a particular experience, whether of conversion or of baptism or of sanctification or some other, are children of God. But, whether it is limited to a gathered group or whether it includes all men, the notion of brotherhood cannot by any stretch of ethical elasticity be delineated according to racial ancestry. Even those who cling to a conception of brotherhood which limits the interpretation of sonship in accordance with a stipulated sacerdotal or ecclesiastical rite, nevertheless subscribe to the belief that every person who fulfills these conditions of sonship is a child of God and their brother in Christ. Not the narrowest of the hard-shell sects, not the most arrogant of the Roman churchmen, not the bluest of the blue-blooded Protestants, can find a substantial ethical basis for drawing the line of Christian brotherhood on the basis of race. Indeed, the inclusiveness of the Christian family applies *a fortiori* to those who hold to some theological or ceremonial limitation of brotherhood; because every man, regardless of the chemicals in his epidermis, who fulfills these conditions is automatically one of their fellowship. And throughout the rest of the church (which is most of it), the fundamental notion on which there is absolutely no disagreement is the universal Fatherhood of God and the universal brotherhood of all men.

The nontheistic Humanists might appear to be an exception to this general agreement; but they are passionately committed to the belief in universal brotherhood. That they do not add to brotherhood its corollary of Fatherhood is a matter of their own choice. Their belief in, and practice of, the notion of universal brotherhood commits them to the elimination of racial caste, just as completely as do the convictions of the honest theist. There is not one island of theological thought or ecclesiastical practice in Christendom which can legitimately claim the ethical right to draw the lines of Christian fellowship in accordance with variations in skin color.

5. JUDGMENT

The ethical teachings of the prophets and of Jesus speak not only of a God of love who is the Father of all men. They not only evoke the affirmative attitudes of fellow feeling and social solidarity. They also speak of the stern judgments of a righteous God who cannot be disobeyed with impunity: *Quod severis metes.*

This truth, that men violate the moral demands of human relationships at their own peril, is not merely a polite notion with which to titillate the Sunday morning sensibilities of churchgoers. It is written large in the pages of history, in the rise and fall of men and of peoples. It is inevitable that this should be so. Brotherhood is not optional: it is in the nature of things. A God who requires of His sons the affection and conduct of brothers toward brothers is no sentimental Heavenly Daddy with whom we become pleasantly chummy, in exchange for the currency of fine phrases. God is a Judge who is neither deceived nor mocked.

There is no need to stress the element of fear implicit in this fact. Guilt and shame sweep upon the sensitive conscience as one contemplates the travesty of love and brotherhood which our racial patterns tolerate. The judgment of God falls upon us as we disregard the plain dictates of conscience and openly violate the demands of brotherhood.

And just as there is general agreement in Christendom over the basic idea of human brotherhood, so all Christendom accepts the truth that the moral order is violated by man at his own peril. None who calls himself Christian would care to deny that human relationships are carried on under the moral judgments of an ethical order. The whole genius of an ethical monotheism is bound up in the fact that immoral men stand under the condemnation of a morality which they have violated to their own hurt. Our difficulty is that, while we give theoretical assent to the idea, we postpone the day of ethical action until the irreversible course of history has carried us beyond the point where affirmative action is creative. Man persists in his sin—in this case, the sin of race pride —knowing that he does so at the certain risk of violating the moral order; but he disregards the day of reckoning until it is too late. Toward that day of reckoning, the movement of the hours carries him. Nothing that Jonathan Edwards implied in his famous sermon on Sinners in the Hands of an Angry God is too strong as an expression of the divine judgment which inevitably descends upon men who will not form their lives ethically.

The truth that man violates the moral nature of things at his own peril has been evident through the centuries; but it is a truth which has been permitted to stay in the area of idealistic discussion. It needs to be translated into ethical specifics rather than being left in the area of moral generalities. There is some peril in this translation of the general to the specific: men do not always know surely what the righteous act may be. Yet the risk must be taken. We cannot be more wrong than when we refuse to obey God at all. When we are clear that God the Father requires of us the affirmative affections and considerate conduct of brothers toward brothers, we have no hesitation in affirming that the denial of the brotherhood is a violation of His will which brings inescapable judgment upon us.

6. HOPE

The Christian gospel does not end with the declaration that man, a sinner, stands under judgment. We know that we are sinners; but the gospel begins, not ends, with that affirmation. The Christian expectation is that man can be saved from sin. The perfectionist school of American Christianity immediately assents to this hope; but it is not necessary to be a perfectionist to give assent. It is necessary only to be a Christian.

Nothing but a perverse misreading of the facts of human nature can justify the gloomy despair with which some persons deny the hope of salvation. Both Christianity and science affirm that *man goes contrary to human nature when race prejudice is permitted to establish a caste system.* The manner in which scientific findings underscore the ancient ethical truth that mankind is one, will be discussed later in these pages. At this point, we are stating the ethical judgment. For nineteen centuries, the Christian religion has affirmed that all men are made of one blood, to share one destiny, to serve one duty. Unity of the Christian community is the Christian expectation. The statement of this hope in terms of ethical and religious purposes is a climactic truth of the moral judgment. It is the cross planted squarely in the center of damnation. So great a hope, so dearly bought, cannot be disregarded. This generation of white men—or some other—may try to disregard it; but the relentless processes of history will not render the verdict in their favor. Whatever remnant of mankind survives the judgment of history upon the sins and errors of this generation, will know the meaning of the redemption that is in vicarious suffering—for it is human nature to fulfill the expectation of the creation.

7. THE INSTRUMENTALIST APPROACH

In speaking of brotherhood, judgment, and hope, we have followed the customary method of Christian theology, deducing our ethical insights from theological postulates. The vast majority of professing Christians follow that method, and we have been interested in pointing out that they are thereby committed to an unrelenting revolutionary attack upon the system of color caste.

For that somewhat smaller, but by no means inconsiderable, group of Christians who do not use the deductive method, a parallel analysis may be suggested. The instrumentalist approach brings us out at the same ethical insights and moral commitments in matters of race as does the deductive approach. The matter is not so readily summarized in a few phrases for the various instrumentalists as it is for the absolutists; but we can suggest something of the common ground on which most instrumentalists stand. That ground, strangely but significantly, is common also to the absolutists. With antipodal methods, the deductive and inductive processes agree in ethical insights in matters of race.

The instrumentalist looks at people and at the social process. He sees what happens to people, in the violation of human values, the warping of personalities, the thwarting of altruistic purposes. He sees a boy in a brown skin denied the opportunities enjoyed by a boy who is less deeply pigmented. He sees the arrogance of the white and the bitterness of the black which that disparity evokes. The more he observes and experiences what color caste does to people, the less he likes it. As the theologian is "against sin," so the instrumentalist sets himself against the destruction or stifling of human values.

Through experience, the observation of experience, and reflective analysis, the instrumentalist arrives at a position which flatly challenges the continuance of caste. Whether he speaks of the "worth of human personality," or of "the continuity of process," or of "creative experience," or of "the reconstruction of experience"—or however he phrases his thought, the instrumentalist, with his concern for human welfare, is driven to reject color caste. Caste denies the "worth" of the majority of human personalities: caste carries forward as a destructive component of the continuous social process: caste interferes with creative experience: caste denies the possibility of the reconstruction of the modes and patterns of human conduct along lines that give expression to the creative potentialities of man.

The conscience which is instrumentally constructed is no less a foe of caste than is the conscience which is deductively established. That this is so is attested by the fact that not one of the leaders of instrumentalist philosophy or theology or ethics stands today in defense of a racial caste system. Many, if not most of them, stand in the forefront of those who take up the cudgels of ethical insight against racism. The fact that they have no snug haven of remote theological postulates in which to find sanctuary when their ethical values are threatened, the fact that they find the values of the ethical struggle in the struggle itself, may tend to make them even more vigorous than their absolutist brethren in condemning color caste. They must rise at once and do battle in defense of their ethical values. They do.

8. The Inner Dimensions

The outline sketch of the dimensions of our dilemmas cannot conclude without touching on the inner dimensions, where choices both of value and of method play a definitive part in determining the results of ethical struggle.

It is relatively easy to speak in righteous indignation, demanding the elimination of color caste in accordance with the Christian conscience. It is also relatively easy to find in the demands of contemporary society sufficient justification for individual and social failure to obey the inner voice. It is not difficult to do either of these things separately; but it is painfully difficult to be aware of the disquieting demands of conscience and at the same time to know well the stubborn facts of a caste-controlled world. Yet, in plumbing the depths of the ethical struggle, we give new dimensions of meaning to the Christian life.

It is only as we refuse to take the easy *either . . . or* of choice between the self-righteousness of the ethical prophet and the unrighteousness of the conformist; it is only as we maintain the strenuous tensions of conflict between the demands of the Christian ethic and the hindrances to obedience to it, that we plumb the depths of the ethical struggle and begin to understand its significance.

It is necessary to recognize that ethical preachment by itself is often a means of escaping the demands of the Christian life—just as unethical action in its turn nurtures an ultimate pessimism about the Christian hope. We have need, therefore, to be hardheaded and softhearted at the same time, and continually to keep both these perspectives, if we wish to see the full dimensions of the dilemma of conscience. Either of these approaches will, by itself, result in gross perversions of the virtues with which it begins; but the use of both processes as interacting parts of a single effort will help to correct the inadequacies of either when taken by itself.

Suppose I were to speak only in behalf of justice. Surely justice is desirable? Can I not, then, speak for it? May I not be permitted to be hardheaded in the relentless struggle for righteousness? Not unless I wish to run the risk of corrupting the struggle for righteousness into a defense of self-righteousness. To be sure, justice is part of the Christian ethic, and the demands of justice must be pressed relentlessly upon us all. But when I give myself without reserve or qualification to the struggle for justice only, I become not only hardheaded but hardhearted as well. In denying the other dimensions of the Christian life, I narrow everything to one single perspective. Knowing (and knowing rightly) the rightness of the cause I espouse, I stand in constant danger of arrogating to myself the righteousness of the cause. I end up not by achieving justice, but by assuming self-justification.

Moreover, as I work single-mindedly for justice, I do not serve the ends of justice either. The more vigorously I fight for the rights of the disinherited and the dispossessed, the more stubborn the opposition becomes; and my insistence on justice prevents the resolution of the struggle in any other terms than those of preponderant power. Fighting for justice, with all the righteousness of the cause to support me, I do not get justice. I get a compromise based on pressure and counterpressure; and I leave slow-healing wounds of bitterness and hatred.

Worst of all, as I struggle for justice for minorities in contemporary society, I marshal the arguments and facts which appear to support the demands for equality and fair play, hurling these at the majority. And in so doing I become an unwitting supporter of the subtlest and yet most effective of all forms of race pride—the assumption that the Caucasian mind is the final arbiter of justice. In trying to prove to the white man that other races merit justice from him, I am supporting Caucasian egotism, tacitly accepting the premise that the majority mind is the final bar before which it is necessary to prove the case for evenhanded justice.

And finally, if I am successful in making a good case for the rights of the minority man before the bar of Caucasian judgment, even though I increase the opposition of the Caucasian by that fact, I do something equally inimical to the member of the minority group. By proving the righteousness of his cause, I feed the pride of the minority man, making him in his turn as insufferably arrogant as is the white man against whom I have been arguing. Pride is an unbeautiful thing in any man, and if the fruits of the struggle for justice are the bitterness of pride in both contending parties, the struggle itself must be scrutinized. It must be recast in terms calculated not to produce the spoiled by-products of racial arrogance in either the majority or the minority man. I must abandon the effort to justify the ways of justice.

If, instead of this, justice is accepted as the overarching structure of the whole scene of life, with all men alike standing under the judgments of God, I have no need to prove to the Caucasian mind that justice should be meted out to all the races of men. I have only to appreciate the tragic plight of the arrogant members of any race who may feel that they can disregard the demands of justice with impunity. But I will be able to see matters in this perspective only if I combine the insights of softheartedness with those of hardheadedness. I must not only feel the blaze of righteous anger over injustice: I must also feel the tragic poignancy of the fate of sinners—of whom I am one. This I cannot do as long as I insist on being hardheaded, and hardhearted as well.

The same argument applies if I am tempted to disregard the demands of hardheadedness and to build my efforts only in terms of softheartedness. The belief that love will take care of everything, that brotherly affection can be induced in the hearts and lives of all men so that injustice falls away as easily as the snake slips out of last winter's skin, is the root of much misleading sentimentalism. It overlooks the fact that the serpent has a new skin, and goes on about his regular business, smiled upon by the same benevolent sun whose warmth encouraged him to shed the old skin. I may not, therefore, expect to meet the demons of racism successfully merely with the sweet smiles of sentiment; for, by itself, the effort of love is corrupted in much the same manner as are the struggles of justice when taken by itself.

If, in love, I work only for brotherhood, I do not get it. I get something far short of it—paternalism. I get an easy compromise based on the continuing assumption of the superiority of the dominant group, and the accommodation of the subordinated. I feed the arrogance of race pride and rivet the chains of caste upon the enshackled. Brotherhood, taken by itself, is thus corrupted in me to become paternalism; and the effect upon society is not to change iniquitous and unjust patterns but to give the sanctions of Christian sentiment to the shockingly unchristian patterns of a racial caste system which is sicklied over with the sweet benevolences of kindliness. The insistence upon softheartedness thus results in softheadedness as well. It is difficult to say which is more objectionable—to be hard of heart or to be soft of head; but it is clear that to insist upon either softheartedness or hardheadedness to the exclusion of the other is to court the danger of becoming soft in both or hard in both.

Justice and brotherhood are twin virtues. More correctly, they are inseparably parts of a single moment of experience. They may not be separated without violence being done to both. They must be held together if the true proportions of the tragic dilemma of conscience are to be appreciated. Every time we sharpen the ethical judgment by clarifying the demands of conscience, we increase the tension and difficulty with which the human spirit seeks to embrace at one moment the demands of both equity and empathy; and it is this tragic tension with its consequences which, as it cries for easement, impels us to act.

9. CONSCIENCE AND EQUALITY

It is a curious fact that men often take greatest pride in the one thing for which they can rightfully claim no personal credit—ancestry. Having made assertions of personal merit derived from his choice of ancestors, a man is then forced to defend an uneasy conscience with particular vehemence, the blatant defense exposing inner uncertainty. His refusal to be softhearted toward other men condemns him to harden his heart and pervert the rightful affection and reverence for his own ancestors into a harmful and destructive pride of ancestry. At the same moment, he dares not reject the prudential demands of his own family and group interest by denying the validity of all such ties, lest such hardheartedness should evoke its companion softheadedness. If he can combine the virtues of affection and intelligence, and can struggle manfully at one and the same moment both for brotherhood and for justice, he may then see the meaning of equality as something more than mere justice and something other than sentimentalism.

Perhaps "equality" is not the word to express the resulting attitude. It might better be called "high indifference" toward race. The Christian conscience, in its serene moments, when matters are viewed steadily from the double perspective of justice and brotherhood, recognizes the fact that pigmentation, whether of hair or of skin, has nothing to do with status before God and ought therefore to have nothing to do with status amongst men. It is not necessary to defend the "equality" of red heads. Why should it be necessary to demand the "equality" of brown skins? Even in its clouded and perturbed moments, the conscience still clings to the affirmation that all men are equal before God. Then, in God's name, why not also equal among men?

But to ask the question that way is to fall into the error of fighting for justice only, ignoring the values of brotherhood. It may be acceptable, for example, to condemn the false pride of Nazi racism which has told us that the tall, blond Nordic (as tall as Goebbels and as blond as Hitler) is the master race. But the man who does the condemning is in danger of establishing his own form of pride in equality as a substitute for the racism he rejects. He becomes insufferably arrogant over his own lack of arrogance, prideful over his own lack of pride. To escape from this danger, he needs to cease arguing for the equality of all races, and merely to act on the assumption that racial identity makes no difference. If he ever permits himself to lapse into the vocabulary of equalitarianism, he refuses to affirm it in the spirit of belligerence which shouts, "I'm as good as you are!" He quietly affirms, "You are as good as I" and promptly forgets the whole matter. An affirmation of a high indifference toward race makes it possible for him to stand squarely, humbly, and unashamedly on the simple fact of the common humanity of us all.

CHAPTER II

DESPAIR

"One ever feels his two-ness—an American, a Negro; two souls, two thoughts, two unreconciled strivings; two warring ideals in one dark body, whose dogged strength alone keeps it from being torn asunder."

—W. E. B. DuBois (1903)

MEN whose minds and hearts are at war within themselves cannot make a clear and final choice. We halt between the fears that bedevil us, and nurse the pride that stifles the fears. Torn by the disintegrating experiences of a caste-ridden society, the white man and the black alike are unable to rise above the tragedy of the dilemma. We are prisoners of Giant Despair, locked in Doubting Castle.

1. THE INNER CONFLICT

"At bottom, our problem is the moral dilemma of the American— the conflict between his moral valuations on various levels of consciousness and generality. The 'American Dilemma' . . . is the ever-raging conflict between . . . the valuations . . . which we shall call the 'American Creed' . . . of high national and Christian precepts, and, on the other hand, the valuations . . . where personal and local interests; economic, social, and sexual jealousies; considerations of community prestige and conformity; group prejudices against particular persons or types of people; and all sorts of miscellaneous wants, impulses, and habits dominate his outlook."[1]

As long as the individual clings to his Christian ideals while at the same time conforming to color caste, there is no escape from this inner tension. It is not merely that society is divided

[1] Gunnar Myrdal, *An American Dilemma: The Negro Problem and Modern Democracy*, p. xliii. Harpers, 1944.

into a multiplicity of conflicting interests and contradictory values, and that life in a schizophrenic society tends to make schizophroids. The conflict of values goes on within the individual person as well. With peculiar poignancy, the individual white man feels within himself the warfare between profession and practice which he shares with his social institutions. Two general streams of experience interweave in this shifting pattern of uneasiness.

One general stream of experiences is made up of those which increase his moral disquiet because of his personal ineffectiveness and feeling of futility in the face of race patterns. The color line zigzags, and he must zigzag with it. He feels that he must not send his children to a school where too many of the "other" group are present; he must not welcome persons of another race to the church he attends; he must not agitate for a change in employment policies in the plant where he works; he must not speak up in union meetings on behalf of minorities; he must not ride in the wrong section of the bus or the wrong car of the train; he must not use the terms of polite address to non-Caucasians in the presence of other Caucasians, or tip his hat to a lady of color; he must not sell or rent a house to a non-Caucasian purchaser in a "good" neighborhood, or refuse to sign a restrictive covenant which his neighbors are signing; he must not nominate a Negro for political office or expect the school board to employ Chinese teachers even in mixed schools; he must not ask for non-Caucasian policemen, judges, and jailers; he must not at any time in his public life expect to be free from the demands of the code of white supremacy.

Many of these things he may wish to attempt; but he is afraid. He fears that the personal cost will be too great. It does little good to cite the experience of individuals who have successfully broken loose from the chains of caste. He fears that he will lose caste if he violates the demands of his role as a member of a racial caste. He thinks his neighbors will not let their children play with his. His business associates may begin to shun him. His wife may not be invited to play bridge. Dinner invitations will dwindle and then cease. His job may be endangered—particularly if he holds a position subject to public pressures: a minister, a teacher, a political appointee. Former friends might pass him on the street without speaking. Some few close friends might try to reason with him "for his own good," and failing to convince him, they might sorrowfully desert him, lest they also should lose caste by associating with him. Whispers might follow his progress through town. People would peer from behind drawn shades. Tradesmen would be cold—or overly cordial to his face and otherwise behind his back. The possibility of physical violence, though it is the least of his actual worries, is a not too remote contingency: he knows the manhandling that has come to certain others who have violated the code of caste. He fears that if he were to choose to live outside the canons of color caste into which he was born he would be called upon to pay a price beyond his ability to pay.

Whether any of these possibilities would become actualities, he does not know. He does not care to find out. To most white persons, the threat of the loss of caste status is an effectual bar to unconventional behavior and opinions. They feel that they have much to lose and little to gain, either for themselves or for their brothers across racial lines, by refusing to conform. They may even feel that if they are to be able to do anything at all to harmonize race relations and to improve the opportunities of the submerged groups, they must meticulously obey all the requirements of caste. Strategy reinforces the fears which demand conformity.

All his desires for security and self-respect and the esteem and affection of friends urge him not to violate the code of white supremacy. In his serene and less-clouded moments, the white man sees something of what has happened to him; but he is like a squirrel in a cage, running desperately just to hold his position. It never occurs to him that if he stopped running the cage would stop revolving.

A better metaphor sees the white man held in the vise of caste while the smoothing plane of conformity shapes his prejudices and habits. If the process goes against the grain, the vise is tightened and the planner reverses the direction. Stubborn knots of ethical resistance are removed and plugged with a synthetic substitute which matches the more amenable grain. Sanded and polished, he is fitted into the furniture of American life. How can the wood rise up and smite the carpenter?

So, also, with the member of the minority racial group. From childhood, he has been taught conformity to caste as the price of survival.[2] His fears, ordinarily expressed as a strong prudential concern for survival and for the avoidance of embarrassment, keep him from too boldly challenging the color line. If he were to break through his inhibitions, he anticipates that the whole weight of the dominant group would descend upon him to thrust him back into his "place." He learns the habits of accommodation, adjustment, "taking low," knowing when to grin and drop his gaze to the third vest button of the white man, when to be polite, when to appear foolish and confused. In time, he may grow so accustomed to this status that he looks with apprehension upon any threat to change the established routines. He resents the "agitator" in either racial group. He is ready to defend the caste system that cradles his dearly bought security.

If he is a "race leader," he rises in some public gathering where "white friends" are present to say that he fully understands and sympathizes with their desire to look down upon Negroes. "Every man has to have someone lower in the scale to look down upon," he says. "That is his way of keeping his own self-respect. If the tables were turned, and the Negro was on top, we would look down on you in just the same way." He does not mean these words as a threat. It is his way of quieting antagonisms, currying favor, making his own path a little less difficult by affirming his conformity to caste.

[2] For illustrations of the point, see Edwin R. Embree's *Thirteen Against the Odds*. Viking, 1943.

The patterns of accommodation to caste are not identical in the majority and minority groups, nor are they identical in each of the several minorities; but the system takes its toll of the ethical sensibilities of both majority and minority group members.

A second general stream of experiences in which the individual feels the conflict of conscience and caste comprises the things which are not his own personal experience, but which he shares vicariously. A white man may live in a town or section where there are few members of racial minorities. But he reads, and he hears. The riots of Los Angeles or Detroit or Philadelphia or Alexandria may be a thousand miles from him; but he feels them as a blot on the honor of his nation. He is shocked when he reads that the legislature of another state evades the decision of the Supreme Court of the United States on the white primaries by hastily repealing every statute having to do with the primary elections of the state. He shares the humiliation of mankind when Marian Anderson is denied the courtesy of singing in Constitution Hall. He thinks he has discovered a religious reason for going to prize fights, because he believes that the professional ring is the one place in American life where absolute equality reigns and merit is the measure of achievement; and then he reads the biography of Joe Louis,[3] and comes out of the book with his fists clenched in frustrated anger. He hears that irate farmers in New Jersey force a relocated Nisei to leave, and he can only sit by his radio and listen.

He feels the hurt of all these things, and many more. They become his own experiences through vicarious sharing. And whether he feels resentful or indignant, or whether he becomes calloused in conscience, inured to the harassing details of the continuing story, and begins to sigh instead of grinding his teeth, he feels frustrated and defeated. He may not accept the caste system by giving open assent to it; but, what amounts to the same thing, he ceases to resist it. He writes a letter to the editor, another to his congressman, and goes fishing. Per-

[3] See Embree, *op. cit.*

haps in the serenity of nature he can forget man's inhumanity to man.

The vicarious experiences of the minority man under color caste are much more intense. Always, as he reads of things that have happened to other people of color, or listens to swift-flying whispers of some new tragedy, he has the sensation that "it" has happened to *him*. Both as the possible next victim and as a member of the group that suffers because of pigmentation, he feels the weight of every discrimination. If the white man of sensitive conscience feels the burden of vicarious experience, much more so does the colored man.

The minority man does not always extend his vicarious empathy to members of racial minorities other than his own. Often, he may seize the opportunity temporarily to rise above his misery by riding the majority band wagon when a member of some other racial minority than his own suffers. The Chinese merchant in Sacramento profits when his Japanese competitor goes to a concentration camp—so he puts on his store window a sticker provided by the Native Sons of the Golden West, whose red, white, and blue legend demands: "No More Japs In California!" The Negro resident of San Francisco hears that the Mexican population of Los Angeles is having a hard time, and he finds secret satisfaction in the fact that there is one place in America where, at least for the moment, someone other than a Negro is getting a bad deal. The ties of common suffering do not always prove stronger than the emotional impulses to identify himself, even for a fleeting moment, with the majority group. But the inner contradictions which he feels in the act intensify his own sense of frustration, finally increasing the difficulty with which he maintains a stable equilibrium in his new role as a sympathizer with the upper caste. The security he sought proves to be expensive.

The minority man is strongly tempted to deny his sympathies when the victim is a "poor white." The long-standing bitterness between the lower economic strata of the two castes, which is glossed over with an easy day-to-day adjustment, beneath the surface of which lurks the constant possibility of antagonism, sets a caste pattern which is stronger than class feeling. But while this antagonism provides an emotional catharsis, it serves to complicate and to intensify his own inner conflicts and tensions.

Whether the experience is direct or vicarious, and whether the individual is Caucasian or non-Caucasian, the ethically sensitive person comes cumulatively to have a feeling of frustration and futility in the face of color caste. The moral confusion of national life becomes the inner perplexity of his soul. He stands on the brink of ethical despair.

Unless he is made of sterner stuff than most men, or unless his ethical conscience is kept alive by contacts with rarely sensitized spirits, or unless he has the support of a group of likeminded men and women, the Caucasian in this situation begins seriously to question the basic tenets of Christian faith. Is it, after all, an obligation of the Christian to live as a brother to *all* others? May it not be that the Christian ideal can be viewed "practically," with a hardheaded sense of what is possible and what is impossible in this world? Failure to narrow the gap of inconsistency between ideals and practices thus leads him to doubt the ideals themselves. Frustration breeds moral cynicism.

But he cannot easily surrender his Christian commitments. He knows they are right and good and true. He has been taught them from childhood; and although he never (or seldom) has been called on to make a bold stand for his convictions, he knows that the great martyrs and prophets of the past have done so. That, too, is a part of his tradition. Is the age of the martyrs past? Or is it only fools and saints who seriously try to live in accordance with the Christian ethic? At any rate, he consoles himself, the fundamental ideas of the nation are soundly Christian. We have written into our constitution, in the Bill of Rights, and in certain amendments since that time, as well as in the Declaration of Independence itself, our fundamental belief in the equality of all men. Perhaps, with the passage of time, things will get better.

And yet, if they do get "better," will that not bring more problems than it solves? I may then have a Chinese neighbor. Negroes will swarm all over the streetcars. Some dark-skinned boy will meet my daughter in college. Suddenly, the emotional tensions are focused in a grim reaffirmation of old shibboleths. The inner conflict which I could not resolve now finds its release in being vented on a scapegoat. White supremacy may not be fully Christian, I tell myself, but if the white race is mongrelized, there won't be anybody left to *be* Christian. We must maintain white supremacy at any cost. "At *any* cost?" queries conscience. And the struggle begins all over again within me. At long last, unable to sustain the tension of this inner conflict between principle and practice, I begin finally to despair of the Christian ethic itself.

So, also, if I am a minority man. Unless I have greater spiritual resources than most men, I run the hazard of loss of faith in the Christian enterprise. It goes without saying that I have little enough confidence in the religious affirmations of the white man. My daily experiences contradict the faith which the white man affirms without practicing, and (rightly or wrongly) I hold him and his fellows responsible for the caste system. Much more serious, however, is the gradual loss of my own faith in Christian values. That loss may come suddenly in some bitter experience, or it may come like a creeping paralysis of the spirit. Beset by the double doubts of faith in others and in myself, I am sorely tempted to cast Christian values aside. If I hold to them, I am reminded of the fact that my white brothers on their side of the caste line are not matching my adherence. "Don't play yourself for a sucker," whispers the imp. Why should I? The seeds of moral cynicism fall on fertile soil.

Whether for the minority man or for the Caucasian, failure to resolve the inner conflict of conscience leads through uncertainty about ethical ideals to an open doubting of them, and finally to the abandoning of ethical standards in favor of some more easily sustained position. When, because of long failure to practice the ideals of democracy and Christianity, he begins clearly to doubt the validity of the ideals themselves, and when the voice of conscience will not be stilled, the tension becomes unbearable. He is then ready frankly to discard the bothersome ethic, in order to achieve inner peace. He adopts a new system of valuations. He may not do it all at once in a grand style. More probably, he does it piecemeal. The compromises increase, until the struggle tapers off at a level of tolerance. He has given allegiance to pagan gods.

The white man goes through this process of ethical defeat leading to moral defeatism, and is ripe for fascism. He gives his allegiance to a Leader who symbolizes the pagan virtues —virtues which are easier to practice than the ethic of Christianity. New tensions supplant the old, and he now ceases to be a passive victim of the race problem; he is an active agent in making that problem worse. Moral cynicism has laid the foundations for an horrendous structure of fascism based on white supremacy. He now worships at the shrine of racial arrogance. All the old frustrations are gone; he gives himself to the pagan gods with zeal. Or, if he does not find a release through allegiance to some pagan Leader, he may resolve the tension through complete cynicism or otherworldly escape. In his passivity he thinks he is merely neutral; but actually he lends his support to the fascist effort. The blossoming of a score of fascist and neofascist movements in all sections of the nation within the past decade testifies to the reality of such ethical despair.

The minority man, when he abandons his ethical standards under these pressures, is tempted to find refuge either in otherworldliness or in some brand of fanaticism. Doctrinaire communism or, more commonly, some form of race chauvinism, beckons to him. The solace of an otherworldly religion, which evades the ethical problem by transferring the ethical struggle to a celestial level, leaving no immediate ethical demands for daily living, entices him. He may match the arrogance of the white racist with an arrogance of his own, or he may duplicate the passivity and irrelevance of the white escapist, permitting his own passivity to encourage the coming of the Strong Man and the reign of terror. He has accepted an ultimate futility.

The amazing thing about American race relations is not that their even tenor is so frequently interrupted by unsavory incidents. It is not the increasing decrepitude of the caste structure and the cracking of the color bar. It is that the bitterness and frustration of the defeated in both castes does not more often break over the controls. The inner tensions which the minority man feels are more intense than those of the white; but both are real. The white man is fighting against his own conscience, and he hears the voice of the colored man reminding him of the struggle in which he meets with only partial success. The minority man is fighting for the conscience of the white man without succeeding, and without the support and co-operation of the group for whose conscience he fights. The inner tensions resulting from such ethical struggle are of a kind few white persons have ever known.

Upon the minority man in America, the burden of this psychological strain is made heavier by the fact that he is always conscious of his double status as a minority man in a white man's world. The essentially tragic character of this predicament is well expressed in *The Souls of Black Folk*:

"It is a peculiar sensation, this double-consciousness, this sense of always looking at one's self through the eyes of others, of measuring one's soul by the tape of a world that looks on with amused contempt and pity. One ever feels his two-ness—an American, a Negro; two souls, two thoughts, two unreconciled strivings; two warring ideals in one dark body, whose dogged strength alone keeps it from being torn asunder."[4]

[4] W. E. B. DuBois, *The Souls of Black Folk*, p. 3. McClurg, 1903.

ie tensions which, at long last, the Caucasian is coming to
.el in all their inescapable insistence and dynamic fury have
long been sustained by the minority man.

2. THE COLLECTIVE CONSCIENCE

There is a sense in which it is not possible to lay an ethical
judgment upon the collective conscience of a nation. Only as
it is grasped by individuals does it become a living reality.
There can be no collective change of attitudes and practices
except as that change is made in each member of the collec-
tivity. This change may not necessarily come in all the members
of a group at the same moment of time; and it seldom is carried through in any one individual to completion at a single
moment. It is an uneven movement, in which some individuals
move faster than their fellows, and the progress of an individual is irregular, sometimes marked by retrogressions and
nearly always partial and incomplete.

At the same time, we are justified in speaking of a collective
conscience. The accepted norms of social behavior, the guides
of conduct which control the minimal standards of daily life,
express a collective judgment of the way things "ought" to be.
This is not merely the sum, or the average, of the standards
espoused by the individuals who make up the nation or the
racial group. It may be lower than certain individuals would
place it. More commonly, it is much higher than the standards
accepted by individuals in their more intimate and personal
relationships.

There is an observation which we shall find substantiated in every
aspect of the Negro problem, that the ordinary white American is more
prejudiced, the more closely individual and personal the matter is.
When he becomes formal, and, particularly, when he acts as a citizen,
he is very much more under the control of the equalitarian national
Creed than when he is just an individual worker, neighbor, or
customer.[5]

[5] Gunnar Myrdal, *op. cit.*, p. 384.

The standards of the nation (as differentiated from the performance of the nation) are supposed to control social institutions and collective behavior. These standards are tacitly accepted as the rightful controls for the processes of justice, the definition of economic opportunity, the degree of access to educational and cultural facilities, the patterns of housing, and many similar matters. They are collective standards.

Over against these collective standards is to be set the picture of actual group behavior, a pattern of color caste. The conflict between collective behavior and collective conscience establishes a dichotomy in society which is as sharp and as devastating as is the conflict within the individual. We have referred to the fact that a schizophrenic society begets schizophroid men; we are now ready to push the thought one step further. The tyranny of social patterns over the individual soul has been noted. We now observe that the conflict within the individual conscience cannot be satisfactorily and finally resolved unless and until the conflict in the social conscience, which sires the inner dichotomy, also is resolved.

This does not lead to the conclusion that we are involved in a vicious circle through which we cannot hope to break. Precisely the opposite is true. The individual is largely formed by social experiences, and social experiences follow the general pattern of arrangements prevailing in the caste of color; but this does not destroy the hope either of personal escape or of social transformation. It leads to the conclusion that when we recognize the manner in which the caste system contradicts the collective conscience we are thereby forced to attack caste itself in order to extricate the individual.

We are not now saying that the only cause of race pride is an iniquitous caste system; but what we are insisting upon is that, when men are forced to grow up from infancy to maturity in a caste-controlled society, they are forced into the pattern of attitudes which such experiences teach them. Man's tendency toward pride and selfishness is sufficiently strong without the deliberate cultivation and nurture of these potentialities through established social institutions. The great indictment of social sins lies not so much in the fact of their sinfulness as in the fact that they lay on the hapless individual the tremendous social pressures which make it difficult to obey conscience and easy to evade it. Every moment of voluntary acquiescence in the continuance of caste is a violation of the prayer, "Lead us not into temptation."

We shall not resolve the conflict in conscience, either individually or socially, except as we resolve both together. That is why the conflict in the collective conscience is of such importance. And that is why we cannot escape the conflict by any means other than resolving it. That, also, is why we cannot longer bear the conflict. The tensions in society have now come to such strength that they threaten to tear the social fabric asunder, thereby paralleling the disintegrating effects of the inner tensions each of us knows. The conflict cannot be escaped except as it is resolved. Both individually and collectively, we stand at the crisis that calls for decision. One form which that decision has too frequently taken is a profound despair of the whole Christian ideal.

3. How the Issue Is Joined

Just as the individual finds the tensions unbearable, so, also, the elastic limits of the social process have been reached. Something will break. Historians of the future will look back on this generation and record that the social tensions of racism with conscience became too great, and that Americans moved, for the second time within a century, toward an irrepressible conflict. We shall not grasp the critical character of this hour of history unless we see it as a moment as decisive as that tumultuous decade which followed the Dred Scott decision and led to the fratricide of the Civil War. The snapping of the cords of the social fabric can already be heard. The social crisis is revealed in the straining of relationships between racial groups in every part of the nation and throughout the world.

The conflict is coming. We move toward it with acceleration and crescendo.

This conflict will not be joined on purely class lines. The frantic efforts of one important section of the labor movement to capture the allegiance of racial minorities is effectually countered by the obstinate refusal of another wing of labor to admit minorities to equality within the movement. The race issue, which helped to split the Knights of Labor half a century ago, promises to cut through the contemporary labor movement and prevent any clear identification of class and caste.

The issue will not be joined along lines of religious denominationalism. There is no wide divergence between the churches in matters of racial exclusiveness today; and the few local institutions which practice racial inclusiveness are scattered through several denominations. There is no close correlation between theology and racial attitudes, no close correspondence of ecclesiastical type and racial pattern. There is little promise that the future will see whole denominations standing in support of caste, with other denominations unitedly attacking it. The race issue splits the church today just as it did a century ago.

The issue will not even be joined on strictly racial lines. There are too many Caucasians who, when the issue is forced, will refuse to stand for white supremacy, and there are too many members of minority groups who, in the time of testing, will be unable to throw off their chains. If there were an international war on race lines, our own nation would be sharply divided and civil war might be an accompaniment of such global conflict. That pattern would be repeated in South Africa and in other parts of the world where caste sets the races against each other within a particular nation.

Within the United States, the crisis might conceivably find issue in a second Civil War, even before it is joined on a world scale; but the geographical ambivalence of the race issue today in America makes such an eventuality unlikely.

There are too many persons in the North and West who share the fascist and racist dogmas of some Southerners; and there are too many Southerners who share the democratic and Christian desires of some Northerners and Westerners for the race issue to become the basis of a geographically clear-cut fight without the stimulus of an international war to force the issue. The dispersion of the racial minorities in all parts of the nation also militates against a too neat geographical delineation of the line of cleavage. There is a certain amount of irresponsible talk which alleges that we are "ready to fight another war over this business of race equality." Fraught with grave import, this is nevertheless to be recognized primarily as a form of emotional catharsis which is symptomatic of the tightening of the inner tensions of conscience. Civil war is only a possibility, not yet a probability, in this nation.

More conceivably, the issue will be joined in all parts of the nation in measures short of civil war. The Congressional debates will become hotter, obstructionist tactics of certain blocs more obstinate and provocative. Legislative steps may be expected—and much depends upon which sort of legislation is supported by majority vote, whether to tear down or to buttress color caste. At the present time, the weight of the Constitution and of judicial processes is on the side of racial equality. We may anticipate that legal pressures will be used in support of citizenship rights and against restrictive covenants on residential housing, to break down segregation in education and in many other areas. This legal pressure against caste will stir up counterpressures from the defenders of caste, which pressures may express themselves principally in extralegal activities and overt violence, unless the democratic process is converted to fascist purposes. In the period of readjustment following on the end of the war and demobilization, there may be an epidemic of race riots. If these riots come, they will be surface indications of the deep contradictions of society, as well as indices of the lack of successful attempts to correct the evils from which the tensions derive.

It is possible that far-visioned and courageous action under-taken speedily may avert some of the rioting and bloodshed through precautionary measures to stem violence wherever it breaks out. The second threatened "Zoot Suit" riot in Los Angeles was averted because the police threw a *cordon sanitaire* around the entire Mexican and Negro districts, keeping the white hoodlums and troublemakers out of the section until the fever pitch of mob violence had passed. The police of many a large city have been going to schools designed to train them in handling race riots. More courageous and far-visioned would be a program designed to correct at least a few of the funda-mental ills from which racial antagonisms spring.

But whatever forms of overt violence and pressure we expe-rience (or manage to avert), we shall not be able to evade the crisis of conscience that is revealed in the contradiction of the Christian ethic by the caste of color. The choice before us is inescapable. If we do not choose between white supremacy and Christianity, we shall ultimately despair of Christianity. Mean-while, the march of world events will not wait on boondoggling tarradiddlers. If, in despair of ethical action, we refuse to act, we shall be given legitimate grounds for despair. That is why Myrdal says we must "do something big, and do it soon."[6] It may yet be that, if our mood of tragic despair is sharp enough, we shall act to correct its causes.

4. HOPE IN DESPAIR

There is one matter which gives great hope in spite of the despair that is upon us. That is the remarkable change in the moral climate within which our decision must be made.

A century ago, the defenders of caste in its then form of slavery were quite certain that there was no ethical difficulty whatever in taking the stand in support of white supremacy. The Reverend J. C. Postell, speaking in Orangeburg, South Carolina, in 1836 said of slavery:

[6] Myrdal, *op. cit.*, p. 1022.

It is not a moral evil. The fact that slavery is of Divine appointment, would be proof enough with the Christians that it could not be a moral evil. . . . It is the Lord's doings and marvellous in our eyes and had it not been for the best, God alone, who is able, long since would have over-ruled it. It is by Divine appointment.[7]

The literature of the slavery controversy is replete with statements of this sort, which make clear that the then defenders of white supremacy had no compunctions of conscience about the ethics or the religion of their stand.

Today, all that is changed. Only occasionally does a writer appear in print with the unashamed statement that racial discrimination is not a moral issue. Hardly a church conference, in the South or elsewhere, adjourns without passing some sort of resolution indicating that it is uneasy in conscience over the racial tensions and the treatment of minorities. The present mental atmosphere within which the race question is discussed is best summed up by Myrdal:

The American Negro problem is a problem in the heart of the American. It is there that the interracial tension has its focus. It is there that the decisive struggle goes on. . . . At the bottom of our problem is the moral dilemma of the American.[8]

However deep the despair of moral frustration, there is great hope in the fact that the basic character of the race problem is now recognized for what it is—an inescapable moral problem.

[7] Quoted in Trevor Bowen's *Divine White Right*, p. 107. Harpers, 1934.
[8] Myrdal, *op. cit.*, p. 1.

CHAPTER III

DEFECTION

"The white man is the custodian of the gospel of Jesus Christ."
—United States Senator Bilbo, speaking before the Mississippi
Legislature (1944)

THE affront to the Christian conscience carried in these
words of the senior Senator from Mississippi is an amazing revelation of the end result of a process of defection.
Readers uninterested in tracing the outlines of this story
through the centuries of the Christian tradition may wish to
skip this chapter; but if there is any hope that men may learn
from history, the main incidents of the Great Defection are
worth putting into the record.

Indeed, Christians of this present century too often tend to
jump from the New Testament to the present moment in one
grand glide of historical ignorance, disregarding the costly
and meaningful experiences of other centuries, ignoring the
record of development which alone can explain the aberrations
of today. How could it have become possible for a professing
Christian to win the applause of his fellows by asserting the
curiously revolting version of the faith that is carried in the
words at the head of this chapter? The answer to that question
is an entire volume in itself: in a few pages here, we summarize
the more important aspects of the story.

Generally speaking, Christians agree that the faith was pure
and undefiled in New Testament times, but that it lost its pris-
tine purity at a specified historical period. Protestants are accustomed to date the corruption of religion at the donation of
Constantine or the edicts of Theodosius. Catholics point to
the Reformation as the time when Christianity fell. There
may be some truth in these analyses which read history in terms

of black and white; but, at least with reference to the racial composition of the church and the attitude of Christianity on the race question, the story follows quite different lines.

There never has been a time when the church was free of controversy between inclusiveness and exclusiveness: it is this controversy which is the ethical nub of the problem of race today. Standing before his home-town people, Jesus of Nazareth pointed out that they, the Israelites, were not the only chosen ones of God. For his pains, he was threatened with death by violence. Before him, the prophets had initiated the struggle of universalism for victory over particularism.[1] New Testament times were bedeviled with the division between Jew and Gentile, between cultured and uncultured, between slave and freeman, between Greek and barbarian. Some of the sharpest words in the Epistles are directed against the exclusiveness of particularism. To understand the modern church in its perverse identification with the heresy of white supremacy, it is useful to trace the warfare through the centuries.

1. THE EARLY CHURCH

There is no precise parallel in earlier Christian history for the present racial heresy that infects Christianity: the notion of "race" as we know it has been too recently injected into history. It is scarcely a century and a half old. The present controversy over racial allegiance of Christians cannot be "settled" merely by citing Biblical passages or earlier rulings of the church. The words may be similar, even identical, but the controversies of earlier times had a different import. [2]

[1] Let the interested reader begin with Amos 9:7, and follow the story through the Bible.

[2] To appreciate something of the difficulty implied by this comment, consider the single example of I Peter 2:9, where Christians are referred to as "an elect *race*, a royal priesthood, a holy *nation*, a *people* for God's own possession." The writer of this epistle argues that Christians "in time past were no people, but now are the people of God" (v. 10). The proof-text method of settling doctrinal and practical controversies finds in this example a pretty enough confusion: "race," "nation," and "people" are used interchangeably. Moreover, a consideration of the meanings of these terms in the first and second centuries

At the same time, although there is no precise parallel either in the terms of earlier language and our own or in the situations of the two periods, there are consistent threads of meaning to be uncovered. In the Hellenistic world (excepting only the Jews and Christians in it), the important line of cleavage that divided one people from another was neither racial nor religious nor governmental nor geographical: it was cultural, distinguishing between the "Greeks" and the "barbarians." Everyone who shared the Hellenistic culture, no matter what his ancestry or religious affiliation, was looked upon as a Hellene, a "Greek." Others were barbarians. Under the empire, the distinction between citizen and foreigner was essentially this cultural line. Political forms and procedures followed the cultural line instead of determining it. The Graeco-Roman, or Hellenistic, culture was both the tool and the badge of empire. Greek in the East and Latin in the West, together with all that is implied in the use of these languages and the corresponding thought forms and artifacts, made up the culture complex which identified the Hellene as distinguished from the barbarian.

In this world, the Jews made up an island of exception; and from the middle of the first century, Christians (either regarded as a variant form of Judaism or, later, as a new religion) also began to be an exception to the general pattern. Christians therefore began to speak of themselves as a "new race" or "new nation," *using these terms interchangeably to mean the same thing.* [3] This is, perhaps, why the Epistles do

---

reveals that in no case did they carry the meanings in the biological, political, and sociological sense which these words convey in the twentieth century Western world.

[3] Cf. Eusebius, *Ecclesiastical History*, I, iv, 2; IV, vii, 10, 14; I, iv, 4. In these passages, "ethnos" and "genos" are used interchangeably by Eusebius, and are translated by Lake and McGiffert (in the Loeb Classics and the *Post Nicene Fathers*, respectively) interchangeably and without consistent relationship to the Greek word. Thus, for example, Eusebius writes, "neon ethnon"; and Lake translates "new race," while McGiffert, with equal fidelity to the original meaning and probably greater fidelity to the contemporary parallel usage, translates "new nation."

not use the word "race" in talking about what we today call "race." What Paul did—and what is far more significant than a mere denunciation of racial divisions and distinctions—was to attack the divisions that were threatening to divide the church, and to declare that none of these could legitimately divide Christians. There could be neither Hellene nor Hebrew, barbarian, Scythian, slave nor freeman. No one had the right to shut another out of full fellowship because of *any* sort of difference.

The significance of this revolutionary view of humanity is seen more than two centuries later in what happened to Constantine when he was converted from paganism to Christianity. The line of demarcation between citizen and foreigner for the entire Graeco-Roman world (except for the Christians and Jews in it) was cultural, not ethnic. But for Christians, it was neither ethnic nor cultural: it was religious, cutting across all other lines and rendering them meaningless. When he became a Christian, Constantine accepted this new insight. He abandoned the prevailing attitude of *Romanitas* toward barbarians, thereby bringing them within the protection of the inclusive religion instead of shutting them outside the protection of the gods of the *polis* and the *civitas* as formerly they had been. He welcomed the Germanic tribes, giving these former barbarians a status of moral and social equality within the empire.

Theodosius I completed the work begun by Constantine (after a brief interruption by Julian the Apostate). With his double policy of political federation (*foederatio*) and biological fusion which encouraged intermarriage of Hellenes and barbarians, Theodosius carried out the obvious obligations of an emperor who professed to believe what the fourth century Christian was universally acknowledged to believe—that there could be no arbitrary distinctions amongst Christians.

That these attitudes of universalism in the empire did not always appear to non-Hellenistic peoples as a shining invitation to equality is another matter. The cruder, less developed Germanic and Celtic peoples of Central and Northern Europe tended to be flattered by the new universalism of the empire, and to respond favorably to it. The more advanced peoples of Africa, Egypt, and the Near East were not complimented in the same degree: they tended to resist the new doctrine, resenting the paternalism implicit in its use, preferring freedom and autonomy to the specious universalism of imperial control. As a result, the nationalistic struggles of these established peoples of Africa, Egypt and the Near East against the dominance of the empire forced them to reject the Church of the Empire as well: the new universalism was stillborn. The "new race" notion of Christianity did not appeal to the peoples along the eastern and southern shores of the Mediterranean: to them, it was a cloak of political imperialism and dominance.

This confusion was inevitable because of the fundamental confusion of method in Constantine's actions. He sought to use, according to his own statement, "the secret eye of thought" to achieve religious unity, while at the same moment using military force to achieve political unity. Just how difficult it was for subject peoples to recognize the working of the "secret eye of thought" at the moment when they were being ground beneath the iron heel of empire, we shall shortly see. But the universalism of the faith was recognized in theory even in this moment when it was denied in defection.

2. THE SYRIAC (NESTORIAN) CHURCH

Even before the harsh imperialism of empire was glossed over with the inclusive spirit of the "new race" Christianity, an important section of the church had broken from the body of Christendom and gone its way. The oldest schismatical church of Christendom, once mighty and widespread in its power and influence, the Syriac (Nestorian) Church is today a pitiful remnant of its former self. If there were not undisputed evidence of its former power and extent, the handful of Nestorians left today would scarcely lead us to credit the story. One patriarch now rules a few families in Kurdistan, "the last tragic remnant of a Church whose history is as glorious as any in Christendom."[4] Its missionary outreach was flung from the Mediterranean to the Pacific. A succession of martyrs hallowed the soil of Persia with their blood when Shapur II played the part of an eastern Diocletian. At one time, this church ordained bishops for India, Herat, the Samarkand, and for China, with its easternmost bastion planted in Han-balik (modern Peiping).

The particular heresy of the Nestorians was not primarily a creation of the Syriac Church; but its acceptance and growth in the East and in Persia were very largely a corollary of its rejection by the Church of the Empire.[5] What the Church of the Empire declared to be heterodox was almost automatically guaranteed an acceptance as orthodoxy by the Syriac Church. Standing on the remote fringe of the empire, it was the first to break away from the imperialism of the centralizing church, using the Nestorian controversy as the issue on which the break was made.

And with the separation of the Syriac Church from the Church of the Empire, all contact and communion ceased. When an emissary, one Rabban Sauma, came from the Nestorian Patriarch to visit the Pope in the thirteenth century, the twelve cardinals who received him (the Pope having just died) had never heard of the Syriac Church and were completely ignorant of its vast expansion throughout the Far East. This Rabban Sauma was a native of Han-balik, and the Patriarch of the Nestorian Church was himself a native of the same city. He then had twenty-five metropolitans under his direction, in Persia, Mesopotamia, Khorasan, Turkistan, India, and China, with a total of some two hundred bishops, each with a separate see. In cutting itself off from the Nestorian Church, the Church of the Empire had lost contact with the greatest missionary outreach of Christianity previous to the nineteenth

[4] Adrian Fortescue, *Lesser Eastern Churches*, p. 17. London: Catholic Truth Society, 1909.

[5] *Ibid.*, p. 54.

century—not excluding the Roman Catholic missions in the New World and the Far East.[6] When the Nestorian Church was lost to Christendom, an inclusive circle of fellowship which might have been drawn around Asia was broken. The defection had begun.

3. THE AFRICAN AND EGYPTIAN CHURCHES

It was from Africa[7] that Tertullian spoke for the Church of the Martyrs, defying the Roman Empire in words that were not idle boasts, but were borne out by those who were sawn asunder and stopped the mouths of lions.

> We grow up in great numbers, as often as we are cut down by you. The blood of the martyrs is the seed of the Church. We are of yesterday, and yet we have filled every place belonging to you—cities, islands, castles, towns, assemblies; your very camps and companies, palace, senate, forum; we leave you your temple only.[8]

Boasting an apologist like Tertullian, an organizer like Cyprian, and a saint like Augustine the theologian, the African Church once covered what is now Tripoli, Tunisia, Morocco, and Libya. It was reported to have had 579 bishops presiding over as many separate dioceses, spreading the length of the southern shore of the Mediterranean from the Libyan Desert to the western promontory of the continent. But of that once powerful church, the only traces which remain today in the whole of that area are the crumbling ruins of ancient cathedrals, skeletal reminders of once flourishing life. The whole of the African Church apostatized to Islam in the seventh century.

Much the same thing happened in Egypt. There, the church

[6] A. C. Moule, in his *Christians in China Before the Year 1550* (Society for the Promoting of Christian Knowledge, 1930), has painstakingly and scientifically garnered the fragments of the record into an imposingly convincing mosaic.

[7] Throughout this section of the chapter, "Africa" is used in its ancient sense, to refer to Proconsular Africa, the area we now refer to as "North Africa," west of Egypt and north of the Sahara.

[8] *Apology*, xxxvii, L.

had spread from the delta to the headwaters of the Nile, and fanned out into a missionary movement into Abyssinia. It boasted of a distinguished line of patriarchs, theologians, and teachers; and by the seventh century it was the accepted religion of practically the entire population of Egypt. The power and vigor of the Egyptian Church had been shown in repeated defiance of the Church of the Empire with its seat in Constantinople and, as at the Synod of Ephesus, which the losing party dubbed the "Robber Synod," in completely dominating conciliar decision. Yet, when Islam arose like a cloud out of the Arabian Desert, it swept across Egypt and on to Africa, completely enveloping the once powerful Egyptian Church, leaving only the sad fragments of Christianity to survive in the present-day Coptic Church. What lies back of this double tragedy, in the loss of the Egyptian and African churches from Christendom?

No single, simple explanation is satisfactory. History is essentially complex, and simplified analyses do violence to historical fact. Doubtless the less rigorous moral code of Islam induced many less saintly Christians to prefer the yoke of the Prophet to that of the Christ. Probably a more important element was the decline of inner vitality within the Christian Church when it ceased to be the Church of the Martyrs and became the religious arm of the empire. Certainly, also, Islam had a greater holding power than Christianity when once it gained a following; for its law of apostasy, which inflicted the death penalty on renegades, gave its perpetuation the double guarantees of faith and fear. But this would hardly have stopped Christians from maintaining a faith for which they had gladly suffered martyrdom under the pagan empire. It was not fear alone that led them to give Islam an open welcome.

Perhaps more important was the appearance of Islam in its early years as a sort of Christian heresy rather than as a non-Christian religion. Its use of the Judaeo-Christian tradition gave it an initial acceptance with other Christians who might themselves also be out of sympathy with the centers of orthodoxy: between Islam and the Coptic Church of Egypt there was undoubtedly the fellow feeling of one heresy for another. But after due allowance is made for all other factors, the great growing and holding power of Islam amongst the peoples of the Egyptian and African churches was found then, as it is now, in the fact that Islam has no race complex. The facts bear out this assertion.

It is commonly believed that the principal point of controversy between the centers of Rome and Constantinople, on the one hand, and the churches in Egypt and Africa, on the other, was theological. In reality, both the Monophysite heresy in Egypt and Donatism in Africa were theological fronts for the fight against imperialism.

It was the old national feeling, the old hatred of the Roman power lurking under the dispute about one or two natures in Christ. As soon as Marcian died (457) the storm burst. They [the Monophysites] drove the soldiers from the temple of Serapis and there burned them alive; they murdered Proterius, and set up as Patriarch a fanatical Monophysite, Timothy the Cat.[9]

The East had its Monophysites, following after an earlier opposition to Arianism (when that had been the faith of Constantinople). In the West, Novatianism was followed by Donatism as the theological front for the struggle against imperial domination. In the East, the imperial party in the Egyptian Church was called "Melkites," or "King's men." They used Greek (sometimes Latin) but never Coptic, in their liturgy and preaching as well as in their conversation and ordinary transactions. But the Monophysite Church spoke as Copts, held that their Patriarch was independent of the government and of the Melkite Church, and made internecine warfare both verbally and physically. Their strong-arm men, the *parabolani*, were on call, and on at least one occasion settled a synodical decision with the use of muscles and clubs, taking the life of at least one opposing bishop. When Constantinople

[9] Adrian Fortescue, *The Orthodox Eastern Church*, p. 14. London: Catholic Truth Society, 1907.

countered with the use of troops, the Copts retreated, the
Patriarch going into hiding in the headwaters of the Nile,
secretly ruling the Coptic Church. It was from such an exile
that he was welcomed back in safe-conduct when the followers
of the Prophet swept the troops of Constantinople out of
Egypt.

It might have appeared that the Egyptians were ready to
welcome any ruler in place of the empire; but their firm stand
against the Persian invasion (six hundred fortified monasteries
being successively leveled by the Persians and their defending
monks being put to the sword with great slaughter) denies
this possibility. There is no record of a great popular uprising
in Egypt when the Persians sought to replace Constantinople.
The monks resisted fiercely; the masses were indifferent to the
new conquerors who pressed their march up the Nile as far
south as Syene.[10]

The end of the Persian invasion restored the empire for a
brief Indian summer of dominance in Egypt, during which the
controversies between Melkites and Monophysites went on,
climaxed by the exile of the Monophysite Patriarch in the
Upper Nile, from which vantage point he encouraged the
Coptic opposition to the empire. Then the real invasion struck.

Al-Makrizi, Arab historian, whose writings are the principal
authority for our knowledge of the situation from this point
on, makes clear that when the Muslims took over in Egypt,
they found the country

filled with Christians who were divided between the governing body,
consisting of Romans from the army of the master of Constantinople, the
King of Rome, whose opinions were those of the Melkites, whose number was about 300,000; and the other part, consisting of the great mass
of the peoples of Egypt, called Copts . . . a mixed race, so that it is no
longer possible to distinguish whether any one of them be of Coptic,
Abyssinian, Nubian, or Jewish descent. . . . Between these and the
Melkites, people of the State, was so great an enmity that they hurt

[10] Cf. Walter F. Adeney, *The Greek and Eastern Churches,* p. 573. Scribners,
1908.

each other by betrayals, and even mutual murders took place. . . . They were properly the people of the land of Egypt, of its upper and its lower part. . . . The Copts sought to make peace with Amr on condition of paying tribute; and he granted this, confirmed their possession of land and other properties, and they helped the Muslims against the Romans till Allah drove these in flight and expelled them from Egypt.[11]

One of Amr's first acts on making conquest of Egypt was to send a letter of amnesty and safe-conduct to the Coptic Patriarch, Benjamin, permitting his return to the Lower Nile, probably in recognition of the part he and his fellow Copts had played in helping to eject the troops and supporters of the empire. The entire holdings of the Melkites were turned over to the Copts: the Church of the Empire ceased to exist in Egypt.

The story is amenable to many interpretations; but in whatever interpretation is made there must be included as a primary datum the fact that the anti-imperialistic antagonisms of the great masses of the Christians of Egypt were a principal motivation, expressing themselves first in several centuries of ecclesiastical warfare and finally in an open espousal of the Muslim in preference to the Roman overlord. But they had not similarly preferred the Persians when opportunity presented itself. Why the difference? In accounting for this, the final determinant in the equation, the racial inclusiveness of Islam, as contrasted with the paternalistic arrogance of the empire and the nonaffirmative policy of Persia, must be recognized as the weight that tipped the balance. Offering not only the exchange of one yoke for another (as the Persians had), but also offering the brotherhood of an inclusive religion, Islam succeeded where Persia had failed, in replacing the empire in Egypt. The religion which had identified itself with the imperial aspirations of the Caesars[12] could not claim the allegiance of the subject peoples. Ready for a new government, they welcomed one which was also armed with an inclusive faith. The church which

[11] Translated from the Arabic and quoted by Fortescue in *Lesser Eastern Churches*, p. 225.

[12] "The faith of Chalcedon was Caesar's religion, therefore it was not theirs" (the Copts'). Fortescue *Op. cit.*, p. 183.

had insisted on identifying itself with the empire lost the allegiance of the darker peoples of Egypt. Thus was consummated one part of the tragedy of the seventh century.

The second act of that tragedy was staged in the West, where that Church of the Martyrs for which Tertullian had spoken in fierce defiance against the empire apostatized to Islam in a body. The details differ from the story in Egypt: the essence is identical. In the East, it was a theological front of anti-Arianism followed by Monophysitism: in the West, Novatianists were followed by Donatists in fighting against Rome. In both areas, the church was used as a tool of empire, and the local Christians resented both the empire and its church. The church came as a "civilizing influence," using Greek in the East and Latin in the West to address Coptic speaking Egyptians and Punic-speaking Berbers. To match the *parabolani* of the Egyptian Church, the African Church had its *circumcelliones*—an armed body of fanatical anti-imperialists who supported the Donatists with military power. And just as, in Egypt, the first invaders were not welcomed, so the Africans bitterly fought the Vandals. And finally, just as Egypt welcomed a conqueror who came with an inclusive brotherhood, so African Christians, even more completely, accepted Islam.

The African Christian Church was utterly destroyed. Its adherents became Muslims; its buildings fell into disuse and ruin. Of its once weighty opinions in councils, little remains aside from the magnificent literary legacy of Tertullian, Cyprian, and Augustine. The total elimination of the African Church from Christendom can be charged squarely to the false identification of Christianity with the purposes of empire.

Although the African province, by the end of the fourth century, was the richest prize of the Roman Empire, Africa was never accorded anything more than colonial status. The Punic-speaking Berbers were looked upon as subjects, fit for exploitation. Both the temporal and the spiritual authorities followed this pattern. The symbolization of imperial dominance in the use of the Latin tongue instead of native languages underlined and emphasized the fact that Africans were accepted in the church not as equals but only as subjects.

It would be an assumption unwarranted by facts to conclude that the Church of the Empire, either in the East or in the West, deliberately cut itself off from its Egyptian and African churches because of what we today would call "racial" feelings. Indeed, in both cases, every effort was made to retain the Egyptians and the Africans within the church—and to keep them tractable. What we are justified in concluding is this: the refusal of the Church of the Empire to accord equality of status and consideration to the churches in colonial Egypt and Africa made these latter susceptible to a rival religion and imperium which offered inclusiveness in place of exclusiveness, equality instead of inequality.

With the loss of the Copts and the Berbers, Christianity became, for the first time, a white man's religion. In subsequent centuries it spread throughout Europe, being estopped from growing eastward and southward by the encircling arms of the Muslim pincers movement which ultimately pounded at the gates of Vienna and rested at the base of the Pyrenees. Thus, the loss of the darker peoples from the church, and the spread of Christianity exclusively amongst Northern European peoples, gave our religion its false and specious identification with the white race.

We are not saying that the membership of the African and Coptic churches was "Negroid." The residents of Egypt and of North Africa were Caucasoid Africans, principally Berbers in Africa and an intermixture of Semitic, Ahamic, Nubian and other peoples in Egypt. What we are saying is that all these "darker" peoples, had they continued within the church and had they been joined by the army of the faithful raised up in Asia by the Nestorians, would have made the complete identification of Christianity with white supremacy by men like Senator Bilbo somewhat more difficult.

In these stories we see an interesting refutation of the

sometimes repeated notion that "Christianity doesn't seem to flourish amongst the darker races." This is one of the most engaging forms of the white man's pride of race; but it is not borne out by a survey of the facts of history. When the darker peoples were in the church—up to the seventh century—they furnished at least their fair share of its principal teachers, thinkers, leaders, and spiritual strength. Five of the greatest theologians of the years A.D. 200 to 400 were Egyptians and Africans: Clement, Origen, Cyprian, Arius, Athanasius. The Coptic Church was a strong missionary church, moving out beyond the valley of the Nile to establish the Abyssinian Church, which still survives. The defection of the darker races from recognized Christianity thirteen centuries ago does not prove that only white men make good Christians. On the contrary, it raises the question of whether white men can be good Christians.

Nor is it possible to overstress the importance of this loss. Is it too much to suggest that the slave trade of the sixteenth to nineteenth centuries would not have been so easily possible if the church had not long before that become a white man's religion, putting black men outside the pale of its protective brotherhood? Certainly, it would not have been possible to defend chattel slavery with the excuse that it afforded an opportunity to bring the heathen black man under the gracious civilizing influences of the Christian faith—to save his soul by buying his body, thereby profiting the master in this world and the slave in the next. The whole history of American life and manners might have been profoundly different. It is not unlikely that there might have been no "race problem"—certainly not as we know it today—if, fifteen centuries ago, Christianity had not carried through its rapprochement with empire and begun to look down its nose at the "lesser" peoples.

The church gained an empire and lost humanity. The magnitude of that disaster has been softened by the passing of centuries; but the historical process which culminated in the modern heresy of white supremacy reached a provisional climax in the catastrophe of the seventh century, its greater and more devastating effects being unfolded in subsequent centuries. In the matter of racial inclusiveness, the church did not so much "fall" from an original inclusiveness as gradually lose a continuing battle against exclusiveness. Twelve centuries of identification of Christianity almost exclusively with the Caucasian peoples have all but erased the memory of that earlier, more inclusive church; and thus has arisen in our own day a man who dares to declare that the white man is the custodian of the gospel of Jesus Christ.

4. In the New World

When the Christians fought in Spain against the Moors, they combined their defense of empire and of religion, thus establishing a tradition which served well as a tool of their later conquest of the New World. The story of conquest, exploitation, despoliation, wholesale brutality and robbery, which is the history of the conquistadors in Central and South America, finds its beginnings in the contest with the Moors in Old Spain. In that contest, religious and racial attitudes were welded into a single pattern. The magnificent splendor of the Incas and the Aztecs was fit plunder for men who felt no inhibitions in carrying out their mission of conquest and freebootery. If converted and baptized, the Andean nonwhites of the New World might enjoy a subordinate position in the church; but in it or out of it, the nonwhites were considered to be of a lesser breed, rightfully enjoying a lower status in the eyes of God and man.

By the time the Dutch and English began to build their colonial empires in the New World the pattern was well established. Nor was there a nonwhite segment left within Christianity to cry out against this false identification of Christianity and the new imperialism. There is no blacker spot on the record of the Caucasian (not even the treatment of the Negro) than the two centuries of conquest of the North American continent by white men who slaughtered the Indian in the name of God and religious liberty. There is nothing in the record to show that the Pilgrim Fathers carried their guns on the way to church solely in the hope of sighting a turkey.

Arnold Toynbee has performed a service for us in pointing to the connection between the religious outlook and the imperialistic performance of the English and Dutch.[13] Appropriating with single-minded literalness the Old Testament notion of the Chosen People, the Protestant whites of northern Europe were relieved of any religious inhibitions which might possibly have qualified the rigors of conquest as they subjugated the North American continent. Similar use was made of the Old Testament notion of the Deity as a God of warfare. Thus, religious sanction was gained not merely for wresting the New Canaan from the (red) Canaanite, but also for exterminating the inhabitants to make room for the New Israel. Whatever vestiges of inclusiveness might have survived the great defections of the third and seventh centuries did not survive the Reformation.

It is worthy of note, however, that Catholic Maryland did not treat the American Indian in a manner markedly different from the practices of Puritan Massachusetts or Anglican Virginia. It is to the dissenters, Baptist and Quaker, in Rhode Island and Pennsylvania, not to the dominant orthodox groups, that we must turn to find examples of somewhat more enlightened attitudes. Nor do the Portuguese and the Belgians in Africa indicate that Catholicism necessarily guarantees more enlightened attitudes than Protestantism. The truth appears to be that from the seventh century until very recent times, Christianity in all of its forms has been more or less completely identified with the aspirations of white men in every quarter of the globe: in the Americas, as in Africa and in the Near East and Far East, when Christianity has capitulated to white imperialism, it has gained an empire and lost

[13] Arnold J. Toynbee, *A Study of History*, 6 vols. (Oxford University Press) 1935-1939. For numerous references, consult index in volume iii.

humanity. Only in recent generations has a contrary tendency begun to assert itself in the modern missionary movement, a development to which we now turn our attention.

5. THE BOOMERANG OF MISSIONS

In the nineteenth century, a new form of Christian imperialism developed. It was not always officially connected with or supported by governmental or commercial agencies. In fact, it frequently incurred the hostility both of government and of trader. Here, at least, the inclusive genius of Christianity began to reassert itself, in tentative form, sometimes arrogantly and falteringly. American and European Christianity reached out to the south and east, and offered to the peoples of the world the Good News of Christ.

The "Great Century"[14] of the world missionary movement saw an outpouring of lives and wealth so stupendous as to stagger the imagination. Thousands of the finest young men and women of Christendom went out to the far corners of the earth, carrying the Christian gospel and rendering Christian service. After all allowance is made for the cultural imperialism and arrogant paternalism implicit (and often explicit) in much of the missionary effort of the nineteenth century, and after the connection of missions with the economic and political imperialism of Europe and North America has been fully acknowledged—to our shame—the story of missions remains one of the most heroic records of altruistic endeavor which history has yet unfolded. Not the least important part of the story has been the revival of interest in Christianity and its work which the world mission has engendered in the home churches. The vision of a triumphant church, marching like an army with banners, bringing salvation to all the world, has stimulated the imaginations and awakened the sympathies (and opened the checkbooks) of men and women of the

[14] Cf. Kenneth Scott Latourette, *History of the Expansion of Christianity.* Harpers, 8 vols., 1937-1945.

churches as nothing else has done since the Crusades. We have thrown out the missions boomerang.

When we threw it out, there was no indication that we expected it to come back; but we certainly intended it to go out. The generation which threw out the boomerang was sure of the superiority of its faith, and tended also to be sure of the superiority of Western culture, the righteousness of imperialism, and the divine destiny of the white man to rule the world. With the compelling assurance of its faith, the nineteenth century drew back the arm of its strength and hurled the missions effort across the world. The boomerang made its magnificent swing across Asia, Africa, and the islands of the Seven Seas, awakening a great expectation in the hearts and minds of those who accepted Christianity.

A boomerang comes back. Christians around the world began to look to the homelands of the missionary effort for leadership and light.

What the missionary activity inevitably does accomplish, whether it expressly wills to do so or not, is to bring the world measurably within the limits of a single moral universe.[15]

The missionary carries a gospel of inclusive brotherhood. When his converts begin to take that gospel seriously, he is greatly embarrassed unless he is ready to practice what he preaches. And if the missionary begins to practice the inclusive brotherhood, he embarrasses the people in the churches back home. They sent him out to preach the gospel; but did they expect that they would be called on to practice what he preached? As the boomerang comes swinging back to us, we must catch it or it deals a smart blow to conscience and paralyzes the missionary effort. Either we agree to live by the principles of Christian brotherhood, which we have triumphantly affirmed and gloriously announced to all the world in our missionary effort, or else we stand convicted of one of the

[15] Robert E. Park in the Foreword to *Christian Missions and Oriental Civilization*, by Maurice T. Price. Shanghai, 1924.

greatest moral hoaxes of history. This may not have been fully apparent in the first generations of the missionary endeavor, when it was characterized more nearly by paternalism than by brotherhood. It is apparent today.

The moderator of the Selma, Alabama, Baptist Association has put the matter as pointedly as any writer. The article might just as well have come from any denomination and from any section of the United States. The missionary effort, argued the writer,[16] is faltering, not in the achievement of workers in the field, but in the falling off of money support back home. The reason is not far to seek. People are beginning to see at long last the contradiction in sending missionaries to Africa while refusing to exercise similar concern for Negroes within the United States. Wishing to escape hypocrisy, they seek escape from the dilemma not by becoming active at home but by abandoning the support of the missionary effort abroad.

The clear and present meaning of missions has never been better stated than by Rufus Jones in his chapter in the *Laymen's Missions Inquiry*:

> In every case the missionary as a guest among another race of people must be respectful to their type of culture and of their faith and aspiration, and he must be extremely sensitive not to wound their age-old habits and their achievements. . . . One cannot be a genuine friend and sharer of life without both giving and taking. It cannot be a "one-way" process. There must be mutual and reciprocal correspondence.[17]

This is the essential meaning of the missions boomerang as we have thrown it out, and as it begins its swing back.

It comes back to us not merely as an ideal, but also incarnate in people and expressed in incidents. Teachers in Christian colleges in China always have a period of soul-searching

---

[16] Edward B. Warren, "Why Southern Missions Falter," *Christian Century*, Vol. LI, No. 30, July 25, 1934, pp. 973-974.

[17] Rufus E. Jones, "Background and Objectives of Protestant Foreign Missions," in Supplementary Series, Vol. II of the *Laymen's Missions Inquiry*, p. xxi. Harpers, 1933.

difficulty as they send a promising graduate to America for further study. They take the student aside and carefully try to prepare him for what he will find when he arrives in "Christian" America. It will be different from the mission compound. He will have a "place" and he will be expected to stay in it. What is that "place"? Where are the words with which the missionary teacher can tell the young Chinese that, while she has been laboring to bring the circle of Christian brotherhood to Shansi and Shanghai, there are still a few segments broken from the arc in Demopolis and Duluth?

One particularly embarrassing blow of the missions boomerang is worth special mention. In some instances, the effect of Christian missions has been greatly to stimulate and strengthen the nationalistic aspirations, and therefore to support anti-imperialistic sentiments and movements, among colonial peoples. Korea (Chosen), for example, had a strong nationalistic movement directed toward independence from Japan; and the backbone of Korean nationalism was the Christian Church in Korea, planted and nurtured by Presbyterians and Methodists. In this instance, the European or American observer applauded, since it was Japan upon whom the brunt of the movement fell. But other cases in which Christian missions have stimulated the self-respect of a subjected people afford enlightening examples of the manner in which the Christian ethic, despite all attempts at political control of it, breaks out of institutional molds and germinates wider movements for freedom and equality. The relatively unimportant percentage of the Chinese people who are Christians have contributed to the Chinese nationalist movement the great preponderance of its leadership. In India, the direct and indirect influences of generations of missionary work have been to strengthen the resolve of the people of India to throw off the British yoke. The importance of this particular by-product of Christian missionary effort in India is documented by the requirement placed on all missionaries by His Majesty's Government, that they must pledge themselves to abstain from all political activity or connection with the nationalist movement, on pain of removal from the country. In Africa, the same pledge of political conformity to imperialism is exacted from missionaries, whether it is the British or the Portuguese or some other nation which does not wish missionaries to introduce yeasty notions. This phenomenon of the Christian mission becoming a threat to white imperialism is a source of acute embarrassment to churchmen at home. The missionaries have, in effect, turned the forces of their work against the white supremacy which often characterizes the home base.

Whether this has always and everywhere been the deliberate intent of missionary work is another matter. But, intended or not, the inevitable logic of the position of the sincere missionary ultimately drives him to take a stand that is sympathetic to the aspirations amongst the people with whom he identifies himself. The cultivation of self-reliance, initiative, and self-consciousness in a world of nation-states, together with the spread of education and the growth of numerical strength in the indigenous churches, has meant that, whether intended or not, the missionary effort has built an organization and sired a spirit which have inevitably become a part of the anti-imperialist thrust of colonial peoples. The missions boomerang has come back to smite the imperialism of white nations, as well as to confound the churches.

The growing edge of the Christian enterprise is now on the foreign missions field. It is there that the practical steps toward church union foreshadow the emergence of an ecumenical church. It is there that the problems of industrialism and exploitation have been most vigorously challenged by fearless pronouncement and forthright action.[18] It is there that the paternalism of the missionary venture has been cut away, and brotherhood has replaced it. It is in India, Africa, China, and Japan, in Hawaii and Ceylon, Galangue and Beirut, that Chris-

---

[18] For example, *Modern Industry and the African*, J. Merle Davis *et al.*, Macmillan, 1933; *The Economic Basis of the Church*, Vol. 5 of the "Madras Series," International Missionary Council, 1938.

tian missions have reached the fuller stature of Christian profession. The devolution from Caucasian control to Christian co-operation has gone steadily forward until, by the outbreak of World War II, it could be said that not one of the progressive mission boards was paternalistic in its field operations. The boomerang came hurtling full in the face of an astonished and timid church when, in the early summer of 1944, a Chinese bishop, just off the plane from Chungking, strode into a crowded conference of American churchmen to announce that he had been commissioned by his Chinese colleagues to request the immediate dispatching of half a dozen Negro Americans for work in China.

No man who is even remotely aware of what is going on in the missions fields can repeat the lie that the white man is the custodian of the gospel of Jesus Christ. The real question now becomes: Will the white man measure up to the challenge of the gospel of an inclusive brotherhood? Or will the churches of America and Europe today repeat the default of the third to sixth centuries, leading to another great defection?

CHAPTER IV

DEFIANCE

The resurgence of the inferior races and classes is evident in every dispatch from Egypt, Ireland, Poland, Roumania, India, and Mexico. It is called nationalism, patriotism, freedom or by other high sounding words; but it is everywhere the phenomenon of the long suppressed servile classes rising against the master races.
—MADISON GRANT in *The Passing of a Great Race*, Preface to the fourth edition, 1921.

FRUSTRATION breeds aggression. This generally recognized truth is now carefully documented.[1] This matter would be sufficiently serious if the frustrated individual felt himself deeply wronged but had no support from the idealistic professions of the dominant group; but when the dominant group affirms a creed of equality, and gives that creed the sanctions of its religion, while at the same time denying to large sections of the population access to the benefits of American democracy and the Christian life, the mind of the disadvantaged person ceases to follow the logic of the act. Resentment grows.

The growing rumble of discontent which any reader of the Negro press has known for years; the multiplication of "incidents" in shipyards and factories, in public conveyances and public places in all parts of the nation; the upthrust of an ugly spirit of counterassertion from one or another of the surging masses of submerged peoples—these are an index of the growing tensions within the nonwhite groups. The Negro soldier who trained in Louisiana, met Jim Crow both in the army and on his leaves in town, and bitterly concluded that, since he had been drafted to fight for democracy, the fight might as well begin right where he was, was not an individual incarna-

[1] John Dollard *et al., Frustration and Aggression.* Yale Univ. Press, 1933.

62

tion of evil. He expressed the unbearable tensions of frustration. His death in Alexandria, Louisiana, was as significant an index in the struggle for democracy as it would have been on any other of the battle fronts—abroad or at home. It signified a truth which is borne in upon us with unmistakable vigor and compelling accent: *the colored peoples of the world, including the racial minorities within the United States, are determined, as never before, to have done with white supremacy.*

This determination is directly associated with the sharpening of the contrasts between the democratic pronouncements of the United Nations, on the one hand, and the lack of democratic performance by the white men who settle the policies of most of those nations, on the other hand. The legacy of World War II in terms of race antagonisms sets the stage for momentous decisions. And the somber colors of the backdrop on the world stage forebode a tragic drama, unless the lines are written by men of determination and vision.

No one is surprised by this situation. Both secular and religious voices have been foretelling this day of decision for decades.[2] The Lord of History is long-suffering, but He has regard for Nineveh as well as Jerusalem. If the Jonahs of today are angry over the withering of the gourd vine of world power which sprang up overnight and has continued its shade for three short centuries, they are reminded that God has an interest in other peoples on the earth also. The fact that He sits in judgment on the processes of history is the assurance that white supremacy cannot longer endure. The instability of evil is our assurance of the moral order.

There are some men who still refuse to believe that the days of white supremacy are numbered. When they read lines like

[2] The writings of Madison Grant, Lothrop Stoddard, C. C. Josey, and Charles A. Lindbergh are typical examples of the warnings against the "Yellow Peril" from the secular side. Among more recent expressions from religious writers are those of Pearl Buck, Paul Hutchinson, and Henry Smith Leiper. Twenty years have passed since three books called attention to the matter in religious terms: Basil J. Mathews, *The Clash of Color* and Robert E. Speer, *Of One Blood,* both published by the Missionary Education Movement in 1924; and J. H. Oldham, *Christianity and the Race Problem,* Doran, 1924.

these, they see red and begin to fulminate. That is why it is necessary to measure the dynamics of color in the world scene, that we may know whether these men can be encouraged in their defiance. It is not enough that we remind ourselves that the Caucasian is outnumbered two to one in the world's population.[3] We must also ask what this portends—and particularly, what is indicated if the policy of white supremacy is pursued beyond this present hour?

History has an elephant's memory. One incident which played a major part in bringing on the Pacific phase of World War II, contributing measurably to the frustration that breeds aggression, took place at Versailles in 1919.[4] The proposal was made by an *ally* of the United States and Great Britain that there be written into the Covenant of the League of Nations a provision calling for equality of status and consideration for citizens of all nations, members of the League, with no distinctions being made "either in law or in fact, on account of race or nationality." Largely on the insistence of Prime Minister Hughes of Australia, the British and American delegations brought influence to bear upon the delegation from our ally, Japan, so that the proposal was withdrawn. Mr. Hughes used a polite form of political blackmail, threatening to campaign against the whole League idea in the western United States and in certain of the British dominions where anti-Oriental feeling was ready to be aroused. Under this pressure, the contemplated section on race equality was withdrawn. The Japanese delegates then countered with the suggestion that there be incorporated in the preamble of the Covenant, where it had no binding force, an innocuous sentence calling for the "endorsement of the principles of the equality of nations and the just treatment of their nationals." The adoption of this sentiment, while it would have had no force in international law and would not have been binding upon the member nations,

[3] See above, Chap. I, sec. 2.
[4] Paul Birdsall, *Versailles Twenty Years After,* Reynal & Hitchcock, 1941. See also the chapter on "The Race Demon" in Paul Hutchinson's *From Victory to Peace*, Willett & Clark, 1943.

would have saved face for the Japanese delegates. But when the vote was taken, although every vote cast was cast in favor of the proposal, there were two silent nations at the table. Since the measure did not have the unanimous approval of all nations represented, Mr. Wilson (as chairman) ruled that the measure had failed of unanimous adoption and could not be incorporated in the preamble of the Covenant. The two nations not voting were Great Britain and the United States.

No one can now declare with certainty whether or not the Covenant of the League of Nations would have been ratified even by the nations which did become members had the provision for race equality been included in the Covenant. The conjectural reconstruction of possible historical alternatives is hazardous and unprofitable. But from the perspective of a quarter century of bitter experience, two comments may be permitted: (1) *if* the League notion had to fail on its first attempt, it would have been better for it to die on its feet, standing firmly for a principle, than for it to stagger weakly to oblivion; and (2) if the League were to have had a genuine opportunity for life, the recognition of the basic justice of race equality was a *sine qua non*. The action of the United States and Great Britain in refusing to grant the principle of race equality at Versailles in 1919 meant but one thing to them and to all the world. It meant that these two nations insisted on the principle of white supremacy, and that they were prepared to sacrifice the hope of the peace of the world for that dogma. Their wish was granted.

Whether the policy of white supremacy will be the policy of Great Britain and the United States in the future is not yet clear. To reveal how obscure the probabilities are, it may be useful to set down a bit of recent history, pursuing the prospects of race equality and white supremacy through the war years and into the United Nations conference at San Francisco.

As we follow this development, we cannot forget the promise that a peace built on white supremacy is the guarantee

of tomorrow's global war on race lines. The resentment of
the colored peoples, fed by the arrogance of the colorless,
builds toward that climax. This truth has never been put more
directly than by the author of *The Good Earth*:

The deep patience of colored peoples is at an end. Everywhere among
them is the same resolve for freedom and equality that white Americans
and British have, but it is a grimmer resolve, for it includes the determination to be rid of white rule and exploitation and white race
prejudice, and nothing will weaken this will.[5]

If the white man defies God by claiming white supremacy, the
moral order asserts itself in the calling forth of counterassertion from the nonwhite: the voice of a brother's blood cries
unto God from the ground. Will Cain's answer be the only
reply?

1. CAIN'S ANSWER?

From the time of the announcement of the Atlantic Charter,
on through the weary months of the war, the common citizen
was made repeatedly to wonder whether or not his country
intended to give Cain's answer or some other. The Atlantic
Charter, when it was first published, shone like a beacon light
of bright hope for the darker peoples of the world. But its
announcement was speedily followed by "clarifying" statements from Whitehall and the White House, creating a confusion which can only be clarified by action. Embarrassed over
the evident fact that the darker peoples evidently expected the
Charter to mean what it said, the Foreign Office and the State
Department, properly supported by Downing Street and the
White House, proceeded, step by step, to emasculate the
Charter, removing all racial connotations, making clear that it
was not to apply to India, Africa, the Island Indies, or Puerto
Rico. By the summer of 1944, all notion that any change in
status for the colored peoples of the world was implied in the
Atlantic Charter had been redundantly corrected. The Char-

[5] Pearl Buck, *American Unity and Asia*, p. 25. John Day, 1942.

ter had been quietly buried; Secretary Hull had pronounced a solemn funeral oration in a radio broadcast, and Mr. Churchill had planted a few roses on the grave. During the summer of 1944, the Prime Minister reverted several times to the subject, as though to make sure that there was no resurrection of what was decently buried. And through the winter of 1944-45, both Mr. Roosevelt and Mr. Churchill, with Mr. Eden, went out of their way on several occasions to emphasize that the Atlantic Charter had "just the same significance" it had had when first handed out to newspapermen. The same significance —no more.

The *coup de grâce* had been given to racial meanings of the Charter months earlier in the four prior agreements arrived at before the November-December, 1943, meetings at Moscow and Teheran. As Secretary Hull revealed in a press conference on November 16, agreement had been reached between the governments of Britain, the United States, and the Soviet Union (as preconditions for the Moscow Conference and its Teheran sequel) with reference to the future and disposal of liberated or reoccupied territories, shedding clear light on the actual significance of the Atlantic Charter. It had been agreed: (1) that no decision would be made as to the future of any of the "liberated" territories prior to the end of hostilities in each of these territories; (2) that policing of each reoccupied (or occupied) area would be carried on by the armies in control at the time fighting ceased; (3) that when the decision as to the future of any area was made, it would be made *by the victor nations*; and (4) that any plebiscite or other matters bearing on the "self-determination" of peoples would be taken up for consideration by the victor nations only after they had finished redrawing the map.[6] While Mr. Hull's candor in making public these agreements marks a distinct advance over secret diplomacy, what the announcement actually meant was merely that the Atlantic Charter was dead. The events of succeeding weeks, with the statements of Mr.

[6] Dispatch to the New York *Times*, November 17, 1943.

Churchill and Mr. Eden to Parliament, underscored the meaning which Mr. Hull's disclosure had made plain, so that the
Christian Century concluded that the Atlantic Charter was
now recognized as "the idealistic hoax it should have been
known to be from the day of its promulgation."[7]

And since the Atlantic Charter had been frankly scuttled,
there should have been little surprise when no Pacific Charter
was forthcoming. Mr. Willkie's plea from Chungking that one
be drawn fell on deaf ears. On February 1, 1944, the President issued a carefully written statement defining the ends for
which the United States was fighting in the Pacific:

> Our task in expelling the Japs from Burma, Malaya, Java, and other
> territory is military. We recognize that our British and Dutch brothers
> in arms are as determined to throw the Japs out of Malaya and the
> Dutch East Indies as we are determined to free the Philippines. We
> propose to help each other, on the roads and waters and above them,
> eastward to these places and beyond to Tokyo.

The careful differences in phrasing in this statement are
startlingly clear in the meanings revealed. For some time the
United States has declared that the Philippines shall be free;
and that is reiterated as part of our reason for fighting in the
Pacific. In addition, Mr. Roosevelt's statement made clear
that we were fighting not to free the peoples of Malaya and
Indonesia from the British and Dutch, but to "throw the Japs
out" and restore the white man's empire in the Far East.
There was no longer need to conjecture. Many Americans
had long feared that one of the purposes of our Far Eastern
campaign was to restore white imperialism. After February
1, 1944, they knew.

But they should have been prepared for this statement of
American war aims in the Pacific if they had read the declara-
tion issued after the Cairo conference in December of 1943.
That declaration affirmed that the United States, Great
Britain, and China "covet no gains for themselves and have
no thought of territorial expansion." These nations did not,

[7] Editorial, January 26, 1944, Vol. LXI, No. 4, p. 100.

however, indicate any decrease of prewar holdings or lessening of prewar programs of commercial expansion and penetration. The Cairo statement implied the return to the *status quo ante bellum* which was confirmed in the February 1 statement. No clarifying words, however, came out of the Cairo conference as to the future of the island bases in the Pacific built up by Japan as mandates in the interwar years. This was in accordance with the general notions of the prior agreements of Moscow-Teheran, although the Chinese were not parties to these meetings. Yet, the silence of Cairo regarding the island bases in the Pacific was particularly ominous.

As if to answer our queries regarding the future of the island bases, voices of authority spoke from Australia and from the United States, making claims on the future. Australia asked for a great encircling girdle of island bases "for military safety" and as steppingstones for peaceful penetration of the Asiatic mainland for commercial purposes. Senators and congressmen in Washington declared that the United States must acquire and fortify a vast system of island bases in the South Pacific, echoing the statement of the late Secretary Knox calling for a navy so big that no one would be able to challenge its supremacy in the Pacific Ocean "for the next hundred years." That navy was to have island bases everywhere. The Big Stick policy implied in these many statements was affirmed as a part of presidential policy in the broadcast from Bremerton which Mr. Roosevelt made on the completion of his August, 1944, visit to Hawaiian and Aleutian outposts.

Thus, from two sides of the Pacific, two nations whose policies have historically identified them as believers in white supremacy spoke through responsible representatives in terms which literally sought to make the Pacific Ocean a white man's pond. With a billion men of color living on the western shores of that ocean and on its rich islands, such planning for the future does not reassure the Asiatic peoples. That was the situation as we approached the San Francisco meetings on World Organization.

We came up to San Francisco with little hope that the once

fair promises of the Atlantic Charter would be realized as a result of the war's slaughter and the peacemaking. We knew that the imperialisms of European nations in the Near East, the Far East, and the Pacific were not to be disturbed; and we saw a rising demand in the United States that "for reasons of military security" this nation should become an active partner in the aggressive policy of world domination by the white man. There was, therefore, no reason to expect any change in the situation in Africa, either. Indeed, we were promised that there would be none. Coincident with the invasion of North Africa, the Allied nations through their responsible spokesmen solemnly pledged themselves not to disturb the integrity of the French Empire there. It is a fair presumption that nothing is intended to disturb the imperial interests of any other European nation in Africa—whether British, Portuguese, Spanish, or French. Possibly the Italians would find themselves displaced by some other overlord.

Yet in the whole vast continent of Africa there are but two islands of racial sanity. Except for Ethiopia and Liberia, the continent is owned and operated by and for European peoples. World War II was not calculated to change that situation. Whatever aspirations the black man may have permitted himself to entertain in the directions of freedom and integrity, these hopes would be the measure not of his realization but of his disillusionment and resultant embitterment. Lying like a giant question mark at the feet of Europe, Africa is the home of the world's most embittered and entangled race relations.[8] It may possibly provide the spark to ignite the tinder for tomorrow which the white man is storing up in Asia and the Pacific.

If now we move the spotlight of scrutiny to the Western Hemisphere, we observe that the practice of the theory of white supremacy in the United States is not calculated to win

[8] See *Africa and the Atlantic Charter*, a report prepared by the Phelps-Stokes Fund, New York (1942), in the days when it was still thought by some that the Atlantic Charter was to be used as a guide in establishing policies of dominant nations toward colonial peoples.

friends and influence people to be good neighbors. We habitually call the nations to the south of the Rio Grande "Latin America." This is our shorthand device for escaping the necessity of considering each of the Central and South American nations as a sovereign people in its own right, commanding our respect; and it is also one way of expressing, in euphemistic terms, the fact that all these other nations are alike in differing from the United States linguistically and racially. "Latin," when used in this instance by citizens of the United States, actually means "nonwhite."

With the possible exceptions of Costa Rica in Central America and of Argentina in South America, none of our neighbors to the south can be called "Caucasian" nations. Underlying all of them (except some of the islands in the Caribbean) is the Indian culture; and in some instances (as Peru, where the Caucasians make up only five per cent of the population), the Indian motif is the dominant one. Spanish is the official language of many of these nations; but the largest, Brazil, is Portuguese speaking. French, Dutch, German, and English are used elsewhere. The ethnic composition of the Americas to the south (excepting only Costa Rica and possibly Argentina), including the spreading crescent of the islands of the Caribbean, is an intermixture of a variety of stocks: African, Indian, Asiatic, and European. The few instances of relatively "pure" European settlements are due to comparatively recent migration. The Americas to the south are populated primarily by peoples who are not complimented by being called "white" and who resent any assumption of superiority by the "white" United States of North America.

As long as the United States clings to a policy of white supremacy within its own borders, and as long as this nation lends its support to the white supremacy patterns in Africa and Asia and the islands of the seas, the Good Neighbor policy is doomed to partial success at best, more likely to total failure, and possibly to becoming a profound embarrassment when it backfires upon us. Let us suppose that the United States

State Department were to cultivate the duplicity necessary
to hide from the Americas to the South the truth about Jim
Crow in the States: who will guarantee that our good neighbors to the south will cultivate the gullibility necessary to
swallow the tale?   Hemispheric solidarity, which was once
the keystone of American foreign policy and which is still
an important stone in whatever arch of peace and security
we shall be able to erect, will not be cemented into the peace
of tomorrow by racial practices which are a direct affront
to the peoples of the other Americas.   The Act of Chapul-
tepec pressed the separate stones together; but the cement
of racial understanding is yet to be supplied.

The acuteness of this problem can be illustrated with fresh
vividness.   Let one instance suffice.   The "Zoot Suit" riots
in Los Angeles in June, 1943, were the occasion for editorial
comment in every newspaper of Latin America.   With one
voice they protested that this was "the same type of Hitlerian
racial intolerance against which the United Nations are now
warring."   The National Autonomous University witnessed
Mexico's first open anti-*yanqui* demonstration in years.   That
rioting was finally quieted when the rector of the university
assured the students that President Roosevelt's liberal policies
absolved him of all blame in the recent riots in the United
States and told the students to request the United States
government "by means of a widespread press and radio
campaign, to make the North American public realize that
the people of Mexico, mostly of mixed Indian and Spanish
blood, cannot fight this war with enthusiasm side by side
with a country that harbors racial prejudice."[9]

Wherever on the globe we turned the spotlight of ethical
scrutiny, the question mark of color stood out, as we approached the San Francisco meetings in April of 1945.   North
America, Central and South America, Asia, Africa, Australia,
everywhere except on the European continent; and there
the costliest conflict in history was closely connected with

[9] "Pachuco Troubles," *Interamerican*, Vol. II, No. 8, August, 1943, p. 6.

the notion of a master race which sought to dominate the world.

Then something happened. Some day the inside story of the San Francisco meetings on World Organization will be written. Until that time, one can only record what one learned at first hand in San Francisco. There is little point in trying to assign credit for the constructive steps that were taken. Certainly the results in the United Nations Charter were, in some respects, far better than there was any hope of their being as the meetings opened. In other respects, our worst fears were justified.

Nothing was done radically to alter the world pattern of white imperialism. Long debates over trusteeship came to nothing, as far as the great imperial systems are concerned. Perhaps San Francisco was not the place to expect steps to be taken on this issue.[10] We were told that such matters were not on the agenda, that they belonged properly to the peace settlement and subsequent developments, not to the planning of the structure of the United Nations Organization. So we expected little to be done on the matter of white imperialism at San Francisco. Our expectations were justified.

On the other hand, the Charter drawn at San Francisco marked an advance over the Dumbarton Oaks preliminary document at several strategically important points. Written into the Charter at several points is the statement which the United States and Great Britain had refused to admit into the Covenant of the League of Nations in 1919. The principle of the equality of all persons, without reference to race, color, nationality, language or sex, is explicitly affirmed at least twice in the body of the Charter, where it has binding force upon every nation which ratifies the Charter and becomes a member of the United Nations Organization. For the first time in the history of the world, the principle of

[10] But see the amazingly detailed and courageous analysis of *Color and Democracy: Colonies and Peace*, by W. E. B. DuBois, which Harcourt, Brace & Company published just in time for the meetings.

white supremacy has been openly, clearly, explicitly denied in the name of the peoples of the world and in behalf of social equality.

Moreover, this principle is to be implemented—however feebly—by direct efforts to put it into effect. Under the Economic and Social Council are to be designated commissions, charged with responsibility for putting the ideals of the Charter into practice. The Commission on Human Rights may reasonably be expected to concern itself with the matter of racial arrogance as a violation of the principle of race equality affirmed by the Charter. A commission to be concerned with intercultural education and understanding will bear a heavy burden of educative effort in trying to bring the segmented world to a realization of its essential oneness and interrelatedness. If these commissions have no power to enforce their findings, indeed no power to investigate and make findings, they nevertheless mark a definite step toward the recognition of the full responsibility of the powerful nations for the creation of that justice and brotherhood without which there can be no peace.

2. The Domestic Angle

In the minds of nonwhite America, much that happened during the war years heightened the tensions and increased the feelings of resentment. The largest racial minority group within the United States, comprising approximately one-tenth of the total, felt the brunt of Jim Crow with a sensitiveness increased because of the democratic war aims which the nation repeatedly affirmed. Other minorities, though numerically smaller, shared the experience of Negro America.

This story has been so well documented that it is unnecessary to repeat even its outlines here.[11]   Discrimination

[11] Charles S. Johnson's *To Stem This Tide* (Pilgrim Press, 1943) summarizes the situation as of the summer of 1943 in a dozen areas of tension in all parts of the nation. Carey McWilliams's *Prejudice* covers the matter of Americans of Japanese ancestry, with Galen Fisher's "Balance Sheet on Japanese Evacuation"

in the armed forces, where only 50,000 out of 700,000
Negroes in the army were used as combat troops, only two
squadrons of fighter planes were piloted by Negroes, men
of color advanced in the navy beyond the rank of petty
officer only with extreme rarity, Negro nurses were publicly
humiliated by their superior (white) officers in the presence
of German prisoners of war whom they were assigned to
serve—such discrimination in the armed forces was the most
important wartime irritant of racial feelings. Widespread
discrimination in employment in the war industries, for which
management and labor bore about equal shares of responsibility, were only partly corrected through the achievements
of the Fair Employment Practice Committee. Inadequate
housing in most centers of war industries and the almost
universal practice of discriminatory assignment of such housing as was available were highlighted by the riots in Detroit
in connection with the Sojourner Truth project. Congestion
of travel, with a multitude of incidents, particularly on local
conveyances in war-crowded centers, but also appearing in
interstate travel on trains and buses, increased the general
resentment of the colored peoples. Political disfranchisement, and especially the poll tax and the white primary,
emphasized the Negro's feeling of injustice when he was
denied the right to vote and to hold office in a democracy
which drafted him to die for the rights he could not exercise.
One young man, drafted from college in the middle of his
senior year, summed it up in words which became classic
through repetition and reprinting in Negro circles: "You
can put on my tombstone this epitaph—

(in the *Christian Century*, August-September, 1943), as a valuable discussion of
that aspect of the problem. Walter White's *A Rising Wind* (Doubleday, Doran,
1945), describing what the author saw in the North African and European
theaters of war, is the most disturbing reading coming from any source in a
long time. Articles in the daily press and in periodicals too numerous to list
(of which Wendell Willkie's last published words, in *Collier's*, are a notable
example) have presented the matter of color discrimination to the American
public so that even the blindest must have been aware of what was happening.

HERE LIES A BLACK MAN
KILLED BY A YELLOW MAN
FOR THE PROFIT OF A WHITE MAN."

In modified form, the same general situation prevailed for all other racial minorities in the American scene, with the possible exception of the Chinese and Filipino Americans. The Chinese were suddenly "discovered," in a mild and paternalistic fashion, as desirable citizens—a sharp reversal of the attitude that had prevailed since the 1850's first brought them to our shores in large numbers. But the belated repeal of the Exclusion Act (for China), permitting 105 Chinese annually to come within the immigration quota, is a face-saving device which makes no appreciable change in the situation. And the attitude of friendliness toward Chinese Americans was too much a function of expediency during a military alliance for it to promise lasting changes in the attitudes of white Americans toward Chinese Americans. No restrictive covenants were abrogated in any American city for the purpose of welcoming as neighbors the Chinese who were now officially to be welcomed as citizens. Only the Filipinos appeared to have a genuine guarantee that World War II would improve their lot: they had a promise that the white man would take his foot off their necks and his hand out of their pockets. The date for emancipation was agreed upon.

With the war's end, the halting of war production and the lagging of peace production began to strain tempers to the breaking point. The animosities stored up on both sides of the racial dikes threatened to break through, inundating the nation in a bath of strife similar to the tidal wave that swept the country after World War I. With the spread of unemployment and the drifting of dislocated populations, many (if not most) of the urban centers were desperately throwing up earthworks in the shape of mayors' committees and committees on civic unity. It was impossible to forecast what would happen. All that we could be sure of (and it was enough) as the war ended and peace broke out was that the manner in which color caste dominated the thinking and acting of America during the war period was not calculated to ease the tensions or to give nonwhite Americans a feeling of security and of belonging. Resentment feeds on discrimination. And when Senators Bilbo and Eastland stood before packed galleries to utter their infamous insults and slanders of all nonwhite Americans, even though they thought they were speaking words that would be welcomed by millions of white Americans, they so far exceeded the bounds of decency and fair play that even the white press of the South spanked them roundly. But resentment continued to grow. Cain's answer to the voice of a brother's blood will not be good enough.

Defiance calls forth defiance. Denying the responsibilities of brotherhood, Cain is forced to defy God also. But the defiant cry of a brother's blood also reaches the ears of the Just One. The partial promises of San Francisco and the partial efforts of scattered groups throughout the nation must be expanded rapidly and intensively if the dissolution of civilization is to be averted. If the Caucasian at the peace table repeats the mistakes of Versailles and attempts once more to fasten white supremacy upon the colored world, and if Caucasian America continues to insist that this is a white man's country, it is likely that this act of defiance will be his final tragic act on the stage of history. The atomic bomb is here.

CHAPTER V

DECEPTION

Of all the mean excuses by which men blind themselves to the fact that social and moral forces influence the spirit of man, none is so mean as that which ascribes the difference in behaviour and character to natural, innate differences.

—JOHN STUART MILL

A DEFIANT man is in no mood to be humbled. He therefore adds to his defiance, deceit. He sees no other way to escape despair. The imperious demands of conscience, daily crying for a resolution of his dilemma in terms he is unwilling to accept, drive him through a galaxy of emotionalism, evasiveness, and deception.[1]

1. THE DELUSION OF WHITE SUPERIORITY

The delusion of superiority rests on the fact of supremacy for its proof. It is a curious trick of fate which brought onto the world scene two otherwise unrelated movements at the same moment of world history. Each in its own right had great significance: the two, when coupled in historical process, gave birth to the dogma of white superiority. The Industrial Revolution and the Great Enlightenment are the parents whose union sired the notion of Caucasian superiority. Before these two world events, the dogma as we know it was not in existence.

Under the aegis of the Industrial Revolution, the Northern

[1] Originally, I wrote five additional chapters for this book, covering about half the outlined materials describing these tortuous processes which are seen in contemporary life and thought. The elimination of most of these materials, in the interest of readability, may make for an apparent dogmatism in the present chapter. The supporting argument has been deleted, leaving only the skeleton of assertion.

Europeans and the white inhabitants of North America came into a position of world dominance they had not previously enjoyed. At the same time, political democracy was nurtured by the spread of the teachings of Rousseau and Tom Paine. Thus it came about that the notion of the Rights of Man came to flower at the same historical moment that the white man came to dominate the earth. In the coupling of the two movements, the doctrine of the Rights of Man was perverted into a justification of the rights of white men. Founded in a belief in Natural Law, and buttressed by its utilitarian service to the purposes of white dominance, this dogma was destined to color large sections of American and European thinking. It reached its intellectual apotheosis in the writings of Count Gobineau and Houston Stewart Chamberlain. It was practically applied in the notion of Nordic superiority in Hitler's Europe and in the dogma of white supremacy in Christian America.

The genesis of the dogma of white superiority reveals a fundamental confusion between supremacy and superiority. The first is an undeniable fact of the present world; the second is an invention of the mind to defend the first. Since he now rules the world, the white man deceives himself into thinking that he does so by *right*: he is supreme because he is superior. He then completes the closed circle of false logic by arguing that the superiority justifies supremacy. One hand washes the other.

The ease with which this notion has won its acceptance is exceeded only by the recency of its promulgation. It is a very new thing in the civilized world, and rests on an exceedingly foreshortened view of history. Those who would argue *post hoc, ergo propter hoc* to establish the notion of Caucasian superiority over what Kipling's contemptuous phrase calls the "lesser breeds without the law" can do so only by limiting their view of history to very recent centuries and by disregarding the future. They must wear the blinders of historical ignorance if they are to deceive themselves into believing in the myth of white superiority.

They cannot go back to Charlemagne to the time when the ancestors of the present great nations of Northern Europe were crude tribesmen living in the semibarbarian state of a huntsman's culture. They dare not go back of Charlemagne to the time of the glory that was Greece and the grandeur that was Rome. They must expurgate the editions of Caesar's *Gallic Wars* which they permit their high school children to read, deleting the Roman's assertion that the Angles (who are one half of the hybrid mixture called Anglo-Saxon) are poor material as slaves because they lack the mental abilities necessary for civilization.[2] They cannot permit themselves to recall that a highly developed Mayan culture flourished in Central America centuries before Italians and Spaniards and Portuguese began to swarm over the New World in search of the gold which the Indian peoples used for body ornaments rather than as an object of murder, piracy, enslavement, and conquest. They will ignore the civilizations of Babylonia and Assyria. They will not admit that, while their own ancestors were in goatskins, mother Nile cradled the glories of Egyptian culture. They have no stomach for the truths of contrast between their ancestral lineage and the achievements of China, of India, of Polynesia, or of Africa.[3] All that is stricken from the record. History must begin with the period of white ascendancy; for if he dropped his plumb line into history at any earlier period, the Caucasian would discover quite different contours of racial supremacy. He could then hold to the notion that supremacy proves superiority only if he was willing to grant that superiority is as mutable as supremacy. In that case, he is not talking about the superiority of any biological racial strain: he is talking about a myth.

Coming late on the scene, and inheriting the accumulated contributions of all the civilizations that went before, the

[2] For a discussion of the universality of cultural interchange, see *When Peoples Meet: A Study of Race Relations and Culture Contacts*, edited by Alain Locke and Bernard Stern, pp. 30-81. New York: Progressive Education Ass., 1942.

[3] Perhaps the least well known of all these earlier civilizations is the African. Melville J. Herskovits, *The Myth of the Negro Past* (Harper & Brothers, 1943), tells the story which refutes the widely held superstition that early Negro civilizations were demonstrations of racial inferiority.

Northern European and his American cousin now stand like fantastic Tarzans, beating their breasts and braying to Heaven that they are lords of the earth. The Caucasian did not invent most of the basic devices of civilization: he inherited them from the "lower" (or, better, the *earlier*) races. The wheel, the lever, the smelting of iron, the use of gunpowder, the whole basic mathematical hypotheses and number systems on which technological development rests, the use of an alphabet and a written language, the science of politics and government—all the basic devices of civilization were hammered out on the anvil of experience by peoples who flourished while the white man was still in the cradle of civilized infancy.[4] The moral and ethical insights which are the finest of all his heritages, and which the Caucasian honors in the breach when he talks of his alleged superiority, are inherited from an ancient Oriental culture which flourished in Asia Minor at a time when human sacrifice was still a part of the religious practice of the inhabitants of Northern Europe and the British Isles. The Caucasian who likes to take pride in his ancestry cannot arbitrarily stop at a designated point and refuse to go back to his ancestral beginnings. It is as legitimate to make comparison of his ancestry and that of other groups in the year 500 B.C. or A.D. 100 as it is to make the comparison at the time the *Mayflower* sailed.

If at this present moment of history the northern European cultures stand taller and their peoples see farther than those of any preceding generation, it is in large part because the Caucasian today stands on the accumulated achievements of all these others who have gone before and who have built into the structure of civilization stones which are the foundations for later superstructures. Civilization is an accumulative process in which the latecomer is heir to the achievements of his precursors. It is only in the sense that he has come latest on the stage, and uses all the settings and properties of his predecessors, that the Caucasian can strut his act. His one great point of superiority is that he came late.

[4] Cf. Locke and Stern, *op. cit.*, pp. 25-85, 308-317.

With a curious quirk of cerebration, the white man then turns to look at other groups which appear to him not yet to have reached the pinnacle of civilization. He calls them "backward" peoples because they come to cultural maturity even later than he. Both those who arrived before and those who will arrive later are inferior—the one because they come too soon, the other because they come too late. He alone is superior who rides the car which at the moment is at the top of the ferris wheel of civilization. Others have preceded him, proving their inferiority by going over the crest and beginning their descent, while still others who follow him have proved their inferiority (*as he did not,* a thousand years ago!) by not yet reaching the top.

Another curious piece of deception is the argument that all those who come after will merely appropriate the achievements of the twentieth century Caucasian. This notion ignores the manner of our own inheritance of the accumulations of civilized progress before us. We cannot afford to lose our sense of superiority by acknowledging indebtedness to any lesser peoples.

To argue from the obvious fact of present white supremacy to the fiction of inherent white superiority is possible only if all of human history prior to the past three or four centuries is disregarded, and only if logic is prostituted to serve the intentions of the reasoner rather than to follow the rules of intelligence. It might almost be said that the use of such tricks of intellect is itself a standing refutation of the claim to innate superiority. In any case, the refusal to face facts, and the consequent necessity to misuse logical processes illogically, are recognizable as pathological conditions not unassociated with moral uneasiness.

2. THE DEMENTIA OF WHITE SUPREMACY

Even when he does not cling to the notion of an innate superiority proved by history, the Caucasian finds himself driven to defend his supremacy on some plausible grounds.

His next line of defense is an assertion of white supremacy which becomes a possessive obsession, a form of demoniac possession. Fortunately not supported by scientific investigation, these dementias nevertheless have a remarkable survival power in contemporary culture.

Twenty years ago there appeared a volume from the pen of a Dartmouth College professor which has not subsequently been duplicated. It represents the final effort on the part of American scholarship to give a rationale for the doctrine of white supremacy. This last gasp of academically respectable race chauvinism as it went down for the third time beneath the rising tide of scientific fact is useful as a final exhibition of the dogma of racial superiority in respectable academic dress. It also serves as a portrait of the skeleton of superstition which the scholastic clothing covered, exposing the structure of the great deception. The argument of Professor Josey's book[5] has, of course, been duplicated scores of times by the master race propagandists of the past decade

[5] Charles Conant Josey, *Race and National Solidarity* (Scribners, 1923). The literature of the "supremacy" of Nordics (or Teutons or Caucasians or Aryans or whites) was prolific in the twenties, following World War I. A few of the more important titles: Count Arthur Gobineau, *The Inequality of the Human Races* (London: trans. 1915); Houston Stewart Chamberlain, *Foundations of the Nineteenth Century* (Dodd, 1912); Edward M. East, *Mankind at the Crossroads* (Scribners, 1923); Madison Grant, *The Passing of the Great Race* (4th ed., Scribners, 1921); Ellsworth Huntington, *Civilization and Climate* (Yale Univ. Press, 1919), *The Character of the Races* (Scribners, 1924); Ernest Sevier Cox, *White America* (Richmond, Va.: The White America Society, 1927); Sir Arthur Keith, *The Antiquity of Man* (Lippincott, 1915); Gustave Le Bon, *The Psychology of Peoples: Its Influence on Their Evolution* (London, 1898—reprinted 1924); C. L. Redfield, *Human Heredity* (The Author, Chicago, 1921); Lothrop Stoddard, *Rising Tide of Color Against White Supremacy,* (Scribners, 1920), *The Revolt Against Civilization: The Menace of Under Man* (Scribners, 1922); J. W. Gregory, *The Menace of Colour: A Study of the Difficulties Due to the Association of White and Coloured Races, With An Account of Measures Proposed For Their Solution, and Special Reference to White Colonization in the Tropics* (London: Seeley, Service & Co., 1924); Sir Leo Chiozza Money, *The Peril of the White* (London: W. Collins Sons, 1925); Wyndham Lewis, *Paleface: the Philosophy of the Melting Pot* (London: Chatts and Windus, 1929); and James Denson Sayres, *Can the White Race Survive?* (Washington, D. C.: Independent Publishing Co., 1929.) For a popular running commentary on these notions as shown in the editing and misrepresenting of the news, see the files of any Hearst newspaper.

in Germany and elsewhere, and it has had one distinguished supporter of its general thesis in the British anthropologist, Sir Arthur Keith, who has been effectually answered by his compatriot, M. F. Ashley Montagu.[6] Aside from Sir Arthur, no person of established academic repute in the past two decades in the English-speaking world has attempted to give intellectually respectable defenses to the theory of Caucasian superiority. The doctrine is still widely held by the "man in the street," as well as by a good many men in pews and pulpits, illustrating the lag between scholarship and education.

In the meantime, both the natural sciences and the social sciences have made great strides toward the objective of establishing scientifically validated facts regarding the question of racial differences. The fifteen years preceding the outbreak of World War II saw the publishing of an enormous amount of excellent material in the field of race, race relations, and race differences, climaxed by the definitive work of Gunnar Myrdal and his associates whose research and publication were made possible by a generous subsidy from the Carnegie Corporation.[7] While much remains to be done in pushing even further the advances thus far made, we know enough about racial matters now so that we can reliably affirm that the old lies are lies, and nothing more.

[6] Sir Arthur Keith, *The Place of Prejudice in Modern Civilization* (John Day, 1931). M. F. Ashley Montagu, *Man's Most Dangerous Myth: The Fallacy of Race* (Columbia Univ. Press, 1942).

[7] Gunnar Myrdal, *An American Dilemma: The Negro Problem and Modern Democracy* (Harpers, 2 vols., 1944). Other volumes in the same series, published as parts of the study: Melville J. Herskovits, *Myth of the Negro Past*; Charles S. Johnson, *Patterns of Negro Segregation*; Richard Sterner, *The Negro's Share*; and *Characteristics of the American Negro*, edited by Otto J. Klineberg (all published by Harpers, 1941-1944). In addition to these six fat, fact-packed volumes, there are 50,000 pages of typed manuscript now deposited with the 135th Street Branch of the New York Public Library, representing much of the original data on which these volumes are based. Unquestionably the most important and most comprehensive study of Negro-white relationships yet produced by careful scholarship anywhere in the world, these materials provide a base line from which all research and investigation in the area of race will proceed for a not inconsiderable future. We may rightfully challenge the presumption of any person to speak with authority in the field of race unless he is familiar with the published volumes of the Carnegie Study of the *Negro in American Life*.

The plausible falsehood to which Professor Josey gave classical expression in academically respectable language is summed up in his words:

> The white races dominate mankind. They are the rulers *par excellence*. In the white man the evolutionary process seems to have reached its highest point. He is its culminating achievement.[8]

To make this plausible argument acceptable to the American mind, Dr. Josey insisted that we must be hardheaded and cease being softhearted. He sees our nominal allegiance to the Christian ethic as a principal stumbling block in the way of realizing our manifest destiny. About one-third of his volume is devoted to an attempt to establish the argument that, since the white man is innately superior to all others, it would be a contradiction of the purposes of the Creator and a betrayal of divine intention for the white man to lose his position of dominance.

> Can we expect God to be pleased because we unselfishly act in a way which, according to our best knowledge, will give the evolutionary process a turn in the downward direction?[9]

Not the least ingenious part of Dr. Josey's argument was the way in which he attempted to play the twin bogeys of class and race against each other, arguing that the "white races" are faced with the revolt of their own working classes, and unless the whites are willing to exploit the nonwhites for the benefit of all Caucasian peoples, the rising working classes in the white nations will overwhelm the upper classes. He therefore argues for

> a world organized along the lines of race and national consciousness as better than one organized along lines of economic interest. . . . Do we think it better that the burdens which our laboring classes are no longer willing to bear be transferred to others rather than that our culture lose much of its richness, complexity, and color?[10]

[8] *Race and National Solidarity*, p. 225.
[9] *Ibid.*, p. 223.
[10] *Ibid.*, p. 219.

Thus the double argument in support of Dr. Josey's position was that (1) we must discard the Christian ethic in order (2) to buy the allegiance of our internal proletariat by exploiting the proletariats of colored peoples. The argument itself was quite independent of these supporting notions: it was simply that the white man is superior, and therefore rightfully supreme. Instead of assuming that the white man's supremacy justifies the conclusion that he is superior, Dr. Josey argued that the white man is innately superior, and therefore ought to be supreme.

The superstition of innate superiority rests on the belief that mental, physical, and other abilities are transmitted from parent to child strictly in accordance with the "race" of the parents; and, further, that in the case of each and every member of the "superior" race these native endowments are superior to those of any member of any of the inferior races. This is the superstition, magnified to the stature of a lie, which supports the arrogance of the master race concept. This is the deceit which the Christian ethic denies and which scientific fact declares to be unproved in some cases and false in others. There is today not one shred of scientifically validated evidence to support the superstition of white supremacy as being rightfully based on biologically inherited superiority.[11] We must conclude, therefore, that there is no factual basis on which to rest the defenses for the claims of white superiority.[12]

The conclusion here stated applies not only to the relationship of whites to Negroes, but of whites to other racial groups

[11] In support of these statements, see the volumes of the Carnegie Study (n. 7 above). Otto Klineberg's *Race Differences* (Harpers, 1935) is the most useful single volume in the field of race differences.

[12] For an interesting example of cultural lag due to explicitly stated prejudgments, see the Publisher's Introduction to *What the Negro Wants*, edited by Rayford W. Logan (Univ. of North Carolina Press, 1944). "Long ago," writes Dr. W. T. Couch, publisher's spokesman, "I had to decide which of these views seemed to me most in accord with the facts and most reasonable. In my account I have made no attempt to hide the place where my faith lies" (p. xv). Having made up his mind "long ago," Dr. Couch must defend his prejudgment with tortuous illogic which is brilliantly deployed as he uses it.

as well. All studies of racial abilities published under standards of scientific rigor comparable to that applying to Negrowhite comparisons indicate that the conclusions hold good for all other racial groups also. To the scientist, as to the man of religion, "race" has much the same meaning as "redheadedness." It is an interesting phenomenon of surface pigmentation. It is not an index of innate abilities, or of differences of superiority and inferiority inherited in accordance with racial classifications. The theory of white superiority on which the dogma of white supremacy rests is not a scientific fact; it was a prescientific superstition which becomes a lie when now affirmed by intelligent men who know that the facts controvert their assertions.

This does not mean that there are no differences between *individuals,* both within each group and across racial lines, as to their inherited capacities. Wide differences in athletic ability, mental agility, and the affective life, can be traced in substantial part to inborn biological equipment of individuals—though even here the influence of environment must not be overlooked. The comparative effects of nature and nurture are matters for further investigation, both with reference to individuals and with reference to whole groups; but as far as *racial* differences are concerned, the theory of *innate* superiority cannot permit any overlapping between groups. All Caucasians must, by definition, be superior to all members of all other groups, if inherited racial superiority means anything. If it is possible for an individual in a non-Caucasian group to have intellectual or physical abilities superior to any whites, then those whites are not superior—which denies the assertion of racial superiority.

The dogma of white superiority has been exposed; but it still retains great practical significance, because it controls the actions of the ruling caste and thereby creates sharp differentials in opportunity which are reflected in differential levels of attainment. These differences in attainment are then rationalized into alleged native differences in ability.

The natural sciences have affirmed that whatever differences can be shown to exist are not inborn; and the social sciences have shown how artificial differentials in the environment (principally patterns of caste in the social structure) can account for whatever differences in achievement are now observed.

When we approach those problems on the hypothesis that differences in behavior are to be explained largely in terms of social and cultural factors, we are on scientifically sound ground. If we should, however, approach them on the hypothesis that they are to be explained primarily in terms of heredity, we do not have any scientific basis for our assumption.[13]

In blunt form, the truth of the matter is that the caste system is sufficient to account for whatever known inferiorities there may be in American life. It takes moral myopia for one to argue that the differentials in achievement which are due to a caste system are "proof" of inborn differentials in ability which are supposed to justify the caste system.

Publication of the truth will not automatically ensure the demise of falsehood. Hitler burned books: our congressmen only ban them.[14] Persons having a vested interest in the continuance of racial discrimination will not welcome truth. But the least we can do is to let the truth be known; and since the scientifically validated truths exactly corroborate the ethical insights of the Christian religion, we have a right to expect a ready reception of the evidence amongst men of the Church. Fortunately, Congress does not yet have power to dictate what shall be available for instruction in the Christian Church.

The natural sciences tell us that the concept of "race" has significance only in that it provides a convenient method of classifying the several members of the human family for

[13] Myrdal, *op. cit.,* p. 149. Author's own italics.

[14] *The Races of Mankind*, a Public Affairs Pamphlet by Ruth Benedict and Gene Weltfish, was banned from circulation among the men of the armed forces by a threat made in Congress to cut the military appropriation if the pamphlet was circulated. It contains a readable summary of what every high school child knows about the facts of race.

study. All members of the human family vary in their basic potentialities, but these variations have no relationship to "race." The social sciences tell us that, while biological significance cannot be attached to "race," its sociological significance is great. We turn to a consideration of that meaning.

3. "Race" as an Instrument of Culture Conflict

The *caste struggle* is a conscious fact to practically every individual in the system. The caste line—or, as it is more popularly known, the color line—is not only an expression of caste differences and caste conflicts, but it has come itself to be a catalyst to widen differences and to engender conflicts. To maintain the color line has, to the ordinary white man, the "function" of upholding the caste system itself, of "keeping the Negro in his place." The color line has become the bulwark against the whites' own adherence to the American Creed, against trends of improvement in Negroes' education, against other social trends which stress the irrationality of the caste system, and against the demands of the Negroes.[15]

It is primarily as an instrument and a symbol of culture conflict that "race" has its significance in American society. There is no single cause of racial prejudice and the perpetuation of the caste system. The close interconnection between a large number of causative factors—economic interest, social prestige, prevailing stereotypes, sexual exploitation, compensation to the lower class white for his economic deprivation, to mention only a few—in the race problem is now a well-documented fact.[16] Many factors working cumulatively on each other together produce the caste system and keep it going. The color line is both a symbol of the conflict and a tool by which the conflict is carried on. As the crusader used the cross both as an object of devotion and as a sword, so caste serves the Caucasian both as a tool of control and as an ob-

[15] Myrdal, *op. cit.*, p. 677. Author's own italics. The entire third section of his Chap. 31 discusses the notion.
[16] Cf. Myrdal, *op. cit.*, pp. 75ff., 719ff., 1068f., and consult the index for numerous other references.

ject of intense loyalty. *"Race" means caste* in the culture conflict.

There is nothing mysterious about the way in which these caste controls operate. They differ in intensity on the Negro-white axis as between the North and the South; on other axes, such as the Occidental-Oriental caste line, the differences in intensity are between the Pacific slope and the rest of the nation; other differences of degree follow similar regional patterns. But despite the differences of intensity, and with many minor variations in detail of operation, the caste controls work both to keep each member of a given racial group on his own side of the color line (as that is variously interpreted in each geographical area) and also to serve the discriminatory and exploitative purposes of the dominant caste.

The dominant group alleges (and often convinces itself that the allegation is in fact true) that the differences in status and opportunity between racial groups are due to innate superiorities in themselves and innate inferiorities in others. They use this allegation or belief as a means of consolidating their defenses of caste. Considered as dynamic factors in the social process, these beliefs play a determinative part, quite independent of their truth or falsity. "The caste distinctions are actually gulfs which divide the population into antagonistic camps."[17] Therein lies the real significance of color. As one competent authority phrases it: ". . . to understand race conflict we need fundamentally to understand *conflict* and not *race*."[18]

The doctrine of white superiority serves as a tool both of aggression and of defense in the hands of the dominant group. Believing that all races except the Caucasian are innately inferior to the Caucasian, the white man feels easier in conscience as he compels the "inferior" races to stay in a sub-

[17] *Ibid.*, p. 677.
[18] Ruth Benedict, *Race: Science and Politics*, p. 237. Modern Age Books, 1940
Author's own italics.

ordinate status. Thereby he quiets conscience as he proceeds with economic exploitation, social disability, political disfranchisement, and all the other devices of the caste system.[19] If the constructive forces of social imagination, ethical insight, and religious commitment which Christianity makes available are to be harnessed in the development of a social program calculated to eradicate caste, man's most dangerous superstition must be labeled for what it is—at best a lame excuse, at worst a horrible lie. The last deceitful defense must be destroyed.

4. THE MYSTICAL CONCEPT OF "RACE"

As the natural and social sciences cut away the ground on which the dogmas of racial superiority rest, the defenders of caste must find new ground on which to rest their case. Accordingly, they revert to the notion that a "race" is not a biological group but a "spiritual" group. Those who share the spirit of the master race are master men, members of the "race."

This doctrine has had its clearest formulation in Nazi Germany, where it was developed for purposes of political expediency. As the exigencies of military alliance and global war made it necessary, the master race was expanded to include persons of widely differing ethnic stock, the Japanese becoming the "yellow Aryans." Even before the doctrine had been pushed to that absurdity, *Mein Kampf* had made clear Hitler's contention that "race" is more a matter of *geist* than of biology. The only way that the diminutive Goebbels and the brunette Hitler could include themselves in the "race" of tall, blond Nordics was to make admission a matter not of biology or anthropometrics but of "spirit."

A sinister purpose underlay this elaboration of theory, a purpose which perfectly illustrates the manner in which "race" has its primary significance as a symbol and tool of group conflict rather than as a description of biologically important

---

[19] Chap. VI discusses the nature of the caste system. See also Chap. I, sec. 1.

facts. By defining the Aryans as a race and the Jews as a race, it then appeared possible for the Nazis to establish the pattern of conflict in sharply focused form, using the Jews as universal scapegoats.[20] The Jews are no more a race than the "Aryans" are. Ethnically, the Jews are a heterogeneous group including practically every racial stock known to the human species, with the possible exception of the Australian Bushman. The Jews are a cultural and religious group, not a race. But if they can be called a race, then it is possible to invent another racial group called Aryans, and to set the two over against each other in a pattern of conflict. With the sheep and the goats thus neatly separated one from another, the master race had its necessary mythological basis for the unification of Germany. It then reached out beyond the geographical borders of Germany, and discovered other "Aryans" who shared the *spirit* of the master race, and included them in the spiritual fellowship of the supermen, a mystical union of the world plunder bund.

Back of the Hitlerian use of "race" in this mythical sense lies the work of Gobineau and Chamberlain: the one a renegade French count who made up his racial theories out of his own fertile imagination without any scientific validation, and who confessed that his labor was directed toward proving that his own family tree was rooted in a superior stock; the other an Englishman who exiled himself in Germany and became so popular in his adopted land and culture that he published his *Foundations of the Nineteenth Century* in German, and became known as "the Kaiser's anthropologist." Chamberlain's book seems to have been the only book Hitler ever read.[21] In it, the definition of the "Aryan race" is an evasive matter. Neither Gobineau nor Chamberlain was able to put his hands on a man and say, "This is an Aryan." Neither of them could point to a nation and say, "These are Aryan people." The

[20] Cf. *The A, B, C of Scapegoating.* Chicago: Central Y.M.C.A., 1943.
[21] If one may rely on the internal evidence of *Mein Kampf.* Chamberlain published his book in 1899, the English translation appearing thirteen years later.

Aryan was a mythical being who shared a mythical experience with others of a mythical world. The only definite common element was the "spirit" which the true Aryan possessed. What is really meant by this nonsense is that anybody who is sufficiently arrogant can be called an Aryan, unless he is by birth a Jew. The utter meaninglessness of such a dogma is apparent in the statement of it. This is no biological race, but something like a social club or a religion. Chamberlain's method of "discovering" and identifying an Aryan was to use intuition. He called it "spiritual divination"; and his method (if it may be dignified by that term) he called "rational anthropology." The spirit of the man makes him an Aryan or a Teuton (Chamberlain used these terms interchangeably).

According to Chamberlain, the Teuton is everywhere triumphant. The Renaissance was due to the Teutons of Italy. All the great creative minds of western Europe were Teutons. Paul and Jesus were Aryans, not Jews.[22]

Of all the falsehoods spun into the fabric of racial dogmas, this myth of the "spiritual race" is the least tenable. It permits its dupes to play fast and loose with the truth at any point they desire, and to distort conclusions to conform to prejudices without consulting facts. The character of the Aryan and the non-Aryan (which has come to mean "Jew") are both established by definition, not by empirically verified fact. If it were not clear that this mystical conception of a spiritual race played a major part in plunging the entire world into the vortex of history's greatest war, it would be impossible to believe that any sane person could accept the myth. It may be that sane persons cannot. At any rate, it is difficult to find persons who have for long subscribed to this particular aberration and who have remained sane.

Our interest in the aberration to which we have just been referring lies in the fact that it illustrates the lengths to which racism can go. Robbed of all factual and scientific props,

[22] Otto Klineberg, *Race Differences*, p. 4. Harpers, 1935.

it invents a synthetic pseudo science and conjures a mythology, relying on "spiritual divination." It accepts only its own "science," and burns the books of all others. It uses "race" not to refer to any inherited biological realities, but to identify themselves and their fellow conspirators as superior men. This is the stuff out of which has been compounded the most volatile racial nonsense of the century. It is a potent tool of culture conflict, for all its seeming irrationality.

The party in power can wield this mystical notion with great effectiveness. Just as the citizens and magistrates of Old Salem could use the superstitions of witchery as a basis of hanging and ducking "witches," so those who cling to a mystical definition of "race" can use it. How many million people have been murdered because they were, by definition, non-Aryans, only the Nazi butcher bund knows. The world knows that the dead Jews are numbered in seven figures.

The bearing of the Nazi use of "race" upon the use of that term in America is not far to seek. There are some among us who hold it in exactly the same form as do the Nazis, and who would apply it in the same way if they had the power. A much larger group are those who use the term to apply to physically indentifiable types of the human species, not always being rigid about the exact line of demarcation but following a "common-sense" definition of race. "Anybody can tell a Negro when he sees one," they say. They add also that whether the Jew is a "race" or not, the Negro certainly is.[23] When they use the racial notion in this arbitrary fashion, they are not using scientifically verified facts; they are using irrational mythology, but the point is that they are using a tool of culture conflict which has peculiar potency. Even though the term "race" is given a specious genuineness in American life by being coupled with observable surface difference instead of resting solely on an alleged mystical spirit, the term in Amer-

[23] On the "racial" composition of the Negro caste, see below, sec. 1 of Chap. VIII.

ican usage retains its real character as a tool of conflict. The point is clinched when we observe that in nations like the Soviet Union, where there is the widest possible variety of ethnic stocks, there is no use of the concept of "race." There is no cultural conflict within the Soviet Union to be served by the use of the concept.

But in the United States of America there is a conflict to be served by the concept of race. It is part of the blindness of the upper caste that the reality of this conflict is frequently denied. Necessary fictions are invented to gloss over the facts.

5. FICTION AND FACT

One of the great services now being performed by the spokesmen for the silent billion is the vigorous manner in which they insistently call attention to the growing resentment of the darker races.

Within America, the first rumblings of organized resentment came in the slave revolts, a chapter in American history which white historians generally manage to overlook or to minimize.[24] As a diapason undertone, this resentment has continued throughout the past century, as any person familiar with the thinking of Negro Americans can testify.[25] The fiction of the contented black man in America is fiction. It is kept alive by the demand of white America, and with the permission of a black America that has not yet succeeded in escaping the demands of caste.[26] The white caste demands the acceptance and circulation of the pleasing fiction, partly be-

[24] Cf. Herbert Aptheker, *American Negro Slave Revolts.* Columbia Univ. Press, 1943.

[25] For the story during Reconstruction days, cf. W. E. B. DuBois, *Black Reconstruction* (Harcourt, Brace, 1935). The vast literature of discontent which Negro America has thrown up during the past half century makes an extensive bibliography by itself. A recent noteworthy addition is Richard Wright's *Black Boy,* Harpers, 1945.

[26] "The Etiquette of Discussion" in Myrdal's *American Dilemma,* pp. 36ff., elaborates the idea I must here compress into a sentence. Chaps. 33 to 37 inclusive also bear on the point, especially the chapter on "Compromise Leadership."

cause it helps to impose docility on the colored man by creating the mind set on both sides of the color line which welcomes docility and conformity and partly because the fiction soothes a troubled conscience and guards it from ugly fact. The Negro contributes to the continuance of the fiction partly as a victim of it and partly because he has learned to use it as a survival technique.

In the days of slavery, the technique was called "talking at the Big Gate." Loud conversations were staged in front of the Big House, for the ears of white folks, intended to give listeners the impressions which the speakers knew were wanted. Talk was easy and cheap, and often gained favors in exchange. Such double talk is still in use. It serves to buttress the belief held by white America that all Negroes are happy and contented with their lot. The white man is superior and supreme; the black man is happy in his place. The continuance of both parts of the fiction is essential to the acceptance of either half.

On occasion, the mask of fiction is ripped aside by an ugly event and the shocked and indignant white caste descends upon some hapless member of the submerged group with the uncontrolled fury of outraged righteousness. It is not merely that a colored man is accused of having done a wrong: courts of law could handle the wrongdoer; but something more than justice is demanded by the situation. The colored man has not only been accused of a misdemeanor or crime, he has also broken the idyllic serenity of the fiction of the contented Negro. For one awful moment the white caste glimpses the accumulated venom and hatred of the generations. Psychological security is jeopardized. Supremacy must be reasserted to protect the feeling of superiority. There is another lynching.[27] The white man can breathe easily once again, and return

[27] Contrary to popular belief, less than one-fourth of the lynchings in the fifty-five years during which records have been kept, have been for a sex crime or an alleged sex crime. More than three-fourths of the lynchings have been for other alleged infractions of the code of white supremacy. Lynchings are to be understood primarily in terms of social controls designed to keep submerged

to his interrupted dream that the colored man is happy and contented.

The whole elaborate ritual of race relations designed to preserve the status of subordination of colored peoples is a denial of the fiction of the contented colored man.[28] The complex structure of the Jim Crow laws, accompanied by legal disfranchisement, the one-party system, and other legal and extralegal controls including the threat of physical violence and an occasional lynching to give substance to the threat, show that the white man does not actually trust the pleasant fiction that Negroes are contented and happy in their lot. Much of the furor over the proposed antilynching legislation in Congress comes from the fact that such a law would, if effective, make it impossible to control the lower caste with the threat of lynching. The actual number of lynchings in any one year is not important: that is to say, a decreasing number does not indicate that they are any less effectual as social controls. On the contrary, as long as there are a few lynchings each year, to keep the threat alive, the white caste in effect makes every Negro walk with a noose about his neck, a noose which can be tightened the moment he gets out of his "place." If the Negro in America were content to occupy his designated place, there would be no need of force and legislation and intimidation to make him stay there. The fiction of the "contented darker races" is a lie manufactured out of whole cloth and used to clothe the moral nakedness of white supremacy.

This story could be told in graphic detail that does not permit retelling within the covers of this polite book. It is available in such writings as "The Ethics of Living Jim

---

groups in their "place." Cf. Gallagher, *American Caste and the Negro College* (Columbia Univ. Press. 1938), pp. 383-397, for supporting evidence. Cf. also Arthur Raper, *The Tragedy of Lynching* (Univ. of North Carolina Press, 1933), and Walter White, *Rope and Faggott: A Biography of Judge Lynch* (Knopf, 1929).

[28] Cf. Bertram W. Doyle, "The Etiquette of Race Relations" in *Journal of Negro Education*, Vol. V, (April, 1936), p. 203; also Gallagher, *op. cit.*, pp. 95-96.

Crow"[29] in which the writer tells how, from earliest childhood, he was taught by his mother, with appropriate belabor-
ments, to stay in "his place" if he wished to remain alive in a
white man's world. "Lawd, man," said an elevator operator
to Wright, "ef it wuzn't fer them polices 'n' them ol' lynch-
mobs, there wouldn't be nuthin' but uproar down here!" Or,
one may read Embree's *Thirteen Against the Odds*[30] to see
how large a percentage of Negro leadership got its initial
determination *not* to be cowed in spirit in some childhood experience with the violence of a white mob.

When we enlarge the canvas to complete the picture by
sketching the world scene, the meaning of the American use
of the fiction of a contented colored man is corroborated by
the universal use of that myth to gloss over ugly world facts.
The Boxer Uprising was not an incident without an explanation. The Oriental Exclusion Act (now tardily repealed in
principle but not in fact for one national group as a part of
the game of power politics in the Far East) did not endear
America to Asiatics. The seething discontent which a heavy-
handed censorship attempts to cover in India is matched by
similar feelings in every part of Africa. The fanatical glee
with which Radio Tokyo seized upon reports of racial difficulty in the United States and beamed them toward India
and the Americas south of the Rio Grande is not accidental.
Los Angeles, Detroit, Houston, Beaumont, Sikeston, New
York, Philadelphia, and other American cities have made
headlines in the nonwhite world. American censorship considered it unwise to permit Negro newspapers to reach Haiti
or other parts of the Caribbean during the war years. The
apathetic indifference of the colored populations of Indo-
China, the East Indies, and Burma toward their erstwhile
white rulers as the Japanese drove the British and the
Dutch from Malaya and the Island Indies does not indicate

[29] Richard Wright in *The Negro Caravan* (Dryden Press, 1941), pp. 1050ff.
See also n. 25 above.
[30] Viking Press, 1943.

that they were happy enough over their subordination to
want to fight for it.[31] The exception proves the case: the
heroic stand of the Filipinos was motivated not by their great
contentedness over being in an inferior position, but by their
passionate belief that 1946 would see the United States ful-
filling its promise to grant independence to a sovereign Filipino nation.

The white man, occupying uneasily his pinnacle of control,
consoles himself by telling himself bedtime stories about the
alleged content of the darker races. He uses deception to
hide his despair, deny his defection, and cover his defiance.

6. MORALIZING AS A SUBSTITUTE FOR MORAL ACTION

It is a sound insight which has maintained that the seat of
man's difficulty lies in the ethical realm. It is in his "heart"
that man faces the ultimate decisions and either wins the ultimate triumph or faces the ultimate defeat. The issues of life
come out of the heart for that is where they take shape. In
the warfare between ethical ideals and unethical conduct,
man finds his most challenging battles and wages his fiercest
fights.

But sound insights can be misused. This one has been. It
is not enough to get the heart right; much more than that is
involved, as the sad history of backsliders testifies. How is the
conscience of man to become triumphant over his baser self?
How can the devastating contradiction between moral insight
and immoral conduct be resolved? Exhortation and instruction in moralistic terms are not enough.

The moralizers have long assumed that by redirecting the
aims of men they had completed their job. They were correct
in assuming that aims must be redirected, but their error lay
in assuming that the job was then accomplished, when it

[31] I have said little about French colonial practices, but interested persons may
check the assertion that, at least in the Far East, French imperialism is of a
piece with British and Dutch by reading Thomas E. Ennis, *French Policy and
Development in Indochina* (Chicago, 1936).

was scarcely begun. There is something of the armchair general in the moralizer who exhorts the masses of Christians to get their hearts right with God, and then to go out to face an unchristian world, without giving to them the necessary moral instruction in terms of concrete situations and actual practices. It is not merely that the preacher faces his own inadequacies. The matter goes deeper than that, or else he would give the best guidance he has for whatever it might be worth. It goes back to his own inability to resolve the ethical tension within himself, a tension born of the contradictions between what he knows and what he does. Unable to act ethically himself, he hesitates to do more than exhort his brethren to a generalized, unfocused suffusion of ethical phraseology. Not all armchair generals are cowards; but the kind of cowardice that keeps a man from uttering in the pulpit the significant word of ethical incisiveness is more to be pitied than condemned. In the ethical bankruptcy of the moralizer is the final proof of the ineffectiveness of moralizing.

Here, also, is the key to the perplexing phenomenon of ecclesiastical resolutions. Not infrequently the statements passed with approval in church conferences, synods, assemblies, and the like are far in advance of anything which the individuals who passed them are willing to espouse on their own responsibility. And, not infrequently, these resolutions are couched in such general terms of sweet moralizing that they mean little in the practical world. And when they do manage to become quite specific and practical, these statements tend to concentrate on peripheral and relatively unimportant matters. Thus, a resolution on race will roundly affirm, in no uncertain terms, the fundamental Christian belief in the brotherhood of all men. But when the resolution begins to make application of the fundamental tenets of the faith, it skirts around important matters and lamely winds up by expressing the general hope that, in the near future, the national gatherings of the denomination will be held in some city where all delegates can be entertained with courtesy and comfort.

Something more than moralizing is needed. That something must be found in the field of social engineering, in an effort to reconstruct social structures and patterns so that it becomes less completely impossible for the individual to practice his ethical convictions. But as long as churchmen deceive themselves into thinking that moralizing is enough there will be no genuine effort to make the moral life possible. We do not question the necessity of prophetic preaching and high resolving. We need not less, but more moralizing in that sense. Unless the leadership of Christendom can be awakened, the trumpet will sound an uncertain note. But moralizing is only the beginning of our strategy. With the awakening of the religious conscience, we must find intelligent, socially constructive, fruitful, long-range, and immediate plans of action which are calculated to uproot the iniquities and inequities of racial caste. And we must put these plans into action.

The double task before us is (a) that of sharpening the ethical judgment so that the fuller meanings of our Christian commitment become clear to every one of us in specific terms of changed racial attitudes, practices, and patterns and (b) that of fashioning the workable tools of social engineering and devising the tedious steps to be taken in bringing the day-to-day practices of our social institutions as well as of our individual lives more nearly into conformity with the objectives which the ethical conscience demands. This dual job of education and of social engineering is much more than sermonizing and preachment and book writing. It is high-minded, sincere, personal commitment, plus wise and fearless social action.

The necessity of social action should be clear without argument. No matter how much the individual here and there may wish to live by the Christian ethic, he cannot freely do so in the present American caste system. He is prevented and inhibited at every turn by the patterns of segregation, the laws and customs and pressures of his society, and the resultant inner tensions and fears which frustrate his efforts and weaken his purposes. If he conquers his fears and masters his inhibitions, and openly flaunts the caste system, he is broken on the wheel of social ostracism. He "loses caste," because an outcast in a caste-controlled world. Under these circumstances, social action is the enabling act of Christian living. Exhortation to the moral life, without accompanying social action, is the cowardice of the armchair general who orders a single private to storm the enemy's bastion without weapons, without generalship, and without comrades.

Race is fundamentally a moral issue, coming to focus in the conscience of the white man. But it will not be solved by moralizing. To cling to the deceitful notion that moralizing is enough is to indulge in immorality.

7. SCIENCE AND CONSCIENCE

We cannot longer deceive ourselves. The judgment of science and of conscience converge, making it necessary for him who would be intellectually honest and ethically responsible to revise his beliefs and his action, being both hardheaded and softhearted in his procedure. Parallel columns will summarize the situation:

Science	Conscience
1. There is no scientifically validated evidence to support the superstition that *any* racial group is inferior or superior to other racial groups because of biological inheritance.	1. The essential equality of all men is announced in the brotherhood of the human family and the worth of every personality, regardless of "race."
2. Inequalities in the milieu can produce inequalities in attainment as between the advantaged and the disadvantaged groups: caste, not race, makes the "racial" differences.	2. Arbitrary inequalities of a caste system, which give advantage and opportunity to men on the basis of skin color, are a violation of the brotherhood of man and a denial of God's Fatherhood.
3. When the caste-produced differentials in achievement are used to justify color caste, prejudice and	3. Prejudice, an expression of the sin of pride, is the fruit of exploitation, which unsettles the ethical

stereotype present a closed circle of blind illogic.

4. The primary significance of "race" is not as an ethnic classification but as an instrument of the caste struggle.

5. The eradication of caste in ever-widening circles of individual and social life is necessary to the growth of sanity and decency.

palate and leaves the bitter taste of hatred.

4. The voice of a brother's blood cries unto God from the ground.

5. Social action is necessary to keep moralizing from being a substitute for moral action, and to enable the individual to be more consistently Christian.

CHAPTER VI

DELINEATION

Caste is becoming an expensive luxury of white men.
—GUNNAR MYRDAL (1944)

ONE of the ways to assess the present situation of color caste is to draw up the accounts and strike a balance. Interested in fullness of life, the Christian conscience is becoming increasingly uneasy over the deficit of racial difference, yet few white Americans appreciate fully just how great that deficit is.

1. THE ECONOMIC BALANCE SHEET

To a large number of employers, caste appears to be a profitable matter. This profit is shown in clear financial gains due to depressed wages. Previous to Executive Order 8802 and the establishing of the Fair Employment Practice Committee, it was quite common practice throughout the South (and not too exceptional in other parts of the nation) to pay a lower wage to Negroes than to whites for identical services, or to keep wages in the unskilled brackets low and to keep Negroes in those brackets. Under such a system, the gains to employers were not negligible, due to a double process: all Negro laborers were obtained at a substantial saving over what white men in the same jobs would have cost; and, in the South, the available reservoir of Negro labor acted as a constant threat by which the wages for whites could be depressed below the national level, thereby giving to employers in the South a differential advantage over employers with whom they competed in the North and West. The southward march of capital in the first third of this century, particularly the southward migration of the textile industry, was in no small part due to the enticement of this cheaper labor. The alleged lower cost of living in the South has been used to excuse the admitted wage differential between that section and the rest of the nation; and the assertion that Negroes live more cheaply than whites has been used to defend the racial differential. It is true that labor in the South lives more cheaply than elsewhere: it has no alternative. It is also true that Negroes live more cheaply than whites: they are paid less. But it is circular reasoning to argue that, since the poorly paid man manages to exist on his lesser wage, he should not be paid an income that would enable him to rise above the poverty level.

In many of the war industries, federal policies eradicated the wage differentials between the races; and where this happened, at least for the duration of the war, the wage savings of employers were cut. Nevertheless, in terms of production costs, the employer appears to benefit greatly from being able to employ Negroes at lower wages, and from being able to keep the level of wages for whites lower than they would be if the threat of cheaper nonwhite labor were removed. The southern employer (who is not always a resident of the south) can get his goods onto the market more cheaply than his northern competitor.

But there are other factors which offset the apparent gains of caste even for the individual employer—not to mention the social whole. Generally speaking, an employer gets no more from his laborers than he pays for. When he insists on paying a substandard wage, he gets substandard returns for his wage payments. One of the clearest examples of this is furnished by the system of farm tenancy prevailing on the cotton plantations. Generations of tenancy have reduced the cotton plantation system to the point where it is perfectly calculated to keep the tenant in poverty and to bankrupt the landlord. It does both, efficiently.[1] Work done grudgingly and

[1] *The Collapse of Cotton Tenancy*, by Will W. Alexander, Edwin R. Embree, and Charles S. Johnson. Univ. of North Carolina Press, 1935.

indifferently is expensive, no matter how little it costs the employer. The inefficiency of southern labor is a notorious fact, which is partly traceable to the low prevailing wage; and this applies with double force to the even lower wage and efficiency rate of the depressed Negro worker. That inefficiency is a function of low wages, rather than of geography, is demonstrated by the fact that wherever white men in the South have been given the same opportunities of training and instruction, with the same wage incentives, as their fellow laborers in other parts of the nation they have justified the higher wages with better production records. And that inefficiency is not a function of race is demonstrated by the similar performance of Negroes when their opportunities and incentives have been equal to those of their white fellow workers.

Given similar training and similar incentives, Negroes turn out a day's work either at the skilled or the semiskilled level, as well as in common labor, that is worth what it costs to the employer as he equalizes their wages. Performance in the war industries, particularly the shipyards, is a notable case in point. The experience of many employers like Ford in Detroit and Firestone in Akron has for many years demonstrated the soundness of the practice of equalizing wages and opportunities. Some employers—particularly those whose first experience with Negro labor has come during the manpower shortages of war production, when the bottom of the barrel has been scraped and then scraped again—are inclined to doubt the statement that Negroes measure up to the enlarged responsibilities in much the same fashion as whites do. They quote their shop foreman and superintendents to the effect that the nonwhite workers are "less efficient" or "lazy" or "irresponsible." Few of these employers, however, have ever taken the trouble to check these assertions against actual performance records. When questioned, they can only reply, "My foremen tell me" or "That is my impression."

Unfortunately, lack of race prejudice is not necessarily one of the qualifications for foremen and superintendents—or even for membership in some unions. In cases where both employers and supervisors *expect* to "find" inefficiency in Negro labor, and do not check actual performance, it is possible for advance expectations to become accepted notions without verification. Or, it is also possible that the morale of the work situation can be adversely affected by the introduction of nonwhite laborers, so that assignments are not equalized or various discouragements are placed in the way of Negro workers. The latter may be shifted from job to job too frequently to permit peak efficiency on piecework, or Jim Crow washrooms and eating facilities may appreciably lower the morale of the Negro workers—there are scores of seemingly unimportant or irrelevant things which the caste system can do to make a Negro worker function below par. Only when the entire white working and supervisory force has been carefully educated so that the work situation is substantially identical for all employees, and only when psychological hazards of resentment are replaced by encouragement and co-operation, can the employer be sure that he has a situation which reasonably measures the comparative efficiency of his white and nonwhite workers. There are some labor unions in which nonwhites are not welcome; and white workers have been known to use measures designed to discredit the performance of nonwhites.

It is therefore useful to be able to cite significant examples of comparative performance in situations where (*a*) proper steps have been taken to ensure the equality of opportunity and of incentive and (*b*) accurate checks have been made to measure comparative performance under these conditions. Such a case is the Sperry Gyroscope Company of New York, makers of precision instruments. Before the war, they hired no Negroes. Employment of Negroes began in 1941, with the hiring of a few men as porters and women as lavatory attendants. Some of the porters later applied for admission to the regular 18-month learnership training course for teaching instrument assemblers and specialist machine-tool operators.

The company wisely used a policy of scattering Negroes throughout the entire training course, in all departments; and from that time on, Negroes were admitted directly to the training courses and regularly employed throughout the plants when they completed the course and qualified. By the summer of 1944, Negroes were employed in twenty-eight different occupations within the company. In the production cutback which had come in 1943, the total number of employees had decreased 20 per cent; but the efficiency of Negro workers was such that less than 6 per cent of Negro employees were lost in the cut. Of the total number of colored employees, one-third were to be found in highly skilled occupations, one-third in semiskilled, and one-third in other jobs. A considerable number had become leaders and foremen; and some were in the offices. The president of the company, Mr. R. E. Gillmor, states the conclusions from experience:

The initial employment of Negroes and each subsequent extension of their employment into new categories was received with doubt by the supervisors and, in some cases, by rumblings and even threats of trouble from some groups of white workers. The threats never materialized, the doubts disappeared and were succeeded by friendliness and cooperation in helping the Negro to learn new jobs and to progress to a better one.

A similar change of attitude has taken place in our union—Local 450 of the U.E.-C.I.O. There were misgivings at first but these have disappeared and in their place has come a really sincere and courteous cooperation and mutual respect. Out of our 300 or so shop stewards, 22 are Negroes. One of the stewards is the only Negro in his department, so we have here an example of a Negro chosen by popular vote to represent an otherwise all-white department.

Given equal education and training, the performance of the Negro worker is, on the average, equal to that of other workers. The average absenteeism is slightly lower and the separation rate is lower.[2]

This is not a typical example, because the practices and procedures which the company followed are not typical. Every

[2] R. E. Gillmor, president of the Sperry Gyroscope Company, New York City, in an address before the National Association for the Advancement of Colored People, July 1944, printed in the N.A.A.C.P. *Bulletin*, September, 1944.

effort was made to ensure the removal of all racial differentials in opportunity and incentive. Not as a typical example of what happens when Negroes are employed without discrimination, but as an indisputable demonstration of what did happen in one highly important and exacting industry when *all* color bars were lowered, this experience merits thoughtful study by employers and labor unions. The straightforward policy of nondiscrimination has paid good dividends to the company and to all its workmen. Mr. Gillmor asserted that the company expected to continue the employment of Negroes after the emergency was past, because it pays.

Pioneering demonstrations like the foregoing lead to the notion that the use of a wage differential based on race is only a means of ensuring that the differential in incentive does actually result in lower performance. When the employer abolishes every semblance of caste within his plant— from the initial hiring interview to the final exit interview— he gets substantially equal performance from his workmen regardless of their racial identity; and he gets a definite lifting of the morale of his entire force as the full significance of their democratic inclusiveness is realized.

And when it comes to selling his product, the producer faces the real results of the wage differential in the fact that poorly paid workers make poor purchasers as consumers. No single employer or company stands to benefit by the increased purchasing power of its own employees through a rise in wages, unless the rise is general throughout the area or the nation. Low wages of an area depress the consumer purchasing power of the workers (who are most of the consumers), so that the sale of the total product of industry is sharply limited by low wages. A general rise in real income of the workingman means a general increase in purchasing power for all consumers' goods in the necessities class and of many goods in the luxury categories. The comparatively higher standards of living of the American workingmen as contrasted with the rest of the world is one demonstration of this fact. It is negatively demonstrated by the manner in which caste depresses the wage levels of both Negro and white workers in the South, thereby constricting the consumer purchasing power and cutting the potential markets of producers and merchandisers of the region. The alleged savings which are supposed to accrue from lower wages are thus offset by the restricting of the market. A *general* leveling up of wages, at least to the minimum standard of living for the white workingman of the nation, would expand the potential market for consumers' goods and make for a more healthy economic situation throughout the nation. The individual employer, however, is powerless to make this general change, unless he becomes a vertical combination. The only measure adequate to improve the situation is a general change in employment and wage policies that eliminates the caste differentials throughout the nation simultaneously.

The potential change in consumer purchasing power which the elimination of substandard wages for nonwhites would bring is enormous. Data are not at hand for the precise calculation of the total amount involved, but some index of what might be expected is given in the Carnegie study.[3] Using the Works Progress Administration's 1935 definition of "maintenance" and "emergency" levels of family income and assessing the family incomes of whites and Negroes in the United States, Sterner reaches the conclusion that

the so-called maintenance level ($1,261) appears at present to be completely beyond the means of the general Negro population, particularly in the South.[4]

Although wartime employment markedly altered this situation for the duration, there are strong pressures in the postwar period to return to the types of wage and employment differentials that prevailed in 1935 when the survey was made.

[3] More than 400 pages of carefully compiled statistics and data, which can scarcely be summarized in a paragraph or two, are given in Richard Sterner's *The Negro's Share*, Harpers, 1943.

[4] *Op. cit.*, p. 85.

At that time, in the cities surveyed, both North and South, the majority of Negro families had an income *below* the "emergency" level, while "only 13 to 27 per cent" of the white families were below this emergency level.[5] This is the level below which the data indicate that a family cannot carry on for more than a short emergency period without seriously impairing the health of its members—to say nothing of clothing, housing, education, and the like.

If the caste pattern were abandoned in employment, upgrading, and wage payments, and if Negroes were thus to receive family incomes comparable to whites for the same level of work, training, and experience, the increase in consumer purchasing power of Negro workers would approach at least two billion dollars annually. That increase would be distributed over the bottom of the economic pyramid, where it would be directly reflected in increased purchasing power to consume the annual product of American industry and agriculture. The equalizing of Negro and white wages would also put a solid base under the next phase of development, in which the generally low wages paid to whites in the South, having become the basic level for whites and Negroes alike in that region, can be raised to approach the national level. The southern differential, which helps to keep the region in a colonial status under northern financial and economic domination, cannot be removed as long as whites and Negroes compete against each other to depress the wage level. Neither can the southern differential be removed as long as employers are content to get cheap results from cheap labor. The continuance of caste must be charged up as a costly affair, particularly costly to the southern states. In terms of interregional comparisons, the South is strongly disadvantaged by the working of its caste system. The southern states are poor, enjoying a per capita wealth of less than $1,800 as compared with a national average of nearly $4,000.[6] Negroes

[5] *Ibid.*, p. 87.
[6] Gallagher, *American Caste and the Negro College*, p. 120.

are poor enough in other parts of the nation; but two-fifths of the Negro population is included in the averages cited for the states outside the South. Whites are poor enough in all parts of the nation; but their low income in the southern states where they make up more than three-fourths of the total, is evident in the fact that every one of the eleven states having a per capita wealth of less than $2,000 is in the South.

The difference between the South and the rest of the nation is not one of racial stock primarily; it is primarily rooted in the fact that in the South the caste pattern is used to keep the poorer white man close to the poverty line by dropping the Negro base line below the poverty level. The continuance of this pattern makes the South easy prey for investors and industrialists from the North and the Middle West who have few compunctions of conscience over exploiting the situation which the South itself nurtures. The South does not like to be kept in financial and industrial bondage to New England and the Middle West; but it can climb out of its colonial status only when it unites its racially divided forces. As long as black and white are played against each other, both suffer. Poverty and inefficiency go together; to eliminate either, both must be eradicated. Yet neither poverty nor inefficiency can be lifted without striking off the chains of caste which shackle the Negro in the economic cellar—and hold the white man down with him.

A second general area in which the caste differential is popularly supposed to be an economic gain for the dominant group is in the provision of public services, such as education, libraries, public health services and hospitalization, in those areas where the races are segregated by law or custom in the use of these facilities. The argument on this point has gone through three successive metamorphoses in the past twenty years. Education may serve to illustrate the point.

Twenty years ago, it was argued that the "dual" system of education was a tremendous cost to the South, and one which it bore with stoic patience—a sort of cross-bearing which put a halo of pious sanctity around the practice of segregation. It was admitted that it was a pity that Negroes could not have as good facilities as whites, or at least as good facilities as they were capable of appreciating; but the costs of duplicating all facilities and services was tremendous, and patience was required of all in the face of the manifest impossibility of immediate equalization of expenditures.

The first blow dealt to this myth was the Rosenwald study of school costs, published in 1935.[7] That study showed that in the eleven southern states from which records were obtainable, nearly $40,000,000 annually was then being saved by the refusal to equalize the facilities for Negroes and whites. Another way of stating the clear money savings was the fact that the Negro teacher received on the average only 47 per cent of what the white teacher was paid. If the school properties for Negroes were to be put on a par with those for whites, the initial capital outlay required would have been $240,000,000 for fifteen southern states, not to mention the increased costs of adequate maintenance. Segregation in schooling spells enormous money gains for the states where segregation is practiced.[8] In the light of these facts, the white caste could no longer argue that its "dual" system was costly to it. No responsible writer or speaker since that time has repeated what was, up to 1935, an accepted axiom of the caste system—although the myth is so popular that it dies hard.

The second phase of the argument, in which it was pointed out that, far from being expensive, the caste division of education provided great savings for the white caste, was climaxed by the studies which revealed that not only local and state funds were spared by not being spent for Negroes, but also that federal funds were commonly diverted so that whites profited at federal expense and Negroes were helped little, if any, by federal aid. The Senate Committee on Education and Labor disclosed, in its 1939 hearings, that in the seventeen

---

[7] *School Money in Black and White*, Julius Rosenwald Fund.
[8] For further data see Gallagher, *op. cit.*, p. 119.

states receiving $16,000,000 for Negro and white land-grant colleges in 1935-1936 Negroes made up 25 per cent of the total population between the ages of eighteen and twenty-one, inclusive; yet they received only 5.4 per cent of the federal allotments—one-fifth of their equitable share. Funds allotted for vocational work of less than college grade were likewise diverted for the benefit of whites so that Negroes, who should have received $5,018,824 on an equitable population ratio basis, actually received only $1,926,682—the balance going to whites.[9]

The states concerned also diverted their own funds unfairly—both in making appropriations and in the actual administrative diversion of funds after appropriation. In some instances, this practice of the states goes so far as to deny to Negroes access to opportunities for certain types of education altogether—particularly at the graduate level; and to deny to Negroes many of the facilities commonly provided for whites, such as school buses, or to make provision on a substantially lower and discriminatory basis. Considering only the southern states (for, in this case, the border states of Oklahoma and Missouri do not follow the pattern of discrimination), when the proportionate expenditures for the transportation of Negro pupils is compared to the percentage that these children are of the total population of school age, the ratio ranges all the way from a high of one-third for Maryland to a low of one one-hundredth for South Carolina. In other words, the best state of this region is spending only one-third as much proportionately for school buses for Negro children as for white children, and the worst is spending slightly less than one one-hundredth of what would be an equitable share.[10]

Education most clearly reveals the story of disparities in expenditure by means of which the caste pattern saves the white caste appreciable sums every year. The story could

[9] Charles S. Johnson, *Patterns of Negro Segregation*, pp. 13-14. Harpers, 1943.
[10] *Ibid.*, pp. 15-19.

be told with equal convincingness in terms of all other public
facilities, without great variation from the picture that education gives. Parks and playgrounds, libraries, hospitals, pav-
ing, sewer and water systems, street lighting, fire and police
protection, the voluntary charitable agencies—in all these
the caste pattern dictates discrimination, at a neat saving
to the white caste in terms of initial financial outlay and continuing yearly services. The fiction that a dual system costs
more to maintain, and the South ought therefore to be pitied
for bearing its heavy financial burden without complaining,
is now clearly appreciated as a fabrication that is contrary
to fact. Perhaps it was never meant to be more than a polite
fiction; but its constant repetition over a sixty-year period
gave it such general acceptance that it took a two-year survey
by a philanthropic foundation and a Senate investigation in
its wake to assemble the facts and figures to discredit the
myth.

The third phase of the argument came close on the heels
of the second development. No sooner had it been pointed
out that segregation, far from being an expensive device to
the taxpayer, saved substantial sums of public money by
providing inferior services to the restricted group than it
also became clear that this apparent saving was offset by
another set of costs which could not be overlooked in balancing the account for society. More difficult to calculate in
precise terms, these costs are nevertheless real costs, in terms
of public money expended and of the shrinking of the social
income. Who will estimate the money costs of ignorance
due to poor schooling and the lack of incentive to study even
in the poor school? Who will tell us the money costs which
are due to loss of man-hours through inefficient performance
due to malnutrition, or through loss of time due to sickness
correlated with poverty?[11] Who will give the total sum

[11] The National Health Survey of 1935-1936 (U. S. Public Health Service,
Washington, 1941) provides much raw data from which interested guessers
may make their computations.

spent on sickness because basic public health services for one-fourth of the southern population are inadequate? Wise expenditures for schooling, libraries, public health, play grounds, swimming pools, recreational facilities and programs, and cultural opportunities would do much to reduce the population of the jails, reformatories, and penitentiaries.

The hidden costs of caste go far to offset the apparent profits. If there are substantial money savings from the caste system accruing to the white population, they are swallowed up by hidden costs. What is saved with one hand is spent with the other.

One possible general exception to this whole discussion must be noted: when a particular trade or occupation is given over to a particular racial group, at a substantially lower rate of return than might prevail for that service if there were no caste differential in the wage, the money gains appear to be a clear profit for all except the disadvantaged group (if we disregard the reduced purchasing power of that group, with its depressive effect upon the total economy). Chinese laundries and Negro barbershops are illustrations. Domestic labor is the most significant example. But the passing of the Negro barbershop as white barbers encroach upon what was once an exclusively Negro occupation and the substitution of machine laundering for the hand processes of the small shop indicate that not even such an occupational differential serves as a permanent guarantee of the quick profits of caste against the long-term pressures of Caucasian avarice. The white man moves in and takes over the field formerly pre-empted by a nonwhite group, and then demands a "white man's wage" for the work. Moreover, when other employment opportunities open, as they did during the war period, the collapse of the less well-paid occupations such as domestic labor leaves a gap in the economy that is both irritating and costly.

On the basis of the economic argument, the system of color caste does not make a particularly good showing for itself. It makes a particularly bad showing when the examination is directed to the inclusive question of the *net* profit or loss of the Caucasian caste as a whole. And if the ethical spotlight is thrown on the economic costs to the lower caste, not one sound defense of caste in economic terms remains.

But at the same time there are many *individuals* in the white group who, as individuals, profit considerably through the caste system: the landlord who gets higher rents for less capital outlay and with lower upkeep costs because his property is rented to Negroes; the employer who gets a lower wage cost for his production; the railroad which provides inferior cars and services for nonwhites; the labor union which restricts the labor supply by keeping non-Caucasians out of the union and therefore out of the labor market; the real estate broker who exploits the non-Caucasian buyers because of the undersupply of unrestricted housing; the housewife who pays three to five dollars a week for domestic labor—these are a few of the individuals who profit directly from the caste system. They make a handsome money income out of the prejudices of their fellow Caucasians and the misery of the minorities.

Look at one example in detail, to get a notion of how color caste operates to give a handsome money return to smart operators. In the North and West, where social custom is not strong enough to enforce the caste system without additional props, most cities are now blanketed by restrictive covenants. The Supreme Court has ruled that it is contrary to constitutional rights to restrict the *ownership* of residential property according to race in any way. It has also ruled that it is unconstitutional to restrict the *occupancy* of a home by law, but it has not yet ruled on the matter of using voluntary restrictive covenants signed by property owners restricting the occupancy of homes to certain racial groups. It is "legal" to achieve, through restrictive covenants, what may not be done through state legislation or city ordinance. Many Caucasian homeowners in the West and North have a feeling that they are protecting their property values as they sign restrictive covenants to keep nonwhites out of their neighborhoods. This is a claim which it is difficult to substantiate in the face of the evidence.

It is claimed, for example, that when non-Caucasians move into a neighborhood the property is not kept in good repair, and its value therefore depreciates. The actual fact is that nonwhites are permitted to move into an area only after it has been permitted to run down for several years. Further, the landlords usually spend much less on upkeep costs for nonwhites than for white tenants, so that the already depreciated properties go from bad to worse.[12] Secondly, when a city is pretty generally covered with restrictive covenants except in the ghetto areas, available housing for nonwhites is sharply limited; and any increase in the minority group population means keen competition for housing in the nonrestricted areas. This means that, as restrictive covenants become general over a city, they defeat their primary purpose, for the homeowner learns (too late) that he could sell his house for 10 to 20 per cent more if it had no restriction on it. By signing the covenant that limited his potential market to whites only he has eliminated the highest bidders. Thirdly, if the owner is interested in his house as a home for himself and not therefore primarily concerned with its resale value, the presence of non-Caucasians on his block has nothing whatever to do with the "value" of his home to him, unless he is a victim of race prejudice. In that case, it is not the presence of the Chinese or the Filipino or the Negro or the Mexican or the Jew in his block that suddenly makes his home of less value to him; it is nothing but his own racial attitudes. Restrictive covenants do not protect property values: they merely protect prejudices, at the expense of the property owners.

But someone does profit by the drawing of the restrictive covenant. It is the promoter. In a single West Coast city,

[12] Johnson, *op. cit.*, p. 10.

for example, one man has promoted thirty-seven restrictive
covenants covering some 25,000 properties in the years 1936
to 1944. Each property owner pays a fee of $10 as he
signs the covenant. The fee is to cover various costs of
title search, recording signatures (at 10 cents each), fees
to canvassers who push the doorbells and browbeat the homeowners into signing, and similar expenditures. It costs this
promoter nothing for meeting places as he organizes his
"homeowners' protective associations," for he enjoys the
gracious co-operation of the School Board, which permits
him to use the city's school buildings free of charge. He
turns back 50 cents out of each $10 fee to the association
of covenanters, to form a nest egg with which to be ready
for legal defenses of any possible infringement of the covenant at some future date. After all these expenditures have
been made, the net commission to the promoter runs at about
$1 to $1.75 per property, according to the best possible
estimates. His "spare-time" activity over a nine-year period
has thus brought one promoter something over $35,000 in
contributions from frightened homeowners who thought they
were protecting their own property values. Prejudice is an
expensive luxury.

The other man who profits from the restrictive covenant
is the shyster real estate dealer (as distinguished from the
realtor who follows a code of ethics) who buys up the properties in a run-down white neighborhood, then gets the restrictive covenant lifted, and sells at inflated prices to the racial
minorities who have no choice but to buy where they have
opportunity, paying the enhanced prices.

The caste system pays—and pays nicely—to certain individuals. The rest of us, minority and majority persons alike,
pay for what these few profiteers take. The white caste,
as a whole, profits little and pays greatly for the total social
costs of caste, while a few Caucasians profit at social expense.

Candor compels us to add a fact that is not complimentary
to certain members of racial minorities; but there is no

a priori reason to believe that minority status guarantees absolute virtue. And if we are to be free to discuss the shortcomings of members of the majority group, we must have the same freedom in discussing members of minorities. We therefore note that the caste system is used by some individuals within the submerged groups for their own personal profit in much the same way that it is exploited by individual Caucasians. Nonwhite and non-Gentile landlords and rent loan sharks in many instances rate a preferred position in the gallery of rogues who exploit their fellow race or minority group members in the restricted circumstances of caste.

A second group, who will not be pleased to see themselves listed here, is the professional group of the minorities, they who depend on the caste line for their position and income. The Negro teacher gets her job because there is a segregated school. The Negro lawyer or doctor or dentist whose practice is limited to his own racial group, in addition to being a servant of his own group is in the anomalous position of being a parasite on the caste system. The wide support which clergymen in minority groups have given to the fact of segregation within the church stems in part from their fear that if segregation were abolished they would have no pulpits and no salaries. It must be admitted that their fears are at least partly justified by the attitudes and practices of the white churches which have not yet made clear their desire to have mixed congregations and to use Negro ministers in these churches. While many, if not most of the Negro professional classes oppose segregation in principle, and also oppose it in specific cases outside their own particular field of work, not all of them are busily sawing off the limb of segregation on which they perch in their own special occupational fields. This fact, that many individuals in the segregated group profit directly from the continuance of segregation, shows that the profits of caste to certain individuals in the segregated group match those of individuals in the white group. It also serves to explain why the weight of professional leadership in the minority groups is often thrown in favor of segregation instead of against it.

Only if the minority man feels that he has a fair future in a nonsegregated world will be be likely to champion the abolition of caste. It is asking a great deal of a Negro minister, for example, to require him to give up the possibility of continuing in the service of the church in order to turn over his congregation to a white pastor. Segregation will be opposed by the "leaders" of the minorities in real earnest only when they have the hope that their own futures are bound up in the elimination rather than the continuance of caste. In this respect, as in so many others, there is no appreciable difference between members of different racial groups.

There are, of course, notable exceptions to this rule. There are instances of Negro college presidents who are fighting segregation in an effort to work themselves out of a job; Negro physicians who refuse to co-operate in segregated hospitalization even though they have to give up their Negro patients to white physicians and surgeons at the hospital door; Negroes who wish to teach in northern schools, but who refuse to sanction or support segregated schools in order to get a job; the unsung heroes of the struggle against caste, who refuse to profit from the misery of their fellows. These are the minority coworkers of those members of majority groups who also refuse to lend their support to caste or to mulct their fellow men.

Over against the whole picture of general segregation and discrimination and exploitation by individuals of both groups who take advantage of the color bar to make their own profits, and over against the story of general discrimination in public expenditures, instances like the state of North Carolina stand out boldly as proof that something *can* be done about it. The first of the southern states to adopt a policy of paying equal salaries to white and Negro teachers, North Carolina stands as a mountain of integrity in the midst of a plain of sham and pretense. North Carolina is saying, in effect, that if the white man insists on segregation he has not the right to make the black man carry the white man's burden.

2. Cultural Aspects of Caste

America is greatly impoverished in its cultural life by a system of color caste which denies to many of its potential contributors the opportunity to make their contributions to the enrichment of the common life. If the nation could welcome the contributions of all people, regardless of skin color, we should be immeasurably richer and happier. The point can be illustrated in terms of the Negro, but it is equally applicable to all racial minorities within the nation.

The Negro in the United States has a proud history.[13] A people that has contributed an orator like Frederick Douglass; a soldier like Colonel Charles Young; an educator like Booker T. Washington; churchmen like Bishop Payne and Alexander Crummel; poets like Paul Laurence Dunbar and Langston Hughes; scientists like Ernest Just and Percy Julian; organizers like C. C. Spaulding and A. Philip Randolph; surgeons like Dr. Daniel Williams and Dr. Louis Wright; physicians like Dr. William Hinton, Dr. T. K. Lawless, and Dr. Charles Drew; sociologists like W. E. B. DuBois, Franklin Frazier, Charles S. Johnson, and Allison Davis; political scientists like Ralph Bunche; economists like Robert Weaver; novelists like Richard Wright; musicians like Nathaniel Dett, Harry T. Burleigh, William Grant Still, Roland Hayes, Marian Anderson, Dorothy Maynor, and Carol Brice; actors like Paul Robeson; leaders like Walter White; painters like Henry O. Tanner and Hale Woodruff; and sculptors like Augusta Savage and Richard Barthe, need feel no inferiority

[13] This story is well told by the publications of the Association for the Study of Negro Life and History, and particularly by the writings of Carter G. Woodson.

in American life. And America would have been poorer for losing a single one of these contributions.

All these things we know; but what is not so well known in the United States is that other nations which do not discriminate against the Negro have been enriched by minority contributions in such proportions as to dwarf into insignificance the achievements of the Negro in the United States.[14] There have been great achievements by Negroes in the United States, but these achievements do not by any means represent the whole or even the greater part of Negro achievements in the Western world. And they represent only a small fraction of what the United States might have enjoyed if the caste of color had not prevented many others from making their contributions. There are more Negroes with more wealth and better education in the United States than in any other part of the world outside of Africa; but the Negro in the United States has rarely excelled in any honorable field of human endeavor within our borders.

Consider the field of poetry. America has had a distinguished succession of Negro poets, from Phyllis Wheatley (whose chief distinction is that she was the first American woman in over one hundred years to publish a volume of verses and the second ever to do so) through Dunbar to Countee Cullen, James Weldon Johnson, Langston Hughes, and Sterling Brown. These have all been creditable contributions, and young poets like Margaret Walker promise a continuation of the line; but if the history of American literature were being written, and only the major poets were to be included, it is doubtful whether the impartial historian would include a single Negro.

How different if the history of French, Russian, or South

[14] For the analysis that follows I am indebted to Mr. Arthur Spingarn, president of the National Association for the Advancement of Colored People, himself not a Negro, who gave the facts substantially as I now repeat them, in a Commencement Address at Talladega College in 1939. I reproduce his argument (and many of his own words) with his consent, absolving him of any responsibility for the conclusions drawn.

and Central American literature were being written! Negro poets would have to be included, no matter how short the lists. The greatest poet of all time in Russia was a Negro, Alexander Pushkin, whose writings made him both the greatest poet of African blood and the chief glory of Russian letters. His masterpieces have been translated into almost every language, and the centenary of his death a few years ago was celebrated throughout the civilized world. Cuba's best-loved poet is the Negro, Placido, whose works have gone through countless editions in many countries, and some of whose poems have been translated by American poets from William Cullen Bryant to James Weldon Johnson. The outstanding poet of Central America (who is also one of the most distinguished poets of his generation in the world) is the Nicaraguan, Reuben Dario, who in his best-known work, *Prosas Profanas,* acknowledges his Negro blood. One of the best writers of Spanish lyric poetry is the Negro, Nicholas Guillen, whose works have been published in Cuba, Mexico, France, and Spain, and some of whose poems have been rendered into English by Langston Hughes.

Richard Wright published an excellent novel which rates a position as one of America's finest horror stories, quite outranking Edgar Allan Poe in this respect; but would anyone think of pitting Wright against the Brazilian, Machada da Assis, who is generally recognized as the most important man of letters in Brazil, her chief novelist and one of her distinguished poets, whose collected works have recently been issued in some thirty-five volumes; or with what American Negro shall we compare the West Indian, René Maran, who won the Prix Goncourt (one of the major prizes of French letters), or the Frenchman, Alexandre Dumas, who was universally recognized as not only France's, but the world's greatest writer of romances? And what American Negro dramatist can be compared to Alexandre Dumas fils, author of *Camille*?[15]

---

[15] Some would, at this point, also include the name of the English Negro Robert Browning. According to Ernest J. Simmons (*Pushkin,* Harvard Univ.

Nathaniel Dett, Harry Burleigh, Rosamond Johnson, William Grant Still, William Dawson, and the writers of popular music, such as James Bland, William C. Handy, and Duke Ellington, have composed beautiful music; but when one thinks of *the* great Negro musician, none of these come to mind. It is an English Negro, Samuel Coleridge-Taylor, who is recognized as one of the outstanding musicians of his time, and whose musical settings of Longfellow's poems of Hiawatha are annually performed by choral societies throughout the English-speaking world. No Negro American composer of operas can compare with the Brazilian, Antonio Gomes, either in merit or in popularity. His works have been performed with acclaim in such famous centers as La Scala at Milan and the Metropolitan Opera House in New York City. Or what Negro violinist can we point to in America who has risen to the fame as composer or performer of the Cuban, José White, who was made the concert master of the Empress Eugénie?

It is in the political scene that we find the greatest discrepancy of all. The Negro in the United States can point to a couple of United States senators and lieutenant governors during Reconstruction, a handful of congressmen, and an occasional federal judge. They have been important exceptions to a universal rule of political disability which bars the Negro from officeholding in this nation. They sink into unimportance when compared to the position Negroes have attained in the political life of other countries. A few examples will suffice to illustrate: in one of the British possessions, a Negro became chief justice and was knighted—Sir Conrad Reeves; a Negro, the late Félix Eboué, was governor general of the principal French slice of the African continent; Blaise Diagne, a native African, became a member of the French cabinet; in Panama, a black man has served as president of

---

Press, 1937, p. 11), Browning had Negro ancestry but concealed it. Whether he had Negro ancestry or not, the fact that he passed for white puts him outside the present argument. In that case, he is like Alexander Hamilton in American political life, a man who would have been estopped by caste had he not hidden his ancestry.

the republic; and in the great republic of Brazil, Nilo Peçanha became president of the nation and served with distinction, subsequently serving as secretary of foreign affairs. Only twice in the history of Brazil has any man ever been elected to a second term in the presidency; and one of the men thus honored was a Negro.

If it were necessary, many more instances of the achievement of Negroes in other nations could be cited; but these are enough to illustrate the evidence which supports the conclusion that the Negro has demonstrated that he has every potentiality possessed by any other race in the world, and where he has been given a decent opportunity to exercise his talents, free of restraints and freed from prejudice, these potentialities have become realized facts.

There are those who try to explain the differential in achievement between the Negro in America and the Negro in other lands by arguing that the Negro racial stock imported by the slave trade to the United States was inferior to that which went to other parts of the world. This is another of the pleasant fictions with which the defenders of caste have attempted to evade the accusations of conscience. There is no sound reason for believing that the racial stock in the slaves brought to the shores of North America was different in quality from that which supplied the islands of the Caribbean and the mainland of South America. On the contrary, a common slave trade supplied all. The theory of "selective enslavement" cannot account for the differential achievement of Negroes in North America and in other Americas. Nor is there any basis for believing that the slaves represented any inferior stock in Africa itself.[16]

We are not saying that *because* of Negro blood admixture

[16] The sources of African slaves for the United States: "The largest single group, the true Negroes, were in many cases inhabitants of the great West Coast kingdoms that possessed on the whole a more complex development of government, art, industry, and material culture than the non-literate inhabitants of any other great continental areas. Moreover, the fact that so frequently enslavement was the result of the exigencies of warfare and political intrigue ensured that the slaves were drawn from all strata of African society and even perhaps resulted in weighting toward the upper levels of the social scale." Louis Wirth

these men and women in other nations were superior to their
contemporaries in those countries and in the United States.
All we are saying—and it is enough—is that these persons,
if they had lived in the United States, would have been classi-
fied as Negroes and forced to conform to their lower caste
status. So much time and energy would have been diverted
into fighting the race problem that the remaining fragments
of energy and talent would have been insufficient to raise their
achievement above the mediocrity of other Negro Americans.
If, on the other hand, Negroes in this nation could have
devoted their talents to constructive purposes in a congenial
and friendly atmosphere, rather than having to spend their
genius in a struggle for mere justice, the United States would
have been a happier and a richer land. This great potential
contribution is one which would be a net addition to our
common welfare. Every good poem, every great book, every
fine song, every act of political integrity and sagacity, and
every painting of beauty enriches everyone and has no debit
to balance the credit. In the cultural area, the account of
the caste system must be reckoned seriously in the red.

3. THE "MINOR" MATTERS OF CASTE

In his *Caste and Class in a Southern Town,* John Dollard[17]
reviews a comprehensive catalogue of the "gains" that accrue
to the members of racial groups under a caste system. These
are mainly in terms of a greater sexual freedom for white
men, psychological compensations for inferiority complexes,
and similar matters. They are important, particularly as
matters of concern when strategy for the elimination of caste
is under consideration. In terms of individuals, they weigh
heavily in favor of caste for white men, and heavily against
caste for most white women and for all members of the submerged caste except those who attach themselves as syco-

and Herbert Goldhamer, "The Hybrid and the Problem of Miscegenation," in
Characteristics of the American Negro, edited by Otto Klineberg, p. 261. Harpers,
1943.
[17] Yale University Press, 1937.

phants to the dominant group or who as individuals exploit the restricted opportunities of their fellow members of the minority group.[18]

Considerations of this sort are listed as "minor" matters in the balance sheet of caste only because they are so greatly overshadowed by the total picture of color in the world scene and in the total domestic picture. At the same time, many of the red entries in the ledger are made with the blood spilled for these "minor" reasons.

Moreover, these are the important considerations when the dynamics for changing color caste are to be considered or when the computation is made with a view to casting up the balance for individuals rather than for society as a whole. It is a curious thing that a system which places the whole of society on the red side of the ledger nevertheless gives to so many individuals a differential share of the net compensations. Being less poorly off than their fellows, they account themselves rich. If it were not so, it would be difficult to account for the perpetuation of color caste.

4. ARROGANCE VERSUS AVARICE

The balance sheet of caste is not to be calculated exclusively in static terms, as we have thus far considered it. There is also the dynamic problem: where does caste lead us? Stated kinetically, the dilemma which the Caucasian faces becomes the warfare between avarice and arrogance.

Avarice would prompt the Caucasian to make sure that the racial minorities in the United States have a higher standard of living, the better to support an increased prosperity for the nation as a whole, becoming better customers and swelling the profits of those who manufacture, sell, and lend. But arrogance will not permit the Caucasian to see this happen; he prefers to see the nonwhite stay in his "place"

---

[18] For the story of what sycophancy among certain so-called "Negro leaders" can do—even to espousing fascism—see J. Saunders Redding, *No Day of Triumph*, pp. 119-138. Harpers, 1942.

rather than to gain the profits of increased well-being at the expense of a narrowing of the chasm of separation.

The clearest illustration of the conflict of avarice and arrogance comes in the relationship of business interests in the United States toward the development of industrialism in Asia, Africa, and South America in the postwar period. It is quite probable that every effort will be made by American, British, and Australian business and financial interests to promote the rapid industrialization of China, some parts of Africa, and, to a degree, India. The white nations will help the darker peoples to go through an industrial revolution which will compress into a couple of decades the progress which took a couple of centuries in Europe and the United States, and which was carried through in the interwar years with amazing celerity in the Soviet Union. Such a development will mean handsome profits to the commercial and financial interests of the Caucasian nations, and will also be welcomed by the darker peoples. But the strengthening of the darker peoples of the world industrially, while it will serve the avarice of the Caucasian, will conflict with the impulses of arrogance. The stronger the pigmented peoples become the less tenable does white supremacy become. In pursuance of his avaricious impulses, the white man cuts the ground from under his arrogance, leaving it supported by the props of pride which tomorrow's giants of the Eastern world can brush aside like cobwebs.

In any alignment of the peoples of the world along the racial spectrum, with the whites against the darker peoples, the most favorable attitude which the white nations may expect from Russia is neutrality. The manner in which the Asiatic nations are already looking to Russia for leadership does not strongly argue that the Soviet Union would refuse to participate in such a conflict—on the side of the pigmented peoples and against the white supremacy that she totally rejects.[19] The Office of Population Research of the League of Nations published in 1944 its estimates of the future

[19] On the racial attitudes of the U.S.S.R., see below, Chap. IX.

population of Europe and of the Soviet Union,[20] which indicate that in the next quarter century the male population
of effective military age in the Soviet Union will have increased from thirty millions to over forty-three millions, while
the comparable figure for the rest of Europe is a net *loss*
of five millions. "The gain alone for the U.S.S.R. is
larger than the 1940 manpower of Germany, the Soviet
Union's closest rival in Europe."[21] No careful estimates of
the probable increases in the populations of other parts of
the world are now available, but Myrdal comments that

the population expansion of the whites is now slowing down, absolutely
and relatively. . . . The colored nations, on the other hand, are just
entering the first stage where expansion is likely to be pushed by an
increasingly improved control over death. The whites will, therefore,
from now on become a progressively smaller portion of the total world
population.[22]

The whites of Western Europe and of the American hemisphere extremities, with a present total of slightly over half
a billion, growing less rapidly than the colored world, with a
present total just under a billion and a half, would by 1970
be outnumbered at least three to one, with Russia failing to
support the Caucasian cause.

It is this conflict into which the warfare between avarice
and arrogance will lead us. We insist on dominating the
darker peoples, and at the same moment we insist on strengthening them in order to make profits. If the policies of white
supremacy continue to force the darker races into a common
bond of hatred toward the lighter, the issue will eventually
be joined in a horrendous struggle for world dominance in
which World Wars I and II will be mere curtain raisers.
That war would begin where the second has left off, the
atomic robot bomb being the mildest of its weapons. Quite
apart from the possible outcome of such a conflict, the stu-

[20] Frank W. Notestein *et al., The Future Population of Europe and of the Soviet Union.* Princeton, 1944.
[21] *Ibid.,* p. 132.
[22] *An American Dilemma,* p. 1017.

pidity of cupidity stands exposed in such a policy as this which leads us to insist on the satisfaction both of avarice and of arrogance.

The same analysis applies to the situation within our own national borders, particularly in the southern states, except that the immediate probabilities of development are the reverse of the international scene. Generally speaking, the South has preferred poverty with race pride to race equality with plenty. Only by preferring poverty to plenty has the American South been able to justify its racial discrimination; and only by continuing to pay the price of poverty can it hope to maintain its system of racial inequality. Yet, there are signs that avarice may outrun arrogance. Particularly among the poorer whites, the feeling is growing that it is time to make common cause with Negro labor against low wages in both North and South. Gentleman Jim Crow is coming out at the elbows. He may yet decide to swallow his pride. It butters no bread.

In these terms, the relatively petty questions of caste etiquette, eating taboos, and the like become insignificant. Arrogance has a very short life before it, for avarice has been appointed executioner. To cling to arrogance while giving free reign to avarice is to commit suicide. There is but one problem before the Caucasian: how, rapidly and completely, to divest himself of his racial arrogance so that he may be able in tomorrow's world to live on a basis of equality with all the peoples of the world.

In the business world, bankruptcy leads to foreclosure. The Christian religion has always maintained that precisely the same thing is true in the ethical realm, that ethical bankruptcy leads to the destruction and collapse of an immoral order. If this is not true, then the notion of a God of Justice and Brotherhood is erroneous, and the whole concept of a moral order must be discarded or radically altered. But if it is true, then man errs grievously in putting his faith in the continuance of color caste.

CHAPTER VII

DECLINE

... if the Nordic race will gather itself together in time, shake off the shackles of an inveterate altruism, discard the vain phantom of internationalism, and reassert the pride of race and the right of merit to rule.

—MADISON GRANT (1921)

WE CAN move in two general directions—upward or downward. Lateral movement amounts to backward movement, as the stream of history leaves us behind. In the next chapter, we shall examine two possibilities of advancement. In this chapter, we examine five varieties of the dogma of white supremacy, each of which is calculated to promote, in varying degree, the decline of Christianity.

1. THE EXTINCTION OF MINORITIES

This must be regarded as one of the live options of the future, if the clash of color is permitted to go forward unchecked. The fate of several million minority peoples in occupied Europe under the Nazi regime is sufficiently clear warning of what the racist spirit can do when it is unleashed. Making all due allowance for the possible exaggerations of atrocity stories, it remains true that a consistent effort has been made by the Nazis to kill off all Jews they could corral in certain sections of Eastern and Southeastern Europe. Under the protection of racist dogmas, the systematic extermination of a "racial" minority has been a principle of program and practice for the "'master race." It could conceivably happen here.

Various devices have been used in the process of extermination. The simplest process is that of shooting. It is expensive, costing at least five cents a round for ammunition; but there are vast stores of munitions left from the war; and five cents a life is not too exorbitant a price to pay.

There are other methods of extermination. Starvation and its cousin, malnutrition, are gaunt specters which have been employed with considerable success by the Nazis in Europe and the British in India. In its less obvious form of underfeeding it has long been a tacit part of the American caste pattern. Failure to provide adequate medical and hospital facilities is a part of the same general pattern of letting the nonwhite population die off. The infant mortality rate among Negroes in ten southern states runs from 50 to 70 per cent higher than among whites in the same states, due in large part to the lack of medical and hospital facilities and prenatal care and instruction for Negroes.[1] Sterilization is advocated by some, as a means of eliminating all minority peoples in one generation. It has the advantage of not involving any actual murder of persons now living; it merely murders the unborn generations. Particularly favored by certain pseudo scientists under the guise of "eugenics," this notion was proposed also by a delegate at the 1944 national convention of the America First party in Detroit. The presidential candidate of the party, the Reverend Gerald L. K. Smith, asked that the proposal be referred to committee "for careful study and recommendation."[2] Lethal gas chambers established at convenient points would perhaps be the most humane means of exterminating minorities in a relatively short time. Humane measures would have the advantage of arousing less opposition among the sentimentalists; but they would have the disadvantage of not satisfying fully the sadistic impulses of those racists whose fanatical espousal of white supremacy leads them to believe that only when all nonwhites are dead can there be security for the Caucasian.

[1] Gallagher, *American Caste and the Negro College*, p. 124.
[2] According to Associated Press dispatches.

If it were undertaken as an announced policy of the white peoples (and it is difficult to see how it could be carried through without announcing it), such a program of pogroms would not be handicapped by the necessity of attempting to conceal the evidence. It would be unnecessary to build great furnaces for mass cremation of bodies, as the Nazis are reported to have done in Poland.

There is, of course, the little question of what the non-white nations of the world would be doing while the purge was on in the United States. It might be necessary to take care of the rest of the world first, before turning to our internal racial proletariat.   But men whose minds are made up to the extermination of racial minorities within the United States and Europe can hardly be expected to give too serious consideration to the possibility that Asia, Africa, and South America might attempt to intervene. The plight of white minorities in Africa and Asia could be "taken care of" by temporary evacuation of whites, preliminary to the systematic use of the atomic bomb to depopulate completely the continents of Africa and Asia. Moreover, there would be little point in exterminating the nonwhite minorities within continental United States unless white America were prepared to carry through the process of extermination in the rest of the world.

The fantastic character of this nightmare does not remove it from the list of options before us. It is the logical consummation of the doctrine of white supremacy, and the defenders of white supremacy never tire of telling us that they are coldly logical. Whether they consciously admit it or not, this is the logical goal toward which the supporters of white supremacy are working. In any final showdown between racial groups, they would prefer extermination of the colored peoples to the subjugation of the whites. The occasional lynching or race riot in this country is only a suggestion of what the believers in white supremacy have in store for the minorities if and when it becomes necessary to act on a comprehensive scale. Mass extermination has been used on a small experimental scale in the United States—first and foremost in the treatment of the American Indian. The failure to follow through in that process means that the Indian on the reservations is not now vanishing. His numbers are increasing again. The experiment was not completed. Another precedent for the process of mass extermination of troublesome minorities is found in some parts of the South during Reconstruction. In a single parish in Louisiana, after a Negro hunt in the seventies, more than two thousand brown bodies were gathered for burial.

A frank appraisal of the extermination method of maintaining white supremacy must lead us to conclude, however, that at the present time it is advocated more for purposes of emotional catharsis than as a serious proposal for immediate action. Troubled in conscience, the advocates of white supremacy are known to declare on some occasions that the only answer to an intolerable situation is to shoot the minorities. "The only good Indian is a dead Indian" is a slogan that could be revived and used against any minority.

2. Expulsion and Colonization

There are those who argue that the initial mistake was made when the minorities were brought to America. They would rectify that mistake by sending non-Caucasians to other parts of the world. Senator Bilbo of Mississippi is the most vocal advocate of the deportation of all Negroes. He usually speaks of "voluntary colonization," and endeavors to make it clear that he is moved solely out of consideration for the good of the Negro. Since this is a white man's country, the Negro has no future here; for his own good, let him go "back to Africa" where he can rule his own destiny without white interference. It is touching to see a man who so unselfishly devotes a major section of his political career to agitation for the welfare of Negroes via the *Black Mayflower* route to Africa. Mr. Bilbo claims to have more than three million *Negro* signatures in support of his proposal. The *Congressional Record* is liberally interlarded with the Senator's speeches in favor of colonization—particularly do these speeches appear in the sections carrying "extension of remarks," designed for free mailing to constituents. He quotes Abraham Lincoln (who at one time favored colonization). Usually he selects Liberia as the future home of all Negro Americans. He reached the crowning insult of his career (at least up to this writing) in a speech from the floor of the Senate in the spring of 1944 when he confessed that he was willing not only to send all Negroes to Liberia, but also to make Mrs. Roosevelt "queen" of the Negro nation.

Colonization has long been a favorite daydream of white Americans who want to get rid of the "race problem" by dumping it on some other shore. The proposal was advocated before the Civil War as a means of getting rid of all free Negroes, who were looked upon as a threat to slavery. In ante bellum days in the North, the controversy between the abolitionists and the colonizers was one of the hottest issues. The American Colonization Society was itself split in two by the abolitionist issue.

Just after World War I, the prospect of colonization was transformed into a shining hope through the activities of West Indies-born Marcus Garvey. Advocating pride in blackness and exhibiting a masterful insight into the methods and uses of mass propaganda, Garvey built a militant movement of Black Nationalism which had a sizable following in the early twenties. He started the Black Star (instead of the White Star) steamship line, raised considerable sums of money, and stirred up the hopes of colored America in a return to Africa which is paralleled in American history only by the fervor of the more intense political Zionists of American Jewry. When the first and only vessel of the Black Star line ran into grief on her maiden voyage under the new ownership, and Garvey finally landed in jail charged with using the mails to defraud, the movement collapsed. But it left behind a legacy of pride in blackness that had never before been as intense a possession of Negro America as a group. Yet, in psychological terms, the movement known as Garveyism was the reaction of the office boy who says, "You can't fire me; I quit!"

Serious practical considerations stand in the way of any successful consummation of the venture of colonization if it is undertaken. First, there is the matter of selecting a site in Africa. That continent is now owned and controlled by European nations, except for the tiny Liberia and remote Ethiopia. To expect that these two small territories could absorb thirteen million Americans is absurd. And it is equally unrealistic to think that Britain, Portugal, Spain, Belgium, or France would welcome immigrant Americans in any large numbers in any of their colonies or dominions. The uneasy control they now maintain over the African population would be jeopardized by a flood of liberty-seeking emigrants from American oppression. While it may be romantic to some to think of a *Black Mayflower* setting out for Africa, it is unrealistic to dream of it without visioning the inevitable preparation to wage war against one or more of the present European owners of that continent.

Secondly, assuming a place to which emigrants could go, there is the question of deciding whether the colonization is to be voluntary or enforced. If it is to be voluntary, the trickle of emigrants would be considerably less than the annual increase in the Negro population of the United States. The only possibility of using colonization as a "solution" of race matters in the United States would lie in the readiness to use the army to enforce it and the navy to carry it through. Men like Mr. Bilbo may be presumed to be intelligent enough to know this, even though they speak publicly only of voluntary colonization.

What this really means is that, if the voluntary colonization of a few Negroes each year were going forward, men like Bilbo could then say, "If you don't like it here, go to Africa." They do not face the grave disruption of American life and economy which any such mass emigration would involve, particularly in the loss of a great reservoir of cheap labor. The necessity of building and policing concentration camps for thirteen million people awaiting deportation is no little matter. Thirteen millions are somewhat more than the 112,000 handled by the War Relocation Authority when Japanese Americans were evacuated from the West Coast. The barbarities of the slave trade would pale by comparison with the operations of the fleet for compulsory evacuation of Negro America to Africa, making the return more barbarous than the coming.

Thirdly, assuming a place to which to send the colonists and the machinery for enforcing the expulsion, there remains the nice matter of identifying "Negroes." Would we send to Africa only those persons now living in this nation who have actually come from Africa? A single ocean liner would carry all of them. Would we then send to Africa only those persons now living in this nation who are of unmixed African descent? That would leave seven to nine million "Negroes" in the nation. Perhaps we would then insist on sending out of the land every individual who had one Negro ancestor anywhere in his lineage? That would make serious inroads in many of the First Families.[3] Then where, between the extremes of unmixed Africans and unmixed whites, shall we draw the line? And with the indefiniteness of existing (or nonexistent) records of parentage, a matter which has been a source of embarrassment to many a draft board which has not wished to pry too deeply into the ancestry of "Negro" registrants, are the advocates of colonization ready to ex-

---

[3] A certain southern legislator, speaking against an especially severe antimiscegenation bill, is reported as having said that if the definition of "Negro" incorporated in the bill were accepted there would not be enough white people in the state to pass it. See Louis Wirth and Herbert Goldhamer, "The Hybrid and the Problem of Miscegenation," in *Characteristics of the American Negro*, edited by Otto Klineberg, pp. 301-302. Harpers, 1943.

pose their blood relationships in order to denounce their cousins? If they are unwilling to expose the actual degree and extent of "white" parentage in the case of each and every individual "Negro" (which would mean parading family skeletons down a thousand Main Streets), the supporters of compulsory colonization are faced with an impossible task of identifying all persons in America who have any non-white ancestry.

In addition to the practical matters standing in the way of colonization, an ethical question may be raised. Amongst all the racial and national groups in the United States, the Negro had the most urgent invitation to come to these shores. If we must think in terms of getting rid of unwelcome immigrants, the Negro is the last to leave. The Chinese, Japanese, Filipino, and Spanish-American peoples whom we brought to supply the needs of the labor market also belong here as "invited" residents, not intruders. Is the white man to use the cheap laborers only when he wants them, and then to send them away, as a small boy sucks an orange dry and throws the skin in the street? It is beside the point to admit that employers who want cheap labor will strongly oppose the deportation of any sizable number of racial minorities. It is a nice ethical question whether the moral balance lies with those who would deport the minorities or those who would keep them here and exploit them. Both proposals fall so far short of minimum standards of decency and justice that the Christian conscience rejects them.

Finally, as far as the Negro in the United States is concerned, it is ludicrous to speak of sending him "back" to Africa. He cannot go "back" to a place he has never been. In the thirteen million persons who make up the Negro group of America there are only about one thousand who have come from Africa.[4] The Negro American is no more "African" than is the white American. The only culture he has is an American culture. His language, religion, dietary and

[4] Myrdal. *op cit* p. 120.

clothing habits, political outlook, and patriotic allegiance are all American. He is as much an alien to Africa as is an Irishman or a Chinese or a Swede. When one looks at the successive waves of immigration that have come to America, and compares Negro immigrants to all others, these facts stands out: (1) the immigration of Negroes began in 1619; (2) since that time, white immigration has continued and still goes on, while Negro immigration stopped a century ago; from which we conclude (3) that the Negro is the "oldest" racial group in the United States with the exception of the American Indian. If we wished to give the country to the people to whom it "belongs" because of length of residence, we should deport everybody except the Negro and the Indian.

The expulsion proposal for solving the problem of minorities is applied to other groups than the Negro. The Joint Immigration Bureau, which is particularly active on the West Coast and sends its lobbyist to Washington, strongly advocates the deportation of all racial minorities *except* the Negro. They are not happy over the presence of Negroes, but they are willing to accept the original error which brought them to America. All others who are nonwhite must be sent back to the countries from which they or their ancestors came. The sympathizers with this movement were particularly active during the time that Japanese Americans were removed from the Pacific slope. Speakers made the rounds of luncheon clubs and women's meetings, getting resolutions passed and petitions signed. They would deport all racial minorities from America except Negroes—beginning with the Japanese and Americans of Japanese ancestry.

A neat proposal was advanced in the columns of the San Francisco *Chronicle* over the signature of H. S. Darlington on July 6, 1943. Beautifully simple, almost to the point of genius, it would solve two problems with one master stroke. First, proposes Mr. Darlington, let us shoot all Japanese now inhabiting the islands of the Japanese homeland. Then, let us send to repopulate the depopulated islands all our Negro citizens. By their loyalty to the American cause they have demonstrated their merit and deserve such solicitude. We would, of course, keep a few of the islands for strategic military and naval outposts, in order adequately to defend the loyal Negro Americans who would continue to merit our guardianship. Mr. Darlington's proposal is a logical combination of the salient features of the first and second proposals for maintaining white supremacy.

3. PATCHING AND PERFECTING THE CASTE SYSTEM

Most persons who today believe in white supremacy in the United States put their energies behind this proposal, the maintenance of the status quo through perfecting the controls of caste. And it is here that the stature of the opposition to Christianity merits special attention.

The supporters of caste are no irresponsible demagogues bellowing in the Cave of the Winds on Capitol Hill. These are no crackpot pamphleteers, no writers of whimsical letters to the editor. These are the substantial and insubstantial people—the citizens and preachers and bank clerks and shop committeemen, the corporation directors and small farmers, the big people and the little people who have grown up under a caste system and have accepted it as one of the *given* things of the universe. These are not "bad" people; most of them are normal, quiet, industrious, good people. Most of them are ashamed of the excesses of enthusiasm of their more outspoken compatriots like the senior Senator from Mississippi or former Governor Talmadge of Georgia. They do not like to hear too much talk about race relations and white supremacy; they are uncomfortable in reading books and articles and pamphlets that bring up the problem. All they want is to be let alone to enjoy life as they found it. They want to live and let live. They believe in tolerance, and insist that they have no prejudice against anyone. Their spokesman is the junior Senator from Mississippi, whose words are quoted at the head of Chapter I. Frequently one hears their position summarized in words like these:

I have nothing against any colored person, and I don't see why he should have anything against me. I have never harmed a colored person in my life. Why, we always had a colored cook, and I played with a Filipino boy in school. I think that each one of us, white, yellow, brown, and black, should stay in his own place. If we do that, there won't be any trouble, and everything will come out for the best in the end.

One of the things usually overlooked by people who say it will all come out in the wash is the fact that *we* are the wash. If the import of world facts reviewed in these pages is correct in any degree, then the washboard is a rough one, and the soaps are calculated to smart.

This is one of the times when the cleansing of society is accelerated by the tempo of world events, and the irritation of washday tempers is increasingly apparent. The readiness to riot is in Boston and San Diego, Miami and Minneapolis, Mobile and Detroit. It is in the remote rural districts of the Deep South and crops out in the remote pockets of the Rockies.[5] The apprehensiveness of jittery whites is well summed up by a white woman of culture, refinement, and high social position in the city of Houston, Texas, who rose in the forum period of a race relations meeting to accuse the speaker of "starting a race war." She went on to say that she believed this war would break out "right here in Houston," and concluded by saying that she had bought a pistol and was practicing in her own back yard, to be ready. Many an editorial in the yellow press and many a cracker

---

[5] Lest this rhetoric be taken for unsubstantiated assertion, a citation or two will suggest the facts: Wallace, Idaho, has not permitted Orientals to stay in the city for generations. Cullman, Alabama, has now taken down a sign of which its better citizens were ashamed; it read: "Nigger, don't let the sun set on you here." In Guerneville, California, a notice went up on the post-office bulletin board demanding that persons of Japanese ancestry be forever excluded from California.

barrel conversation at the crossroads country store are matched by many a long argument in the smoking rooms of the Pullmans and the corridors and committee rooms of Congress. People are apprehensive.

Being apprehensive, they are not ready to sit quietly by and witness the disintegration of established social patterns. The individual gets his psychological ground in his society; and any threat of change to that society is automatically a threat to his own psychological stability.[6] He needs to be neither a knave nor a fool to feel restless and upset, even vindictive, when proposals are made for radically altering the basic structure of the society in which he moves. The slightest deviation from the accustomed etiquette of caste becomes, for him, the cause of acute inner unrest. He justifiably feels that in maintaining the established pattern of race relations he is defending something real and valuable to him. He does not need to have the additional psychological incentives connected with a grandfather who fought and died for white supremacy. He feels that he must fight for it or lose the very basis of his own personality. This feeling does not need to be phrased explicitly. It is what he calls an "instinctive" reaction, because it has been his reaction from earliest childhood.

That is why many persons, in talking about racial relations, adopt an indirect and cautious approach. They do not want open discussion, because it unsettles people. Even those who are most anxious to see a change made will often insist that the "indirect approach" is the best way to work on race matters.

Educators, reformers, and journalists with liberal leanings in the South have a standard text which they recite to please one another and the visitor. Everything can be said in the South if it is said "in the right way." . . . I have listened again and again to the pronouncements of this theory of Southern indirectness from liberal white Southerners who have been most anxious that I should understand, not only the aesthetics,

[6] Muzafer Sherif, *The Psychology of Social Norms.* Harpers, 1936.

but also the pragmatic purpose of this escape machinery. . . . I have
sensed the high subjective pleasure of this persistent balancing on the
margins and the corresponding pleasures of the less liberal audience in
being teased but never affronted by the sore points. I have come to understand how a whole system of moral escape has become polite form in
the South. This form is applicable even to scientific writings and,
definitely, to public discussion and teaching on all levels. It is sometimes developed into an exquisite and absorbing art.[7]

The natural result of this whole frame of mind, which power-
fully controls the thought patterns of all persons who grow
up in the acceptance of the caste system, is that the problem
of race is never met squarely if it can be treated obliquely.
Whenever possible, it is assumed to be "settled," not a fit
subject for argument as to its mutability. There could be
no better intellectual defense of caste than to have every
discussion of it proceed from the premise that it cannot be
changed.

So firmly does this notion fix itself on the mind of the
member of the white caste that a recent writer, a man of
liberal reputation and scholarly standing, tells us that the
only way to make any headway at all in race matters is to
begin with the assumption that the race problem is insoluble.
Here are his words:

No notable improvement can be achieved, in my opinion, unless the
ground is cleared by a recognition on the part of both whites and
Negroes that (a) the problem is incapable of solution and (b) the
issue of segregation must not be called in question.[8]

If we make this initial concession, he argues, we shall
then be able to do much to ameliorate the hurtful aspects of
the caste structure; but we must begin with the "candid
acknowledgment that the Negro question is insoluble." To

---

[7] Myrdal, *op. cit.*, pp. 36-37. (Having been guilty, myself, of producing one
book which conformed to these canons of the etiquette of caste, I am speaking
somewhat more bluntly in these present pages. B. G. G.)

[8] David L. Cohn, "How the South Feels About the Race Problem," *Atlantic
Monthly*, January, 1944. The succeeding quotations from Mr. Cohn are from
the same source.

support this contention, Mr. Cohn then brings forth the intermarriage red herring, demanding as a second "candid acknowledgment" the concession that the heart of the problem can only be reached by admitting that the race question

is at bottom a blood or sexual question. The whites are determined that no white in their legal jurisdiction shall marry a Negro, and this is the law of all the southern states. They are equally determined that white women shall not have physical relations with Negro men except, when discovered, upon pain of death or banishment inflicted upon one or both parties to the act.

And the argument is concluded, as far as Mr. Cohn's written statement is concerned, with his insistence that these two basic acknowledgments lead directly to a third concession regarding the Negro question:

If it is insoluble, the issue is confused and harm is done to race relations when leaders on both sides, out of sentimentality or refusal to face the fact, pretend that somehow it is capable of solution.

If his readers are ready to grant Mr. Cohn's "candid acknowledgments," his own readiness to return the courtesy is quickly given. He will not contend that this is justice or democracy which he is advocating.

Let us not delude ourselves. This is less than democracy. But there is no section of the country in which at some time other minorities, as well as the Negro, have not been discriminated against. There is no government—indeed, no organized religion—which has not at some time compromised with the logic of its own institutions. . . . No one can view the position of the American Negro without a sore heart, a troubled conscience and a deep compassion. Nor can one view the position of the southern whites without sympathy, for they are the sum of their inheritance and their environment, and act according to their lights.

Thus, although Mr. Cohn agrees that the caste pattern largely molds the attitudes of the people who grow up under it, his remedy is not to suggest the changing of these patterns but only to insist that the social order of the South has been based upon the maintenance of the "color line," and nothing—not even the horrors of Reconstruction—has been able to shake its foundations.

Mr. Cohn's argument is illuminating and useful, not only because he states a thesis with which many readers will agree, but also because he demonstrates the tortuous manner in which the "troubled conscience" seeks every avenue of escape except that of *moral* action. His article is a gem of condensed and cogent persuasion in defense of caste. He admits that he is not arguing for democracy, being disarmingly frank about it and insisting that this is only what men of every age and clime have done in compromising with the "logic of [religious] institutions."

The real significance of the article comes, however, in the direct threat that it packs. Mr. Cohn directly warns all well-meaning persons to stay clear of tampering with the color line unless they are ready (as he puts it) to see "the country swept by civil war." And the ethical import of his argument is carefully stated when he argues that he knows that this is something less than democracy, but that it is all that can be hoped for in "any foreseeable time." The article might be understood to be a blanket defiance of all attempts to transform the caste structure in America, or it might be interpreted as one of the final gasps of a decadent social system. I prefer to view it as an explicit statement of the truth that the caste system can be defended only by a frank abandonment of democratic and Christian ethical standards.

The problem before the defenders of caste, if they wish to do anything more than fight a delaying action, is one of convincing white America that it ought to give up its professions of political and economic democracy, and deny the ethical standards of the Hebraic-Christian tradition, in order to be able with a clear conscience to support color caste. The effective patching and perfecting of the caste system waits upon the discarding of democratic and Christian standards

ATION Sy

and practices. The American racist comes out at exactly the same point at which his Nazi cousin emerges: the church, and the religion it ought to represent, must be regarded as Enemy Number One of the racist.

When the case is so convincingly argued by the defenders of caste, we who oppose it in the name of religion and democracy are spared the necessity of stating the argument.

4. THE FORTY-NINTH STATE

Just as the colonization movement called up its counterpart in Garveyism, so the argument for the maintenance and perfecting of the caste system calls forth Black Nationalism as its natural companion. In the past two decades, many Negroes (and some liberal whites who think of themselves as champions of Negro rights) have fondly toyed with the idea of establishing somewhere within the confines of the United States a haven for black America. In effect, they say, "You can't segregate us; we will segregate ourselves!" The idea is popular among some of the younger intellectuals, but is not limited to them.

Just where the Sepia State is to be located has never been agreed upon. Sometimes the southern half of New Jersey is selected; sometimes the southern half of California (Los Angeles included). One of the wildest proposals has been that the United States annex Lower California from Mexico and deed it to Negro America. The problem of location has never been solved by the Black Nationalists any more than it is solved by the Bilbo colonizers. It is to be a forty-ninth state carved out somewhere: they are a little vague as to just where.

One of the clearest and most carefully worked out of these proposals appeared in a book by James S. Allen,[9] in which full details of location and organization for the forty-ninth

[9] *The Negro Question in the United States.* International Publishers, 1936.

state are elaborated. By gerrymandering his counties on the basis of census data, Mr. Allen was able to piece together a continuous series of counties running from central Virginia in a great, downsweeping crescent to the heart of the Delta country in Mississippi, in which the 1930 census gave a net 51 per cent majority of Negro population. Included in the proposed Black Crescent were many counties which had less than a majority of colored people; but the mathematical majority of 1 per cent was established by Mr. Allen's use of only such few of these counties as were necessary to serve as connecting links between other counties where Negroes approximated 50 per cent, together with those few counties in which they outnumbered the whites. In Mr. Allen's argument, this Negro state is to be the Negro Soviet in the coming Soviet America. Aside from his book, I have seen in print no serious scholarly proposal for establishing the Sepia State. Nevertheless, it continues to be a pleasant pipe dream of some intellectuals.

Millions of whites would welcome the proposal to put all Negroes into a permanently circumscribed area. Some might be sorry to lose a ready supply of ghetto labor, as the not infrequent irritation of some southern whites over the northward and westward migration of Negroes testifies. On the whole, however, white America would heave a mighty sigh of relief if it could believe that the segregation of all Negroes in a separate state would solve the problem of caste and free conscience of its tensions. There might be disagreement over the site; but the middle of the Arizona desert or the thinly settled portions of Montana and Wyoming might do. If Indians can be put on reservations and if Japanese Americans can be segregated in the mountains, why not Negroes?

We can be fairly certain of one thing: Negroes themselves will never willingly be segregated in one gigantic mass. Only by force of arms could they be compelled to accept even the most lush agricultural and industrial heart of America as compensation for the indignity of enforced complete segregation. The young intellectuals do not speak for the people on this issue.

We can, I believe, be equally certain that if white America ever worked itself into the frame of mind necessary to consummate such a process of completing the segregation pattern with geographical finality, that mind set would point toward the duplication of the Tule Lake and Topaz patterns for Japanese evacuees and the bleaker Indian Reservations (making sure that there was no oil on the lands given to Negroes, as there was on in the land the Cherokees got).

And if the ethical conscience may be permitted a word on the proposal, despite its academic character, that word is one of unqualified condemnation. No matter what name is used, segregation is segregation. It establishes patterns of conflict and misunderstanding and hatred. It makes more problems than it solves. It denies the impulses of brotherhood and perpetuates in magnified form an injustice which it is powerless to correct.

5. PARALLEL CIVILIZATIONS

Among white liberals all over the nation, and especially in the South, this proposal has widest acceptance. It also claims the allegiance of many Negro leaders. It was first given full formulation by Gardner Murphy;[10] but before that, Booker T. Washington had paved the way in his famous five minutes before the Atlantic Exposition:

In all things that are purely social we can be as separate as the fingers, yet one as the hand in all things essential to mutual progress.[11]

Biracialism, race parallelism, or parallel civilizations, as the proposal is variously called, in simple terms means that each race is to stay on its own side of the color line in all matters that are "purely social," while complete freedom of oppor-

[10] Gardner Murphy, *The Basis of Ascendancy.* Longmans, Green, 1909.
[11] *Up From Slavery,* pp. 221-222. Doubleday, Page & Co., 1900.

tunity is to be accorded to both groups equally, to advance to the limits of their own potentialities, each on its own side of the color line.

The caste line, it is argued, has divided the two groups *horizontally*, putting all Negroes below all whites.[12] Let that line now be drawn *vertically* between the two groups, setting no ceiling on the possibilities of either group to advance upward to the highest limits of its own potentiality, but restricting each caste to its own side of the line in all matters "purely social and racial." This proposal has a distinct ethical advantage over all others named in this chapter, in that it seriously tries to apply the "separate but equal" formula in both of its facets—separation *and* equality. It seems to many liberal Negroes and whites alike that it may be the desired next phase of development in American race relations. It is the growing edge of the Christian conscience at work on race relations. Or, more accurately, it *was* the growing edge of the Christian conscience a few decades ago.

In his great book on *Christianity and the Race Problem*,[13] J. H. Oldham devoted a chapter to "Social Equality" in which he carefully considered "racial and social segregation on the basis of equality of opportunity," concluding that "the experiment will and must be tried, since no other solution is at present within sight."[14] It was his judgment in 1924 that

segregation may not, indeed cannot, be the ultimate ideal. But as a particular stage in the development of the human race it may be the arrangement which on the whole makes for harmony and peaceful progress.[15]

There are, then, two quite different grounds on which biracialism may be advocated, and much depends on which of these two bases is used for the argument and to guide the development: it may be proposed as a permanent pattern of adjust-

[12] For refinements of the patterns of caste configuration, see Myrdal, *op. cit.*, pp. 691-692 and 1381; and Gallagher, *op. cit.*, pp. 74, 81, 86. The line is *not* absolutely horizontal, but tilted on a bias or bent in a crescent.

[13] London: Student Christian Movement, 1924.

[14] *Ibid.*, pp. 170-171.

[15] *Ibid.*

ment or it may be advocated as a necessary and useful transition stage. It is worth examining the proposal from both of these angles.

First, as a proposed permanent adjustment—what is to be said of race parallelism? It has no historical precedent; and since it has never been tried, we have no empirical method of knowing whether it will work. We can observe a few instances in the American scene where an effort has been made to live up to both parts of the "separate but equal" formula, most of which are of such recent origin as not to afford sufficient experience for final judgment. We can only conjecture what the result would be *if* equality of opportunity and incentive, together with absolute social segregation, were to become the accepted pattern of race adjustment in America. But conjecture is swayed by subjective considerations. Are there no facts available?

The facts are that the ethical demands placed upon the more powerful group by the proposed race parallelism are greater than men have yet demonstrated the ability to obey. Oldham put it rightly:

Social separation is in itself a policy which both races can accept. It is possible on a basis of complete mutual respect, and is sincerely advocated in this sense by many of those who favor it. But in practice it is apt to mean not merely separation but discrimination.[16]

This position, as Oldham recognizes, is an irreconcilable contradiction. The "basis of complete mutual respect," if it is genuine, is nothing but the principle of the equality of the races; and the whole purpose of white supremacy is defeated when this principle is granted. Can this notion of complete mutual respect (equality) be expected to rule the conduct of the more powerful group as long as the fact of separation continually invites the more powerful group to renew and perpetuate its exploitation? The white group, holding an almost complete monopoly of power, and constituting a ninety per cent majority

[16] *Ibid.*, p. 172.

armed with that power, would be saddled with the responsibility of acting justly and impartially in the exercise of its
power, to the point of abrogating all differentials between
itself and the nonwhite groups—and continuing to do so with
no other coercion than the persuasion of conscience. The caste
line is to remain unbroken, standing as a constant temptation
to the more powerful group to use segregation as a means of
discrimination. With the sheep continually in the corral, will
no one ever think of shearing them?

This is the nub of the whole dilemma with which the white
man's conscience is continually bedeviled: that he is committed
in principle to the idea of equality of opportunity and equal
treatment of all men, while at the same time he gives his
support to the idea and practice of segregation, which is the
principal tool of caste. It is playing with words to suggest
that the enunciation of the notion of caste parallelism will
make any significant difference in the attitudes or the practices
of the dominant group over any considerable period of time.
A temporary softening of adjustment might be achieved in the
wake of some great symbolic national event; but the ethical
tenacity required voluntarily to maintain the high position of
forbearance from exploitation as long as caste invites avarice
is a quality of saintliness known to St. Francis but to few others.

Race parallelism would make a significant ethical difference
in practical operation only if it were based on substantially
equal access to the power which stands back of the mutual
respect. As Oldham put it:

The world has recognized in regard to individuals that it is not right
or possible for a man to be a judge in his own cause. It is not any
easier for a community enjoying exclusive power to act justly where its
own interests are involved.[17]

The proof of the sincerity of the proposal and of its effectiveness in execution would lie in a willingness to permit an
impartial tribunal to sit constantly on the degree of equality

[17] *Ibid.*

prevailing in the proposed segregated-egalitarian society. No writer who advocates race parallelism has as yet advanced a serious proposal that Negro judges be added to the bench that sits on cases of racial discrimination. The fact that this proposal has never seriously been advanced by proponents of the theory of parallel civilizations suggests that the advocates of the theory have not thought their way through the matter, or else that they do not really mean to eliminate inequality. And the further fact that the entire weight of caste has been thrown against every effort to enforce the legal equalities long guaranteed by the Bill of Rights and the Thirteenth, Fourteenth, and Fifteenth Amendments to the Constitution suggests that something much more radical than race parallelism is needed if the caste structure is to be modified so that equality becomes a fact.

It will help to understand the parallel civilizations proposal if we look at its genesis. The statement of Mr. Booker T. Washington, which forms the basic notion from which the proposal derives, is an amazing sentence when it is analyzed. *It completely ignores the question of equality, and mentions only the degree of separation that is to prevail.* It leaves unsaid much more than it says. It was an effort—and, on the whole, a successful one—to strike a basis of compromise between the two racial groups in the 1890's, but it was aimed at quieting the more violent and vehement forms of antagonism directed toward the Negro, and promised that the Negro would not try to break down the separation of the two groups in things "purely social." By implication, the eloquent silences of Mr. Washington's statement promised that the Negro was ready to accept a subordinate caste position of inequality whenever "things essential to mutual progress" brought the two races together. Whatever equality the Negro was to enjoy would be limited strictly to those times and places when he was by himself—when he was "purely social." The genesis of the notion of race parallelism opens no exodus from inequality.

As formulated and developed by writers and thinkers since

Washington's Atlanta Exposition speech, the "separate but equal" formula has never corrected this initial weakness except in words. The formula has been used to evade, rather than to express, the egalitarian requirements of the Constitution, the American Creed, and the Christian religion. It recognizes in theory the demands of conscience for equality; yet the substance of that equality is denied by the insistence on separation in many areas and the observance of caste in all areas where separation does not prevail.

To clarify the point, let it be supposed that complete equality between the two groups were to be achieved under the "separate but equal" formulation of the caste relationship. What would be the result? *Would it not mean that absolute and complete physical separation in every aspect of life must be enforced?* Under the present caste system, the color line is observed in many different ways, physical separation being only one method of recognizing the race differential.[18] As long as some recognition of caste status is made, it is possible for the members of the two castes to mingle on the most intimate terms. A Negro and a white person may live under the same roof and be "members of the same family"—provided the master-servant relationship is maintained. If, however, the Negro lived in the house as an equal, there would be no way of establishing the separateness. In a caste system, Negroes may work side by side with white workingmen in a construction job; but the Negro is the "helper" and gets a lower wage. If the occupational differential were removed, to give equality of status, then separation must be enforced to maintain the integrity of caste. Many of the "best people" boast of Negro "mammies" who nursed and suckled them, and lament the passing of the "darky" servant class. Under a caste system, the most intimate forms of association and collaboration between the races was made possible, because inequality of status was defined by some other device than physical separation—a

[18] Cf. Charles S. Johnson, *Patterns of Negro Segregation*, pp. 1-230. Harpers, 1943.

uniform, or the use of the first name for the servant, or back-door entrance only; but under the proposed egalitarian society of race parallelism, the striking off of all racial differentiations of superiority and inferiority would demand that each caste stay completely by itself in order to preserve the amenities of equality. That is the clear and inescapable meaning of separate-but-equal: to be equal, the groups must be separate. If and where complete separation is not enforced, then, if equality prevails, the integrity of the caste line is destroyed, and the whole structure of racial integrity which the parallelism formula attempts to protect is destroyed. On the other hand, if complete separation were enforced, is either group ready to face the implications?

That would mean that the white man would have to provide his own servant class and unskilled labor. It would mean the development of two parallel economic and financial structures: two banking systems, two marketing and retailing processes, duplicate factories and mills and railroads, duplicate telephones and communications, two Hollywoods to produce pictures for two sets of theaters, duplications in all phases of economic activity (with the profits formerly accruing to whites from sales to black customers now transferred to the Negro group). It would mean the elaboration not only of separate educational systems, each autonomous; there would need to be two political systems, two judiciaries, two sets of laws each with its own enforcement machinery, a complete duplication of all machinery for taxation and assessment, two dog pounds, complete duplication of all processes of citizenship. In fine, it means the principles of the forty-ninth state, with scores of these little pockets of colored life encysted in the white body politic.

If race parallelism does not mean these things, what does it mean? It demands equality and is sincere about that demand, for therein lies its only ethically sound argument. Yet, is it ready to face the implications of the separation which it proffers as the price of equality?

Race parallelism is not ready to grant equality without separation. That would mean Negroes sitting as judges in the trial of white criminals. That would mean white women serving as servants in the better-class Negro homes. That would mean Negro foremen giving orders to mixed gangs. No; race parallelism rests its willingness to grant equality on its assurance that there will be complete separation; but when faced squarely with the implications of its stand, is it willing to pay the price of complete separation?

Thus it comes about that the advocates of parallelism are usually careful to limit precisely the areas of equality and to insist on separation *only in those areas*—while at the same time insisting that there is not to be separation in other areas, and that there is to be inequality where there is no separation. The classic statement of this idea was quoted by Dr. Oldham:

Sir Frederick Lugard has summarized this view of the relations between the races: "Here, then, is the true conception of the inter-relation of colour: complete uniformity in ideals, absolute equality in the paths of knowledge and culture, equal opportunity for those who strive, equal admiration for those who achieve; in matters social and racial a separate path, each person pursuing his own inherited traditions, preserving his own race purity and race pride; *equality in things spiritual, agreed diversity in the physical and material.*[19]

Sir Frederick's statement was given the standing of careful quotation and public approval by President Harding in his speech in Birmingham, Alabama, in 1921; and during the interwar years this notion of "racial and social segregation on the basis of equality of opportunity" became the principal cliché used in defense of color caste.

That it could never be anything other than a defense of caste is inherent in the fact that it grants equality only in the areas of separation, and refuses to mention equality in "the physical and material." Back of this silence lies a confusing identification between the "physical" as applying to intermarriage and the same term as applying to jobs and living condi-

[19] *Ibid.*, p. 170. (Italics are mine. B. G. G.)

tions. In these areas of breadwinning and housing and employment, there is to be segregation; but it is not the segregation of spatial separation: it is the observance of the etiquette of caste, expressed in occupational differentials or ritual observance such as the use of first names for Negroes and "mister" for whites. It permits the continuing day-to-day intimate contacts of members of the two groups, by keeping the Negro "in his place" as he works beside the white man. In return, it offers the members of the submerged caste the compensation that they may go as far as they like in "spiritual matters," provided they will stay by themselves as they do it. John Henry may work on the railroads, provided he does not aspire to rise higher than section hand on the road crews, fireman on the locomotive, or porter in the passenger services: he may not expect to be a foreman, an engineer, or a conductor. Marian Anderson may be accepted as the greatest contralto of her generation, provided she does not expect that acceptance to be given in Constitution Hall.

The conclusion is inescapable: complete separation of the races by any other device than the forty-ninth state, colonization, or extermination is impossible; and therefore the "separate but equal" formula is unworkable. The white man needs the Negro as a laborer. He needs him as a customer. He needs him to complete the psychological patterns of his own spiritual life. He needs the enrichment of the common life which comes when all contributions are encouraged. What the proposal called race parallelism means is that the Negro is to be encouraged to stay by himself whenever and wherever the white man does not need him; but that he is expected to come to the service of the white man whenever and wherever he is needed, and in the rendering of this needed service he is to forget *both* parts of the "separate but equal" notion.

In the end, what the proposal amounts to is an effort to use a slogan to soften the impact of the caste system upon both racial groups by modifying it in the direction of equality while at the same time appearing to make sure that the integrity of the caste line is not threatened. Stripped to its essentials, the proposal is no permanent plan at all. It is not even a new plan. It is merely a modification of some aspects of caste to permit enlarged opportunities for Negroes in certain marginal fields so long as they stay on their own side of the line, while at the same time they are to cross over the line and continue their caste status at every point where the white caste wants their services. It means neither separation nor equality.

In its thoroughgoing form of complete separation, the proposal of race parallelism is as unthinkable to the white man as to the Negro—the first, because the white man stands to lose too much by it; the second, because the Negro rightfully resents any form of compulsory segregation; and both, because segregation violates the basic unity of the human family and is repugnant to the essential desires for spiritual unity. In its thoroughgoing form of complete equality, the proposal contradicts the purposes of the color line, it places demands upon the altruism of the more powerful group which the latter shows no signs of being ready, willing, or able to assume, and therefore appears to be both bad logic and unrealistic ethic. As a serious proposal for the permanent adjustment of the races, parallelism must be rejected. Its principal importance lies in the fact that for fifty years, since Mr. Washington's Atlanta Compromise, this proposal has provided a convenient and easy escape from the challenge of conscience. White men have been able to say that this was what the Negro asked for; Negroes have been able to say that this was all that could be expected. And in the meantime, the caste of color has maintained itself behind the moralistic irrelevancies.

There is, however, another way in which the argument for race parallelism may be advanced. *Instead of advocating it as a permanent pattern of adjustment, it may be considered as a transition stage toward something else.* It was only in this sense that Oldham saw any legitimate argument for it twenty years ago. It is only in that sense that it has any serious claim to consideration today. If it can be used in such a manner that it works continually to increase equality and to reduce separation, it will have been a useful catalytic agent.

But the important question remains to be asked. If race parallelism is to be used as a transition technique, the question is: transition to what? A more perfect caste structure? If so, it would be the better part of honesty to put the case plainly and say that we advocate race parallelism because it will enable us to keep all the things we want in the caste system while at the same time quieting the hungers of conscience by serving up a new portion of the separate-but-equal stew, the bread and meat on which caste has for generations fed itself. If, instead, race parallelism is advocated as a transition toward a noncaste society, the next question is: what kind of noncaste society?

CHAPTER VIII

DELIVERANCE

Are ye not as the children of the Ethiopians unto me, O children
of Israel? saith Jehovah.

—Amos

NO GENUINE hope of releasing the tensions of
conscience constructively lies in any of the methods for
maintaining white supremacy discussed in the preceding chapter. There is only one direction of movement which promises
deliverance from caste, and that is movement in the direction
of equality.

However, race equality may take one of two forms: amalgamation or integration. Many persons who believe themselves opposed to the equality of the races take that road because they are opposed to amalgamation, and because they believe that amalgamation is the only possible expression of racial
equality. They have never troubled to distinguish between
amalgamation and integration. Rejecting biological amalgamation, they believe that they must therefore avoid racial
equality. Indeed, they tend to reject amalgamation *because* it
enables them to reject equality in other forms. Having made
equality and identity synonymous, they are ready to do whatever is necessary to preserve the purity of the white race in
the maintenance of inequality.

By making this confusing identification of "social equality"
and "intermarriage" they pose a sharp antithesis of choice:
either (1) to stand for equality, and promote biological amalgamation as a means of attaining it, or (2) to reject amalgamation, and therefore to reject all forms of equality between the

races. Faced with this choice, white America overwhelmingly declares against amalgamation and for inequality. Rightly or wrongly, few persons of either racial group in America are openly in favor of marriage across race lines. The white caste is particularly insistent in united opposition to it, and the Negro caste is largely indifferent to it.[1]

1. AMALGAMATION

Amalgamation does not, however, necessarily promise the end of a system of caste based on color. Not, at least, for a long time. Only when the process of biological fusion had gone so far as to place the persons of obviously mixed ancestry in a position of being the majority group, and only after they had succeeded in wresting the power from the reduced Caucasian minority, could there be an end to white supremacy. And the possibility, under such developments, that white supremacy would merely be replaced with a new caste system in which black or brown supremacy is substituted for white domination does not make the future an inviting one. Arrogance is no less ugly when resident in a Negro. The effort to eliminate color caste by eliminating color is not a promising proposal. *It is not color, but caste based on color, that is the seat of the iniquity.*

Nevertheless, amalgamation merits serious consideration as one of the seven possibilities before us, because of the important part it plays in all discussions of race relations. Its primary importance lies in the fact that it is a powerful emotional block to clear thought and constructive action in the field of race. In its emotionalized forms, the antiamalgamation doctrine plays an almost demonic role in the American culture conflict, having become so firmly established in the current thought forms and accepted stereotypes that it appears almost to function as an independent force. Not all white people are equally subject to it; but the white caste as a whole tends to

[1] Myrdal, *An American Dilemma,* pp. 60-67.

reject all forms of equality—"social equality" first and fore-most, and other forms of equality in a scale of decreasing im-portance;[2] and the obsession of the Caucasian caste with the antiamalgamation dogma lies at the root of this matter. Rec-ognizing the stultifying effect of the fear of intermarriage, the opponent of caste is faced with a difficult problem as he tries to overcome the initial inertia of the antiamalgamation doctrine.

The modern Negro leader will try to solve this dilemma by iterating that no Negroes want to intrude upon white people's private lives. But this is not what Southern white opinion asks for. It is not satisfied with the natural rules of polite conduct that no individual, of whatever race, shall push his presence on a society where he is not wanted. It asks for a general order according to which *all* Negroes are placed under *all* whites and excluded from not only the white man's society but also from the ordinary symbols of respect. No Negro shall ever aspire to them, and no white shall be allowed to offer them.[3]

This is the situation that permits the antiamalgamation doc-trine to become the principal emotional driving force which commits the white caste to a defense of its system of control.

If, then, we are to be able to consider the merits and de-merits of amalgamation as a possible social policy, we must attempt to probe beneath the surface emotionalism of an irra-tional defense. We need to ask how much intermarraige and intermixture has already taken place, what conclusions may be warranted by available biological data, and whether there are other considerations which may also help answer the question as to the desirability of amalgamation as social policy.

How much intermixture has already gone forward? What percentage of the American population is of "pure" racial stock, and what percentage is "mixed"? Referring to the peo-ple of the southern states, Cohn claims:

They are, moreover—if you exclude Negroes—the only great racially homogeneous bloc in the United States, being almost 100 per cent native-born Americans of Anglo-Saxon stock, Protestant to the core.[4]

[2] Myrdal, *op. cit.*, pp. 53-57.
[3] *Ibid.*, p. 65.
[4] See Chap. VII, n. 8.

It would be difficult to pack more fallacies of logic and of rhetoric into a single sentence than Mr. Cohn has done in this instance. He confuses religion with "race"; he confuses nationality with "race"; he implies that a hyphenated group, the Anglo-Saxon, is unmixed, and that it is a "race"; and he commits the gross error of excluding the Negro population before he begins to talk about the homogeneity of the area. That the whites are Protestants has nothing to do with their "racial" homogeneity: the proportion of Negroes who are Protestants is even higher than amongst whites of the same area. That the population is "almost 100 per cent native born" does not distinguish them in any way from the Negroes of the entire nation, who are 99.9948 per cent native born. That they are "Anglo-Saxon" does not establish "racial" purity: it establishes the fact of hybridization. And the exclusion of all "Negroes" from the calculation, in order then to establish what Mr. Cohn characterizes as a homogeneous population group, does direct violence to the facts of the census as well as of the family tree. Negroes live everywhere throughout the region, and a high percentage of persons whom the caste system classifies as "Negro" have as legitimate a biological claim to membership in the white caste as in the colored. To claim "race purity" for the white caste because all persons of mixed blood have been ejected from that caste is a trick of the mind which can no longer be permitted to circulate. This is analogous to a father claiming that he had no redheaded children in his home—a truth which covered the fact that he had kept only the blondes and brunettes, sending his redheaded offspring to an orphanage. The white *race* has not protected its purity by ejecting all persons of mixed blood from the white *caste*. It has protected itself from the intrusion of non-Caucasian strains, except in the cases of persons of mixed ancestry who "pass" for white or whose non-Caucasian ancestry was acquired in some manner which history now graciously conceals. But the white race is involved in the parentage of the persons of mixed ancestry just as much as are the members of the minority caste.

There is caste purity in the American scene—in one caste; but racial purity we do not have.

Not all Americans are aware of the degree to which race mixture has already gone. Unfortunately, no finally definitive statistics on race mixture are available, and it will be difficult to arrive at anything more than an estimate. What is accepted as "the safest basis for a present estimation"[5] indicates that the present "Negro" population of the United States probably falls into approximately the following divisions:

ANCESTRY OF AMERICAN "NEGROES"
(Estimated Per Cent)

African ancestry only	22	
African and Indian ancestry	7	
Total "Negroes" having *no Caucasian ancestry*		29
African and Caucasian ancestry	51	
African, Indian, and Caucasian ancestry	20	
Total "Negroes" having *some Caucasian ancestry*		71
		100

The African ancestry of Negro Americans is itself a fairly complex mixture of racial groups, including Caucasoid Africans (Hamitic and Semitic peoples) from northern Africa and the Negroid Africans (Bushmen, Hottentots, Negritos, Bantus, and "true Negroes") mainly from southern Africa.[6] The Indian racial strains in the "Negro" population are from at least a dozen tribes, principally those which once inhabited the southern region of the United States, but not exclusively so. The white racial stocks include everything from the Nordic to the Mediterranean. Each of the three groups noted in this tabulation is, like all other parts of the human race in the world today, a mixture in itself—a mixture of ancestry that

---

[5] Wirth and Goldhamer, "The Hybrid and the Problem of Miscegenation," p. 271. The table of percentages given here is a condensed version of the more elaborate table given by these authors, based on researches of Melville J. Herskovits.

[6] Wirth and Goldhamer, *op. cit.*, pp. 259-260.

reaches back before the dawn of history into prehistory for its origins.

The estimates cited are not given as finally accurate statistical percentages. They may be used only as general indications of the facts of "racial" composition for the "Negro" caste in America. There are, however, "indications that Herskovits's results may well be confirmed by additional investigations."[7] And even though these percentages are only rough indices of general proportions of racial composition of the "Negro" caste, we are permitted to observe that to talk of "race purity" in the light of these facts is to indulge in emotional cant.

If seven in every ten American "Negroes" now have some Caucasian ancestry, by what means can the Caucasian justify his sermons on "race purity" gratuitously directed toward the Negro caste? If the sermonizer is ignorant of the facts, this may explain, but not condone, the egregious insult of his admonitions. But if he knows the facts and still persists in preaching to "Negroes" about "race purity," we must conclude (1) that this preaching quiets his conscience by permitting him to appear as the champion of "race purity" in *both* castes; (2) that the doctrine is accepted by Negroes because it partly compensates for the indignities of an inferior position by playing up pride of racial purity; (3) that the doctrine of racial purity serves to solidify and to consolidate the caste structure. These are the purposes which the antiamalgamation doctrine serves as it is preached in its affirmative form of Pride in Race Purity.

But the facts do not support the dogma. For better or for worse, the white man has poured his germ plasm into nearly three-fourths of the "Negro" caste. Race purity today in the United States is a hallucination: race mixture is a fact. The intermarriage of members of the Negro caste will, in a few more generations, distribute the Caucasian strain rather completely throughout the caste, and the Negro "race" will have disappeared from the American scene, leaving a "Negro" caste made up of Caucasian, Indian (and other) ancestry

[7] *Ibid.*, p. 271.

mixed with African. There is no race purity in the Negro caste. The white man has seen to that.

What about the racial purity of the white caste? It is here that the anxieties of the Caucasian cluster. He is little troubled over the ambivalence of the affections of the male Caucasians who have sired the racial mixture of the Negro caste; but if he can be sure that the white caste is free of the possibility of invasion, he achieves his purposes of psychological security. The white man may deplore the fact of race mixture; but as long as miscegenation does not include intermarriage, the progeny are included in the Negro caste, and disapproval is passive. Active disapproval comes only when white women and Negro men are the active persons in the liaison.

The fixation on the purity of white womanhood, and also part of the intensity of the emotion surrounding the whole sphere of segregation and discrimination, are to be understood as the backwashes of the sore conscience on the part of white men for their own and their compeers' relations with, or desires for, Negro women. These psychological effects are greatly magnified because of the puritan *milieu* of America and especially of the South. The upper class men in a less puritanical people could probably have indulged in sex relations with, and sexual daydreams of, lower caste women in a more matter-of-course way and without generating so much pathos about white womanhood. The Negro people have to carry the burden not only of the white men's sins but also of their virtues. The virtues of the honest, democratic, puritan white Americans in the South are great, and the burden upon the Negroes becomes ponderous.[8]

Because of the pressures which this pattern generates, extensive safeguards have been thrown up to protect the integrity of the white caste. Two of them are worth passing comment.

The first of these safeguards of the integrity of the white caste (though not of the white race) is legislation against intermarriage. Extramarital relationships are not regarded as a threat to the white caste because of the second safeguard: the insistence that all white persons must become members of the

[8] Myrdal, *op. cit.*, p. 591.

Negro caste if they marry across the caste line in states where
such marriage is legally possible, and the universal insistence
that all children, whether of wedlock or not, must be members
of the Negro caste. These two safeguards can be seen in
operation. In thirty of the forty-eight states, marriage of
Negroes with Caucasians is illegal. Outside of New England,
it is possible only in the Middle Atlantic states, and in New
Mexico, Washington, Iowa, Minnesota, Ohio, Illinois, Michi-
gan, Wisconsin and the District of Columbia.[9] Social pressures
combine with these legal restrictions so that, even where interracial marriage might be theoretically possible, the total number of such marriages is an inconsequential dribble in the
annual stream of American wedlock. Marriages do occur in
the states where the law permits; but they are a microscopic
percentage of the total. Thus, for example, Boston, Massachusetts, with its abolitionist heritage one of the freest of
American cities in its attitude toward intercaste marriages, has
witnessed only thirteen out of every ten thousand of its Caucasians marrying Negro spouses.[10]

The second safeguard of the "purity" of the white caste lies
in the fact that, whenever a marriage occurs between a Negro
and a Caucasian, the caste system thrusts the Caucasian spouse
down into the Negro caste and includes all children of the marriage in the Negro caste. The proportion of marriages between
whites and Negroes ("primary" crossings), as compared with
the marriages between persons of mixed Caucasian-Negro ancestry with persons of unmixed African ancestry ("secondary"
crossings) is, by the fifth decade of the twentieth century, relatively nil. The further extension of the Caucasian genes
throughout the Negro caste comes almost entirely through
intermarriage within the Negro caste and through the extramarital relationships of white men and Negro women.

Under the present caste system, the sole threat to the integ-

[9] Wirth and Goldhamer, *op. cit.*, pp. 360-362.
[10] The figures are for the years 1914-1938, and are cited in Wirth and Goldhamer, *op. cit.*, p. 281.

rity of the dominant caste comes from cases of "passing" in which an individual, whose physical characteristics permit, anonymously passes over from the caste in which he was born, to become a member of the white caste. There is no way of knowing how many or how few persons do this. Estimates vary widely, and can be neither verified nor disproved. Whatever urge there is to encourage the passing of individuals from the lower to the higher caste is more a responsibility of the white than of the Negro. It is from the white man that the individual gets his physical ability to pass—not from his Negroid ancestors. And the inequities that shape the desires to escape from the lower caste are not of the Negro's creating nor of his choosing.

In this matter of "passing" we encounter another of the irrational myths that feed phobias but have no foundation in fact. It is the "black baby" myth—the notion that a white person who marries a Negro passing for white may become the parent of a "black" baby. It is possible for a Negroid child to look more like a "true Negro" than either of its parents, *if both parents carry Negro blood;* but it is not possible for the child to be more Negroid than either of its parents if one of them has no Negro blood.[11] A favorite short story plot, particularly overworked by the writers for the pulp magazines, this myth of the "black baby" must be relegated to the limbo of mythology along with the unicorn and the satyr. Whatever amount of passing there may or may not be, it hardly constitutes a grave threat to the integrity of the white caste.

We come now to the second of our major questions about amalgamation: *What conclusions regarding its advisability are warranted by available biological data?* There has been much speculation and not a little pseudo science on this question. Popular novels like *The Clansman* and *The Crisis* (literary items which had a vogue a generation ago, and which

[11] In stating this conclusion, Wirth and Goldhamer summarize the available scientific evidence in the matter, and refer to Hooten and other anthropologists who verify the conclusion. *Op. cit.,* p. 329.

are principally of antiquarian interest today—except as they profoundly shaped the attitudes of many of today's adults) have played up nightmarish phobias about the biological inter-mixture of diverse racial strains, using the fears thus created to buttress the caste system. Facts can be used as corrective antidotes to these poisons.

There are a number of popular misconceptions, many of them mutually contradictory, which may be enumerated in passing. Their refutation is summarized in the Carnegie study. (1) It is alleged that low fecundity results from crossing Caucasian and other racial stocks. There is no proof of the allegation.[12] (2) High fecundity is alleged to result from racial crossings in marriage. There is no proof of this, either.[13] (3) An imbalance of physical parts is alleged to result from hybridization: the large teeth of one parent with the small jaws of the other; or the long legs of the black parent combined with the short arms of the white parent are supposed to put the child at a disadvantage in picking things off the ground. But are there no white children who visit orthodontists? And what about the stereotype which insists that Negroes have long arms and short legs "like apes"? And could not the child just as easily have the short legs of the white parent and the long arms of the Negro parent, thus being at an advantage in picking up things off the ground? Or, to leave theory and come into the realm of observed and recorded fact, there is general evidence from all the annals of anthropometrics which indicates that whatever the racial composition of the parents, the various parts of the body and its organs appear to achieve a general harmonization within which all functions are normally and satisfactorily performed. There are asymmetrical individuals; but this is not correlated with intercaste marriages.

[12] "Certainly it can be said that there is no satisfactory evidence that the mulatto shows a lower reproductive capacity." *Op. cit.*, p. 328.

[13] The 1940 census indicates that southern family size amongst rural whites is greater than amongst rural Negroes. Family size, generally speaking, is correlated with living standards, education, and other cultural, nonbiological factors.

(4) Susceptibility to disease is alleged to be greater amongst hybrids. While some diseases, such as tuberculosis, are known to have a higher incidence in the Negro caste than in the white caste, there is as yet no data to indicate either (a) that the incidence of tuberculosis is higher amongst hybrids than amongst "pure" Negroes or (b) that the higher incidence of such ailments amongst Negroes is not correlated with such factors as malnutrition, bad housing, and poor public health and hospitalization services for Negroes rather than with biological inheritance. (5) There is an "instinctive repugnance" between racial groups, which makes intermarriage a matter of necessary incompatibility. If there were such an instinct, the elaborate laws against intermarriage would hardly be necessary, nor would there be any way to justify that twenty per cent of the lynchings which are laid to sex crimes. If there were such an instinct, the Caucasian would not have given his germ plasm so freely to the Negro caste that seven out of ten "Negroes" have some Caucasian ancestry. If there were such an instinctive aversion, the elaborate ritual controls of caste would not be needed, to keep the Negro in his "place." (6) There is an "instinctive attraction" between the two groups which makes antiamalgamation sentiment and legislation imperative if "race purity" is to be preserved. Aside from the fact that there is no proof for this assertion, the *necessity* of the legislation and sentiment against amalgamation does not arise out of any proved biological inadvisability of such marriages; it stems from the demands of caste. (7) Hybrids are mentally inferior to whites. This notion, together with the notion that Negroes of unmixed parentage are also inferior to Caucasians, has been unable to stand in the presence of scientific research.[14]

We conclude that whatever arguments there may be against marriage of persons from different castes, these arguments are not founded on sound scientific data drawn from verified biological, physiological, psychological, and anthropological research. The evidence to support these conclusions is given

[14] See Chap. V, sec. 2.

in the volumes of the Carnegie study. There appear, then, to
be no sound biological arguments against marriages across
racial lines.

There is a third question, however, on which the judgment
of clear thinking is opposed to marriage across caste lines as
they are now drawn in the United States of America. There
is no sound reason for opposing interracial marriages; but
there is sound reason for discouraging intercaste marriages in
present-day American society.

Marriage is difficult enough in contemporary America, as
the activities of the divorce courts indicate. To increase these
difficulties knowingly and thereby to strengthen the possibilities
of defeat in marriage would seem unwise. In the eigtheen
states where such marriage is now legally possible, persons
who contemplate marriage across caste lines are forced to consider carefully before taking the step. In the preponderance of
the cases of such marriages on record in Boston, the white
spouse has obtained advantages of wealth or of social position
within the Negro caste which were not readily open through
marriage within the white caste. In such marriages, the com-
pensating factors may outweigh the social indignities attendant
upon it, and the chances for success and happiness may be increased by that fact.[15] But the white caste universally rejects
the white partner to an intercaste marriage; and in many cases
the Negro caste is slow to accept the newcomer. Harlem in
New York City now has a sizable social circle which the mixed-
marriage group has created for its own protection. Rejected
alike by the two castes, the mixed-marriage group draws itself
together in a protective social unit.

The children of mixed marriages will almost certainly be
members of the Negro caste, unless they "pass" for Caucasians
or for dark-skinned non-Negroes. That the children will grow
up hating the Caucasian parent for the choice that brought
them into the world as members of the submerged caste is not
a conjecture but a genuine probability. Notable exceptions to

[15] Cf. Wirth and Goldhamer, *op. cit.*, Chap. IV.

the general rule must be taken as exceptions, not as contrary argument.

The character of American society as now constituted is a cogent argument against intercaste marriages. It serves effectually to estop all but a small trickle of such marriages in the states where there is no legislation against them, with the result that the few persons who, in spite of these discouragements, do marry across caste lines are moved by a more than ordinary community of interest, affection, and determination. They appear to be happier and more successful than there is any *a priori* expectation for them to be under the sharp strictures and censure of color caste. A useful piece of research might be conducted at this point, investigating the comparative success of mixed marriages as compared with ingroup marriages, in comparable social and economic brackets.

As far as amalgamation is concerned, we conclude: (1) that there appears to be less immediate probability of the American people consciously adopting the complete interfusion of the two castes as a social policy than there is of the adoption of any one of the five possibilities listed in the preceding chapter; (2) that amalgamation plays its principal role not as a live option of social policy but as a scarecrow to divert attention and thought from the injustices and iniquities of caste; (3) that interracial admixture has gone forward within the Negro caste to a remarkable degree, and may be expected to continue, while the white caste attempts to preserve the racial purity of its caste at the expense of the racial purity of the Negro caste; and therefore (4) that "race purity" in any absolute sense is a misnomer, used to signify "caste integrity" for the whites while denying either racial or caste integrity for Negroes; and thus (5) the basic significance of "race" in the American scene as a tool of caste control is clearly revealed. The conscious effort to achieve racial equality through the encouragement of intercaste marriages appears to be as improbable as (in the opening paragraph of this section, we pointed out) it is ineffective as a means of achieving such equality.

2. INTEGRATION

Sometimes called "cultural assimilation" to distinguish it from biological assimilation, *integration is not to be confused with amalgamation.* The difference between the two lies primarily in their respective attitudes toward intercaste marriage. While the believers in amalgamation are champions of intermarriage as a declared social policy, and while believers in white supremacy are equally vehement in their opposition to intermarriage (albeit as an actual defense of a superior caste status rather than to defend "racial" purity, as we have seen), the integrationist has a high indifference toward intercaste marriage. He knows there is no sound biological argument against interracial marriage. He also knows that at present the caste system exacts a high price from families of intercaste marriages. He further sees that, if caste were eliminated, the only effective argument against intercaste marriage would be removed. He does not, however, advocate the elimination of caste in order to promote interracial marriages, any more than he advocates intercaste marriages now as a means of breaking down the caste system. Knowing these things, and being interested in removing the artificial inequities of the American caste system, he does not permit the bogey of miscegenation to stand in the way of the effort to eliminate caste. That is the negative statement of the integrationist position.

Positively stated, the integrationist position is precisely what the Christian ethic requires—that every man, woman, and child shall be free to enter into, and to contribute to, the welfare of all mankind, without any restrictions or disabilities based on color caste—and without any advantages because of color or the lack of it.

The real significance of color caste lies not in color but in caste. With caste removed, color ceases to have irrational emotional overtones attached to it; it ceases to be a tool of culture conflict. It then becomes merely one of the interesting surface phenomena of which one takes pleasant note. Color then is useless as a basis of exploitation, segregation, discrimination, or any other form of artificial differentiation between individuals and groups. No special advantages accrue to some; and no special disadvantages to others, on account of pigmentation.

Stated concretely, this integrationist position means things like these: (1) in the economic field, employment, upgrading, and wage policies which know no color bar or differential; union membership open without reference to race or color; (2) in the political field, opportunity and encouragement to register, vote, run for office, and serve when elected, regardless of color; (3) in housing, the freedom to occupy a home within one's means, and to feel welcome in the community without reference to color; (4) in educational and cultural services, no separation of pupils and patrons on the basis of color, the employment and promotion of teachers and staff persons on the basis of merit without reference to color, the designing of curriculum and teaching to include the fully rounded experience of the entire human race; (5) in all public facilities, such as restaurants, hotels, trains, and buses, freedom of access by patrons regardless of color; (6) in churches and religious life, an open welcome to all persons of whatever color, both as ministers and as officials and as worshipers; (7) in "social" life, freedom to form one's own friendships and to carry on one's own social life without pressures of any kind based on color or the lack of it; (8) in home life, including marriage and homemaking, the same freedom of choice to act with a high indifference to color. Many other items might be added to the catalogue. These are enough to illustrate the meaning of the integrationist point of view. The integrationist, believing that caste must be eradicated, wishes to build a society in which color of skin has no more significance than color of hair.

Such a notion is, of course, utopian in a sense. That is another way of saying that the Christian ideal does not always seem immediately realizable. But that is not to say that the

Christian ideal must therefore be totally rejected. On the contrary, it argues that, because the ideal is so remote from present practice and from immediately realizable potentialities, the effort of Christian people to realize the ideal must become much more powerful than it has ever been. It is the character of present reality, not the nature of the Christian ideal, that gives the latter a utopian aura. Therefore, to say that the Christian conception of the irrelevance of color sets a utopian notion before us is not equivalent to saying that the ideal is incapable of realization. *The clear and sufficient answer to those who say that there is "no solution" to the problem of race lies in the fact that in many parts of the globe there is no such problem.*[16]

3. A WORD OF WARNING

Some defenders of white supremacy will accuse the integrationist of "advocating miscegenation." This is not true. The integrationist neither advocates nor opposes marriage between members of different racial groups. He would hold that individuals should be free to choose their life partners without arbitrary interference by the State or by their neighbors.

What the integrationist does advocate is the creation of a society in which the problem of marriage between castes ceases to be a problem because there are no castes. At the present time, intermarriage is not a biological problem of "race"; it is part of the sociological problem of caste. With caste eliminated, the problem of intercaste marriage is no more. In the noncaste society, as now operating in parts of the world other than the United States, persons who would have been divided by a caste line in our society marry each other and there is no objection from any source. The only legitimate objection to intercaste marriage comes from the caste system and its defenders. With these removed, there can be no tenable argu-

---

[16] An example of the reasoning we reject: "The various methods advocated by individuals and organizations as solutions of the race problem may be dismissed with brief comment. There is no solution." E. B. Reuter, *The American Race Problem*, p. 427. Crowell, 1927.

ment against such marriage. Neither is there any possible argument *for* "intermarriage" in a casteless society—the very concept of caste, which alone determines what is an out-group marriage, is inoperative. In an integrated society, it will be impossible to marry across caste lines because there will be no caste lines.

The individual who accuses the integrationist of "advocating intermarriage" is unfair both to himself and to the integrationist position. He is unfair to himself in that he continues to subject his mind to the confusing false identification of "racial equality" and "amalgamation." He is unfair to the integrationist in that he permits himself to contribute to, and to increase, a misunderstanding or misinterpretation of the latter's position.

To put the matter bluntly: there is too much at stake in this effort to put the Christian conscience to work against color caste for us to permit the obstructionists to misinterpret or misquote us. We who work for integration of Negroes, Englishmen, Chinese, Mexicans, Scotsmen, Dutchmen, Filipinos, Irishmen, Japanese, Frenchmen, Germans, Italians, Russians, Indians, West Indians, and every other sort of person into a united family of mankind, where no one will suffer any disability or gain any advantage on account of the skin color of his ancestors, and where all are free to contribute to and to share in the richest fullness of life—we integrationists have too much at stake to permit the racists and the race-baiters to tell easy lies. I therefore warn the defenders of caste that they have not the right to lift a sentence or two out of this book, or to disregard the main trend of the argument, and thus to fling the accusation of "miscegenation" against the integrationist position.

If the defender of caste and of the white supremacy that caste maintains wishes to have a summary statement of the position to which the Christian conscience leads me, the position indicated by all that I have written up to this point, here is the statement he may quote:

The intergrationist is indifferent to racial identity, with a high indifference which attaches no importance to surface pigmentation. He wishes to see no arbitrary hindrances placed on any child of God because someone else does not like the color of his skin or the slant of his eyes. He wishes all men to be freed from the fact and the hardship of color caste.

In this possibility the integrationist sees the great deliverance.

CHAPTER IX

DECISION

It should be apparent that the time to come to an understanding on the basis of equality is rapidly running out. When colored nations have once acquired power but still sense the scorn of white superiority and racial discrimination, they are likely to become indoctrinated by a race prejudice much more akin to that of the whites—a race prejudice which can be satisfied only by the white's humiliation and subjugation.

—GUNNAR MYRDAL (1944)

THE present crisis of our culture, of which color caste is a particular malevolent expression, does not threaten the essential genius of Christianity. It merely involves the fate of the present institutions and adherents of Christianity in the Western world. The essential values of Christianity have long since demonstrated their ability to survive the complete collapse of civilizations with which they had become interwoven —although the recollection of the fate of half of Christendom in the seventh century puts a question mark opposite the blithe assurance that nothing can kill Christianity. The Phoenixlike quality of the faith ensures to it a continuing life in some form or other, even though the era of white supremacy draws to a close—perhaps because the present age is coming to an end.

The fall of Jerusalem did not kill the church. The faith and its values survived the demise of the Roman Empire which, by the fifth century, had become almost indistinguishable from the church, so completely were the two intertwined. Feudalism, largely a child of Christendom, waxed old and died; but the faith lived on, and in its new vigor of both the Protestant and Catholic reformations went on to new strength. The Enlightenment and the Industrial Revolution brought the end of one era and the beginning of another; but the Christian faith not only survived the shock of political and cultural upheaval: it profoundly influenced the new order as it grew. In the eighteenth and nineteenth centuries, Christianity experienced the most powerful revivals of its history; and in the nineteenth and twentieth centuries it carried through the stupendous world-wide missionary effort which walked on the feet of the faithful and the consecrated until it reached into every remote corner of the globe with the single exception of the mountain fastnesses of the Himalayas.

Even more significantly, the values of the Christian religion have shown their power of resistance and of regeneration in spite of the persistent hostility of the church to the Christian ethic. If the belief in a God of Justice and in the values of Christian brotherhood can survive nineteen centuries of denial by the institutions of Christianity, they are something more than idle dreams. They must represent the deepest yearnings and highest aspirations of the human spirit. They must partake of the Eternal. And yet, there is that nagging memory of the fact that, when the civilized world centered around the Mediterranean, the white half of the church on the northern rim of that sea permitted itself to be detached from the darker half on the other side of the sea. . . .

And this moment of history is another hour of great decision. Color caste now rules. If the Caucasian, who holds the power, does not decide to end that rule by his own act of volition, he automatically decides to let the crisis move to its own climax. There is no third possibility. The failure to decide against color caste leaves us with the probability that the caste positions will be reversed in the not too distant future, the white man falling into the pit of his own digging. If we are interested in racial equality, the final hour in which we can grasp that prize is now striking. It is conceivable that the Caucasian might manage to hold the colored world in subjugation for another generation or two by the use of overpowering brute force; but if we now set our feet on that path there is no retreat from it. That is why the decision against white supremacy must be made *now*, if it is ever to be made voluntarily by the Caucasian.

Recognizing that the stakes of the present decision are great, we take small consolation in the assurance that the verdict of past history is that no amount of apostasy can completely kill the faith—the torch merely passes to new hands. It is no encouragement to white supremacy to point out that, although racism is suicidal, the Christian faith itself may find rootage in other racial groups as the Caucasian passes off the scene. It is no compensation to us to recall that the timetable of the Lord of History is a long one, and that setbacks have come before. As long as there is any hope of making decisions which can salvage the present hour and ensure a sane future, that effort is worth making. Indeed, it is worth making even though the possibilities of constructive action may appear slight—the smaller the probability the more necessary does ethical action become. These are the considerations that lead us to assess the values which are at stake in the decision we are making.

1. ETHICAL VIRILITY

Even though the day of reckoning were postponed, and the institutions of contemporary culture were to continue for a generation or more in their present form, that would not guarantee the realization of the ethical values of the Christian religion. Nor would it ensure the security of the institutions, which are apparently built on the belief that white supremacy is more important than brotherhood. On the contrary, the continuance of a race-divided church in a caste-controlled society would mean that little of real value was left in the surviving shell of institutionalism.

The painful struggle of religion to achieve ethical vigor is recorded in the Old and the New Testaments. The warfare of the prophetic and priestly strains runs through the whole of the Old Testament and in the New Testament sharply divides sacerdotalism from the ethical teachings of Jesus.

This does not mean that institutionalism, even sacerdotalism, cannot nurture and support an ethical religion. The ethical virility of the Catholic wing of the Anglican Church, stemming from the union of Puseyism with the Christian socialism of Kingsley and Maurice, and coming down to the present hour through the development of the Industrial Christian Fellowship to the climatic achievements of Malvern and of participation in Oxford,[1] argues that institutionalism and sacerdotalism can become powerful vehicles for ethical insight.[2]

It does mean, however, that the church without the Christian ethic is dead—a corpse that needs nothing so much as it needs burial. This statement is masterfully documented by Troeltsch and Toynbee.[3] It finds its classic Protestant American expression in the writings of Walter Rauschenbush, Harry F. Ward, Arthur Holt, and Reinhold Niebuhr. It is cogently stated for the Roman Catholics by Don Luigi Sturzo. An institution which has lost its ethical virility, say these writers, is worse than dead. It cannot rightfully claim to be the instrument of God's purposes, the ark of Christian values.

There is, then, a serious internal threat to the church in its symbiotic identification with white supremacy. Christians interested in saving the church will place this high on the list of the values at stake in the present decision. In addition to this internal threat to the life of the church, there are two outstanding competitors now bidding for world allegiance. These together constitute a formidable threat to the life of Christianity as long as the ethical advantage is granted to them in the continuance of the alliance between racism and

[1] These conferences will be discussed in the next chapter.
[2] Cf. the writings of Charles E. Raven (especially his *Christian Socialism* Macmillan, 1920), of the late Bishop Charles Gore, the Reverend V. A. Demant, the late Father Conrad Noel, the Reverend Percy E. T. Widdrington, Mr. Maurice B. Reckett, and many others. A good single volume is W. G. Peck's *Social Implications of the Oxford Movement* (Scribners, 1933).
[3] Ernst Troeltsch, *The Social Teachings of the Christian Church*, 2 vols. (Macmillan, 1931), and Arnold J. Toynbee, *A Study of History*, 6 vols. (Oxford Univ. Press, 1935-1939).

Christianity. The racial practices of the Soviets and of Islam require a serious word.

2. THE SOVIET TREATMENT OF "RACE"

It is not necessary to ascribe any special virtue to political dictatorship or economic communism in order to point out that under the Soviets "race" has no meaning. Neither do we assume that, since the Soviet system now seriously bids for world allegiance, we must regard it as essentially evil. For the purposes of this discussion of Christianity and racism, we are neither commending nor condemning the Soviet system. Whether economic communism and political dictatorship are desirable or undesirable is an argument that has no bearing on this discussion. In the matter of color caste, however, the ethical and spiritual challenge that is presented to Christianity by the clear and unequivocal practice of the Soviets is inescapable.

In raising this issue, we are not setting the United States and the nations of Western Europe over against the Union of Soviet Socialist Republics. We remember that one of the real possibilities of the future, if caste is perpetuated by the United States co-operating with the world empires of France, Holland, Portugal, Spain, Belgium, and Britain, is a global conflict in which the Russians cannot be expected to support white supremacy. But the political and nationalistic aspects of the possible conflict between the U.S.S.R. and the U.S.A., while they are of great concern to us, are not the matters here under discussion. What we are concerned with here is the fact that, while Christianity professes equality without practicing it, under the Soviets equality of races is practiced. This constitutes an incalculable ethical disadvantage for Christianity if it wishes to obtain the world allegiance of men.

If it be said in response that Christianity is not interested in "competing" with the Soviets for world acceptance, the answer is that, whether Christianity is interested or not, the Soviet treatment of minorities gives it such a clear-cut ethical superiority over Christianity in this regard as to make it more acceptable to at least two-thirds of the world *en bloc*, and to an increasingly large number of persons inside the "Christian" nations also.

If the "white" nations (which happen now to be most of the "Christian" nations as well) insist on white supremacy, they play directly into the hands of a process which not only sets the "white" world against the nonwhite, but also puts Christianity under the ethical handicap of having to masquerade as the defender of a system which contradicts its own basic values. Such a misalliance may then become the deciding factor in uniting the nonwhite world against the Caucasian, as the pressures of economic exploitation and political and military disability are compounded by the racial factor intensified by religious emotions.

What, then, is the Soviet practice with reference to "race"? On the negatve side, the Soviets have legislated against any expression, oral or written, of any kind of antipathy or prejudice between national and racial groups within the Soviet Union. Embracing well over one hundred and fifty ethnic and national groups, the Soviets have made the expression of race prejudice illegal. In the 1936 constitution of the Union of Soviet Socialist Republics, it is written:

Article 123: Equal rights for citizens of the USSR, irrespective of their nationality or race, in all spheres of economic, state, cultural, social and political life, shall be an irrevocable law. Any direct or indirect limitation of these rights, or, conversely, any establishment of direct or indirect privileges for citizens on account of their race or nationality, as well as any propagation of racial or national exclusiveness or hatred and contempt, shall be punished by law.

This basic law is enforced, as dictatorships can enforce laws, with heavy penalties and ruthless completeness. If there are any racial antipathies within the Soviet Union, they are confined to the inner privacy of unspoken thoughts. No one dares to express any kind of racial antipathy openly.

On the positive side, the Soviets have made a thoroughgoing effort to recognize the values of each minority and its culture, however small its numbers. The principle of cultural diversity within the framework of economic communism and political dictatorship makes possible the cultural recognition and encouragement of a multitude of ethnic and national minority groups. It is not merely that the negative job has been done in making sure that "race" constitutes no disadvantage to any person within the Union. It is much more than that. The positive values of each distinctive culture—in language, customs, costumes, dietary habits and tastes, art, literature, drama, education, religion, and the like—are openly encouraged and carefully nurtured (although religion is the last of these cultural values to be recognized and given official encouragement).

There have been changes in Soviet policy in this matter during the quarter century since the October Revolution, which were dictated by the necessity of changing tactics in the light of developing conditions;[4] but the grand strategy of the Soviets with reference to "race" has not altered. Any person, regardless of racial or national identity, who subscribes to the three basic essentials of sovietism (Marxian communism, as interpreted by Lenin and Stalin; the dictatorship of the proletariat, with a one-party political system; and dialectical materialism, as interpreted by the party), stands on an equal footing with any other person. He is accepted, and integrated into the Soviet social and political structure. Moreover, an elaborate machinery for the recognition of racial and national groups, as groups, has been worked out under the Soviet system, as many as two thousand smaller soviets being included in a single larger unit to achieve this purpose of group autonomy within the framework of the Union. Both as individuals and as groups, men find absolute equality of "races" under the Soviet system.

[4] Cf. Jacob Robinson, "The Soviet Solution of the Minorities Problem," in *Group Relations and Group Antagonisms*, edited by R. H. MacIver. Harpers, 1943.

The historical explanation of this fact does not detract from its cogency as a pragmatic demonstration of ethical superiority over a caste-controlled Christianity. That explanation lies primarily in two sets of factors: the historical roots and the practical necessities of strategy.

Historically, there has never been much of what the West calls "race" prejudice in Russia. Under the czarist regime, much the same kind of individual opportunity for acceptance without reference to race or color prevailed as is now evident in Soviet Russia. There were sharp discriminations of economic class and political power, both in secular and in religious life; but racial distinctions had no meaning. Any person who subscribed to the three basic notions of czarism (Russian nationalism, the Orthodox Church, and the monarchy), regardless of his "racial" ancestry, was an accepted member of the czarist regime—in his proper economic or political status.[5] The list of the heroes and great men of Czarist Russia includes men from many of the diverse elements of the vast Russian Empire, from its western border to the waters of the Pacific. In some parts of Czarist Russia, Jews were subjected to violence and to bitter and sharp persecutions and discrimination. Protestant sects did not flourish, and Roman Catholicism made little progress. But these are cultural differences, not racial; and any person who cared to take on himself voluntarily the three basic notions of czarism found that "race" made no difference. In the case of Jews who were baptized as Christians, thus subscribing to orthodoxy, as well as to the other two principles of the czarist trilogy, it sometimes took a generation to achieve complete integration and acceptance; but there was no racial caste system based on color, from which no one could escape. Thus, when sovietism came into power, it had no new principle to force upon an unaccustomed people, as far as race is con-

[5] The fact that Alexander Pushkin's grandfather married "a handsome creole" without in any way affecting the aristocratic standing of the family and that Pushkin himself, who would have been put in the "Negro" caste in America, was Russia's foremost man of letters is an illustration of the social and political irrelevance of "race" in the old Russia.

cerned. It had only to substitute the new trilogy of sovietism for the old trilogy of czarism, and whoever accepted these new dogmas was a part of the new order, just as the conformist had been a part of the old order—regardless of race. The historical origins of present indifference to color in the Soviet Union help to explain it; they do not in any sense reduce the significance of the ethical challenge to Christianity.

Moreover, there are certain important points at which the soviet practice is a marked advance over the czarist practice in the area of race, even though the same ideological foundation continues to serve as the basis of the new structure with its somewhat different architecture. One of the basic tenets of czarism was Russian nationalism. This meant that all other national groups were compelled to regard themselves as subject peoples within the empire. And many of these subject national-ities differed in racial complexion from the Great Russians. The forward strides of sovietism on the minorities question are seen principally in the recognition of national minorities within the Union, a practice which completely reverses the czarist policy. It is incidental that some of these national groups differ from others in racial complexion also; but race, as race, is no handicap whatever to any person or group within the Soviet Union.

The necessities of strategy also serve to support the Soviet practice of racial equality. One of the real problems faced by the young government of the Bolsheviki in its first years was the dominance of the Russians within the Union. The de-Russi-fication of the Union therefore became one of the principal planks in the Communist platform during the first years. The playing up of more than one hundred other nationalities within the Union was a strategically useful device in playing down the significance of the Great Russians. When the Ukrainians and the Karelians attempted to move into the vacuum created by the removal of Russian nationalism, their efforts were speedily scotched through the liquidation of a few well-chosen leaders and the quashing of these nationalistic movements which threatened to take over in place of the dethroned Russian nationalism. It was useful to have a great many other nationalities and ethnic groups, each autonomous, all equal to put over against the Russian, Karelian, and Ukrainian bids for dominance. By the middle thirties, the threats of these rival nationalistic movements had subsided, and by the forties, it had become possible for the Kremlin to add religion to the list of diverse factors which were welcomed and encouraged within the general framework of the U.S.S.R. Muslim pilgrims began to make their journeys to Mecca again—this time at state expense. Christian churches began to operate with the open encouragement of Soviet officialdom. The Soviets thus demonstrated in its final and most conclusive form their indifference to race. They showed that they were indifferent to the religions which the races have espoused.

Critics of the Union are quick to point out that the policy of recognizing a multitude of small ethnic and national units is an application of the old technique of divide and control. They will argue, for example, that instead of permitting the entire Muslim population of the southern and southwestern sections of the Union to come together in a single powerful soviet, a score or more of separate Muslim units were established on the basis of very slight linguistic differences. They will argue, further, that the recognition of every small concentration of a minority people in a separate, autonomous soviet is to be explained more by a desire to make sure that there is no single unit powerful enough to challenge the Supreme Soviet in Moscow than by any sentimental or ethical appreciation of the cultural values of the many minorities. It is, for example, argued that once the score or more of separate Muslim soviets were established, each with its own language, press, and educational system, an enormous pressure for the maintenance of each little subdivision is maintained by the corps of intellectuals and administrative officers whose jobs depend upon the perpetuation of the divisions. Whether these were the motives back of the Soviet action in granting minority autonomy in cultural matters or whether some higher motive prompted the action is beside the point of our present discussion, and in no way affects the fact that under the Supreme Soviet no one feels any handicap or discrimination of any sort because of his racial identity. Everyone who cares to has the option of identifying himself with a soviet of his own ethnic or national group, without in any way imperiling his standing in society or in the Communist party. That fact no criticism can minimize.

Across several hundred miles of borders, the peoples of Europe and of Asia look with interest at the fact of racial equality within the Soviet Union. The Soviet practice looks more enticing to the pigmented peoples, and to the oppressed minorities of Europe, than does the type of society thus far produced under the aegis of the Christian Church in Europe or America or anywhere else.

And within the United States, the matter of racial equality as practiced by the Soviet Union, when contrasted with color caste within the United States of America, constitutes one of the most important ethical arguments of American Communists. We are not raising the question of whether or not the United States should "go communist." What we are saying is that the Christian Church, which includes well over half the adult population of these United States, has not produced an ethical attack on color caste which approaches the vigor and virility of the attack launched by the American Communists.

The Christian Church in America has a few glorious moments in its history. In the days of the abolitionist movement, some sections of the church took a bold and forthright stand, although William Lloyd Garrison went on record to the effect that he got little support from the churches. The Underground Railway was principally managed by men and women of religion in both races. Since the Civil War, however, the activities of several denominations in the field of Negro education have been the only great, continuing, practical demonstration of an interest of American Christianity in the plight and progress of the Negro in this country. And, with a few notable excep-

tions, the schools and colleges supported by the white denominations have conformed to caste rather than challenged it.
Even the colleges supported by the Negro denominations, following the leadership of the Negro churches on which they
depend, have often tended to conform to caste rather than to
wage a vigorous fight against it.[6] And outside of the educational field, the activities of the Christian churches of America
in combating racial caste have been meager, halting, and largely
ineffective. A brief and glorious championing of the abolitionist
cause, a sprinkling of hospitals ("For Negroes Only"), an
occasional educational or cultural outpost of racial integrity
which wages an uneven fight against the encroachments of
caste, the exchanging of "fraternal delegates," the employment of "race relations" techniques calculated to soften the
impact of caste without fundamentally rejecting it, and a long
series of high-sounding resolutions—these are the principal
part of the record of the Christian churches in the face of
American caste. The uncompromising spirit of those who conducted the Underground Railway, fought for the abolition of
slavery, and risked their lives and fortunes in behalf of Negro
education in the early days of Reconstruction has been succeeded by an uneasy accommodation to the caste system. The
record does not compare too favorably with the Soviet achievements in race equality. It is not possible to learn with certainty
how large a following communism has gained amongst American minorities, because such figures are not published. But that
the program of racial equality strongly appeals to Negroes in
the United States is an observable fact.

The same considerations apply to South Africa, and to other
parts of the African continent, where the record of Christianity in combating caste is not too convincing. The complete
capitulation of Christianity to white supremacy in Australia
does not bolster the Christian effort in India, Ceylon, and the

[6] On the colleges, see my *American Caste and the Negro College*, pp. 169-214,
and Myrdal's *American Dilemma*, pp. 739-742, 879-907.

Island Indies, nor on the Asiatic mainland in the Far East. The Soviet practice of complete racial equality constitutes a principal challenge to Christianity's effort to be a world religion without acknowledging the equality of all races.

If we wish to consider the Soviet Union as a world competitor, we cannot afford to give her the superior ethical advantage of our denial of the race equality which she practices. If we wish, on the other hand, to enter into a co-operative and peaceful relationship with the Soviet Union, a principal hindrance to achieving that relationship is this matter of our color caste. The Union of Soviet Socialist Republics now covers one-sixth of the land surface of the globe; and by the time our children are become adults, the two Unions—of Northern Asia and of North America—will be the two colossi astride the eastern and western hemispheres. If we wish to be an enemy of the U.S.S.R., we had best be a strong one. If we wish to be a friend, we had best be a good one. *In either case, we have no choice but to abandon color caste.*

3. "Race" and Islam

In Africa, the Near East, the Middle East, and the Pacific Southwest, Islam runs like a prairie fire while Christianity inches along with glacial slowness. Of immense practical concern to the missionary effort of Christianity, this fact is a matter of interest also to churchmen at home in America.

Few Christians are anxious to admit that Islam has at any point an ethical advantage over Christianity. But when Islam and Christianity meet, nothing weighs as large in the mind of the potential convert as the fact that, contrasted with Christianity, Islam has no color bar. There are no special places in the mosques for white people; there are no Muslim congregations segregated according to color; there are no racial distinctions of any kind within Islam. The father gives his daughter in marriage to another Muslim with complete indifference to the hair texture or skin color of the bridegroom.

In Africa, the strength of Islam is a religious pride that transcends all race, and the weakness of Christianity is a racial pride that breaks up religion. Negroes are being won to Islam on the failure of Christianity to live up to the principles of its Founder on the race problem.[7]

We have referred to the failure of Christianity to hold its own in the face of Islam in the seventh century. For twelve centuries since that time, the world has been large enough for the white Christian to ignore the meaning of his race attitudes in a world where Islam also was present. The shrinking of the globe now means that there is no latitude for compromise today. The white man must choose either to recover the inclusiveness of the religion he professes or to disregard the Christian religion and adopt some Weltanschauung more congenial to white supremacy.

It is the failure to recover its earlier inclusiveness as a reconciling and universal force of Christendom that has made Christianity an ally of white supremacy and a contributor to the ferment in the Near East today. Whether Islam is about to yield to the pressures of current nationalism and to follow in the wake of Christianity by denying its own inclusiveness is not yet clear. There are signs that the Pan-Islamic movement may harden into a new political nationalism, based on race, which may replace the Islam of an international and interracial brotherhood. This emergent Pan-Islamic spirit, which appears about to come to full fruition in a union of the entire Muslim world against the rest of the globe, is one of tomorrow's imponderables; but the decisions of white nations will have much to do with the future developments of Pan-Islam. Wherever white supremacy and Christianity make common cause in confronting Islam, the trends of history indicate that we may eventually expect the subjugated peoples to be welded together in common opposition to their white rulers—and in the name of a non-Christian religion make fanatical efforts to be free.

[7] Samuel M. Zwemer, speaking at the Jerusalem Conference of the International Missionary Council in 1928, as quoted by Basil Mathews, *Roads to the City of God*, p. 68. Missionary Education Movement, 1928.

It is not particularly surprising that the Muslim policy of racial equality now supports the nationalistic aspirations of the peoples of the Near East (and, in part, the Far East, as Mr. Jinnah demonstrates in India). This pattern of conflict can be broken successfully only as the practice of white supremacy is openly disavowed and frankly abandoned by "Christian" peoples.

To be sure, the present crosscurrents of the Near East and of North Africa are made up of a number of factors—economic, political, national, religious, linguistic, racial. It is the increasing cohesion of these sometimes conflicting patterns into one consistent pattern of antagonism toward the dominance of "Christian" white men that is symbolized by the emergent nationalism and Pan-Islamism surging from the Persian Gulf to Dakar. The exploited minority groups are principally Islamic, with an interfusion in Egypt and the Near East of the small but sturdy remnants of the once glorious Coptic Church and an alien planting of small units of the Roman Catholic, Orthodox, and Protestant churches. Political Zionism enters as an additional complicating factor in the Near East, where Arab opposition to it is not altogether different from the general opposition of Islam to all non-Islamic intrusions.

Out of this welter of conflicting ethnic, religious, cultural, linguistic, and nationalistic aspiratons, it is possible that tomorrow may see the emergence of a common unity of purpose directed toward the ejection of the European overlord, as today has seen the cementing of Pan-Islamic loyalties under the leadership of King Ibn Saud. And as long as "Christian" nations insist on the practice of white supremacy, they give the ethical advantage on this point (which is the crucial issue) to Islam, making that religion appear as the champion of the rights of oppressed racial minorities. While it might be argued that to give up white supremacy in Africa and the Near East is to ensure that the white man will be ejected, that ought to be no deterrent to ethical action. At the same time, it is by no means certain that equality would lead to an increase in anti-white sentiment. He who is unwelcome as a master might be retained gladly as a colleague. What is certain is that to demand the continuance of white supremacy in these areas is to create the one condition which is certain to knit together the divergent peoples in a common resolve to be done with subjugation.

If we move the spotlight from North Africa and the Near East and drop below the Sahara Desert to examine the vast reaches of the African continent, together with the empires of Britain, Portugal, France, and Belgium, the same story is told. From Dakar to Cape Town to Djibouti (with the exception of Liberia), the great triangle of Africa below the Sahara is populated by black peoples who are held subject by handfuls of Europeans only through the use of stringent measures of repression. The pass laws, the control of education, the political disfranchisement of the blacks, the establishment of a buffer caste of "colored" people between the white and black castes —here is a picture that sickens the heart of Christendom. Into this ethical void Islam is moving. Today its progress is accelerating. Tomorrow it will be too late to do anything except lament the shortsightedness of the fatal union of white supremacy with Christianity. Faced with that union, the black man will reject Christianity and embrace a religion which practices the equality of an ethical monotheism. Bound up in that step is the possibility of creating the united strength necessary for the ultimate unseating of the white usurper.

Or move the focus of scrutiny across the Indian Ocean to the Far East, and look at the Malay Peninsula and the Island Indies. There are relatively strong Roman Catholic missions in French Indo-China and a lesser group of Protestant converts as well. But the native peoples of the Malay Peninsula are predominantly Muslims; few of them have been baptized into Christianity. Most of the comparatively small number of Christians in the peninsula are Chinese, not Malayans—a curious exception to the general pattern of identification of Christianity with Europeans throughout the Pacific Southwest. The Dutch East Indies present a fairly strong group of Christians of native birth, principally those on islands where Dutch imperialism did not find an already well-entrenched Islam. On the other hand, Java, which contains more than half the total population of the archipelago, is a Muslim stronghold in which the Christian Church can boast only a few thousand adherents, mainly in the remote inland villages.

In India, Islam is far stronger than Christianity, and there is a possibility that Hinduism and Islam may eventually make common cause against Britain. On the Indian subcontinent with its more than three hundred and fifty million people, there is an ethnic and national diversity comparable in complexity with that of the European peninsula which is attached to another side of the Asiatic continent. India has been brought into the semblance of a single political state under the British Raj; but it is now being welded together into a spiritual unity of common opposition to the British. The racial difference between the European rulers of India and the amazingly diverse peoples of India is similar to the situation that prevailed in Syria, Egypt, and Africa in the second to sixth centuries. A darker people, not relishing the overlordship of a lighter, may find the strength to throw off the yoke. An outsider may be invited to do it for them.

The principal gains of Christian missions in India, at least in terms of numbers of converts, have been among the depressed classes and the outcasts, a fact which emphasizes the truth that Christianity *can* grow amongst the darker peoples today, just as it did in earlier centuries, when it ignores all lines of race and caste. Whether this lesson can be learned fast enough to impel the church to break down all barriers of race and caste throughout Christendom remains to be seen.

There are four general possibilities among which we may choose in relating Christianity to Islam. First, Christianity may continue clearly and unequivocally to identify itself with military conquest and economic overlordship by the white peoples of Europe in all lands. In that case, the church must renounce both the principle and the practice of human brotherhood, and stand firmly on the non-Christian practice of white supremacy. Secondly, Christianity may refuse to have any part in the Near East, Africa, or Central and Southern Asia or the Southwest Pacific (outside of a handful of islands off the Australian coast, and that island continent itself), pursuing a hands-off policy toward all Islamic peoples, completely withdrawing from the Islamic world. In that case, if the church were able to wear the blinders of geographical isolation, abandon the missionary effort, and by ethical obtuseness deceive itself into thinking that it had no part in the continuing commercial and military operations of white men in the remote quarters of the globe, an uneasy bed of compromise might be made on which the Christian conscience could toss for a few generations. Either of these alternatives involves the actual denial of Christian brotherhood.

A third possibility is that Christianity, affirming its essential genius as an inclusive brotherhood and therefore armed with the actual practice of racial equality at home and on the mission field, may make a vigorous proselyting effort among Muslim peoples. This would be to follow the spirit of the nineteenth century missionary effort. Whether political expediency (or other considerations) will make such an effort advisable or possible is another question. But this much we know: no effort at proselyting the followers of the Prophet can expect to make a dent in Islam as long as it does not base itself clearly on the equality of all races.

A fourth possibility, which has the support of contemporary trends in the world church, is that Christianity may seek a basis of common understanding and co-operative work with Islam and other world religions, enabling an inclusive circle of common purpose to be drawn around divergent faiths, so that all may work unitedly for the elevation of the life of the common man. Such a departure is clearly impossible unless it be based on a thoroughgoing repudiation of racial inequality throughout Christendom, and on an equally thorough affirmation and practice of racial equality, also throughout Christendom. Race pride makes any missionary effort a sham and holds the church up to shame.

4. THE GREAT GAMBLE

The effort to abandon caste within the United States is fraught with a possibility of the gravest consequences. At the July, 1942, hearings of the Fair Employment Practice Committee in Birmingham, I sat in stunned silence and heard these words from the then chairman of the committee, Mark Ethridge, a southern liberal, a man of integrity and insight, who was made chairman of the F.E.P.C. to promote the process of integrating racial minorities into American industry:

There is no power in the world—not even in all the mechanized armies of the earth, Allied and Axis—which could now force the Southern white people to abandonment of the principle of social segregation. It is a cruel disillusionment, bearing the germs of strife and perhaps tragedy, for any of their [Negroes'] leaders to tell them that they can expect it, or that they can exact it as the price of their participation in the war.[8]

These are not the irresponsible threats of a political rabble rouser. This is the considered and mature judgment of one of the leading white men of the southern states who has long stood fearlessly for racial justice within the framework of the separate-but-equal formula. He was speaking not only for himself but for what he rightly believes to be the sentiment of the great preponderance of the white South. He was also speaking for a considerable proportion of the white population in the rest of the nation, whether he intended to or not. The possibility that the effort to do away with caste may be the means of precipitating grave consequences in internal strife, bloodshed, and social disorganization, and in giving impetus to a reactionary movement which would strengthen fascist and racist tendencies, is one of the inescapable hazards of the venture. The stakes are great.

And from the other side, words of equally compelling force are spoken. Mr. Ethridge spoke for millions of white Ameri-

[8] A.N.P. dispatches, checked for accuracy with the official release of Mr. Ethridge's speech, and with personal notes made at the hearings by the writer.

cans when he said that integration can never be forced upon
them. Spokesmen for the darker races in the United States
are equally uncompromising in their determination to be rid
of racial caste. Here is the voice of the Honorable Hubert T.
Delaney, a Negro, judge in the Domestic Relations Court of
New York City, speaking in the keynote address for the
National Association for the Advancement of Colored People
in Chicago, July 12, 1944:

> These are serious times. If we want the rights to which we are en-
> titled, we must follow the leadership of the NAACP in fighting and
> fighting hard for them. Freedom and equality were never given to any-
> body. We must take them. . . . We of the NAACP know that the good
> people of America are not going to give us freedom. We know we
> must fight every step of the way for it, and we are prepared to do so.[9]

These are not the words of an irresponsible racial chauvin-
ist or an illiterate agitator. This is the careful opinion of one
of the leading Negroes of the nation, who has long stood fearlessly for justice on the only basis on which it can mean
justice—equality. He was speaking not only for himself but
for what he rightly believed to be the sentiment of the great
preponderance of the minority peoples of America. The possibilities that the effort to keep caste may bring the gravest
consequences in internal strife, bloodshed, and social disorganization, and in giving impetus to revolutionary movements
which would strengthen radical totalitarian tendencies, is also
an inescapable part of the choice before us. The stakes are
great, whether we decide to act or refuse to decide.

If we may accept Mr. Ethridge's words, the possibilities of
peaceful victory for the Christian conscience are exceedingly
slender; the possibilities that the Christian conscience will
not be obeyed, and that white supremacy will win the day are
enormous. If we accept the words of Judge Delaney, the possibilities of peaceful permanent adjustment on any basis other
than that of the Christian conscience are exceedingly slender;
the probability that refusal to obey conscience will provoke
the revolt of the oppressed is a real one. Never in the history

[9] N.A.A.C.P. *Bulletin*, September, 1944, p. 2.

of this nation, and seldom since the day when the hope of the world was entrusted to eleven men in Galilee, has so much depended upon such slender promises.

Nevertheless, the question before us is not whether the church has the strength and the insight necessary to defeat caste. Our real question is whether the church can longer compromise itself and its faith over the race issue. Just as the Syriac, Egyptian, Nubian, and African churches rejected the Church of the Empire thirteen centuries ago, so today the vestryman of an Episcopal Church, a Negro, speaks words pregnant with foreboding:

There is another enemy of America which has a great deal of influence about which people fear to speak. I don't fear to speak about this enemy of America because I think I am qualified to speak. I was born among and lived with the enemy for eighteen long years and I know what I am talking about. And that enemy is the majority of your Christian churches in America. . . . We find that in every large metropolitan city in the United States the Negro still lives in a ghetto. He is still discriminated against. He is still denied equal opportunity with his fellow men, and is still a second class citizen. Now I say to you that if our white church is really sincere in its application of its Christianity, it would say that the time is always ripe to advocate the abolition of segregation; the time is always ripe to advocate the elimination of jimcrowism, discrimination, prejudice in the Courts, and abolition of the poll tax. And yet, with few exceptions, I never hear the Church lift its voice![10]

Admitting that the odds against us are great, we are constrained to make the effort. If we fail of accomplishment, we nevertheless begin the ultimate destruction of the iniquities of caste and we write a page of history which may yet be accounted to this generation for righteousness. We cannot do worse than refuse to try, with the lame excuse that the odds are heavily against us. They are human odds. At least let it be said that the effort was made within the United States and the Western Church in the middle of the twentieth century to pass on an honest patrimony of ethical integrity.

[10] Delaney, *op. cit.*

CHAPTER X

DECLARATION

We are asked to turn to the church for our enlightenment, but
when we do so we find that the voice of the church is not inspired.
The voice of the church today, we find, is the echo of our own
voices. And the result of this exprience, already manifest, is disillusionment.

—Fortune MAGAZINE, JANUARY, 1940.

IN THE field of race, whatever else may be true in other
areas, the voice of the church has spoken in a great series of
ecumenical conferences to give the lie to the accusation of
Fortune's editors. Jerusalem, Madras, Oxford, Malvern,
Delaware, Cleveland, and the Laymen's Inquiry have spoken
for the collective conscience of Christendom in a voice that is
like the blast of God's trumpet. Some readers who may have
been upset by the chapters of this book, which may have
appeared to be the opinions of one man, are now brought to
face the collective affirmations of the churches of the world.

1. JERUSALEM

At Passiontide in 1928, there came together on the Mount
of Olives what was, up to that time, the most significant
gathering of non-Roman missionary leaders and thinkers ever
assembled. The conference was planned with the deliberate
purpose of "drawing together the Christians of different
lands and races."[1]

It constituted the first meeting ever held in which the churches of
Europe, North America, and Australia which send out missionaries

[1] John R. Mott in the Foreword to Basil Mathew's *Roads to the City of God.*
Missionary Education Movement, 1928.

were represented in approximately the same numbers as the churches of Asia, Africa, and Latin America which were planted by missionaries.[2]

Thus, in its constituent character, the Jerusalem meeting was calculated to recognize and to symbolize the equal meeting and sharing of peoples from all races and nations.

Moreover, the delegates who assembled on Olivet were

a thoroughly representative body of men and women, who command to a unique degree the confidence of the Christians the world over.[3]

The roster of persons present reads like a catalogue of the great names of world-wide Protestantism. They came from fifty nations, chosen from the leadership of the Christian community in every continent. He would be a bold man who would set himself up as an authority to gainsay the ethical insights of the Jerusalem Meeting of the International Missionary Council in 1928.

Not that any conference is infallible, and not that Jerusalem spoke the final word. No such pretensions were made. But when the record of the assembly and its debates were printed, Dr. Mott was able to say:

Without doubt, if Christians throughout the world act upon the message and the program [here set forth], twenty years hence men of discernment will be able to say that the Jerusalem Meeting marked nothing short of the beginning of a new epoch in the evolution and expansion of the world-wide Christian movement.[4]

The *if* in Dr. Mott's statement was a big one; but the affirmation itself was not too extravagant. The commitments made by the thinkers and searchers of the Jerusalem Meeting were revolutionary in their import. If they had been acted upon, the history of the world would have been profoundly different. Basil Mathews is an old hand at conferences, and he might be expected not to overestimate the importance of such a meeting, or to overstate his case in reporting it. In

[2] Mott, *op. cit.*, p. viii.
[3] *Ibid.*, p. ix.
[4] *Ibid.*

the chapter of his book which deals with the subject of race at the Jerusalem Meeting, he wrote:

In all the writer's experience, no discussion has ever more frankly lifted the lid of reality and looked more deeply into the seething cauldron. No nation's feelings were spared through lack of thoroughly, straightforward speech, yet no one felt hurt, except in the healthful process of having conscience mightily shaken. For the spirit prevailing was that of sharing truth in order to arrive at a better day.[5]

From such a gathering, with such an atmosphere, in the face of such a problem, words of significance should have come. They did come.[6] There were plain words about color caste in America, and about the agencies that were attempting to establish bridges of co-operative understanding across race lines. The festering sore of South Africa was bared to analysis and diagnosis. The relations between Occidental and Oriental peoples on the Pacific slope in North America were analyzed with uncommon candor. The Council heard the words of hope and frustration from China, and saw "What Is Moving in the Heart of India." A careful program of action, based on clearly enunciated principles and pointed in Christian directions, was laid down. It is interesting to look back over the intervening years, and to speculate on what might have been the present possibilities of the Christian life *if* the Jerusalem statement had been acted upon.

The opening paragraph of the Council's statement "On the Duty of Christians" reads:

All Christian forces, and particularly the International Missionary Council, dedicated as they are to prepare for the establishment among all mankind of the Kingdom of God, are bound to work with all their power to remove race prejudice and adverse conditions due to it, to preserve the rights of peoples, and to establish educational, religious, and

[5] Mathews, *op. cit.*, p. 64.
[6] *Missions and Race Conflict*, Vol. IV of the *Reports* of the Jerusalem Meeting of the International Missionary Council, March 24—April 8, 1928. Missionary Education Movement, 1928.

other facilities designed to enable all alike to enjoy equality of social, political, and economic opportunity.[7]

Critical readers may see a weasel phrase in the words "equality of social opportunity." They might argue that this phrase attempts to combine the "equality of opportunity" so dear to the race-parallelism school of thought with the "social equality" championed by the integrationist, without actually supporting either alternative or stating a choice between the two. It is more nearly correct to say that the phrasing is intended to dodge no issues and make no compromises, but to say exactly what it means and mean exactly what it says. "Social equality" is not a matter that can be attained by compulsion. The opportunity, free and untrammeled by arbitrary controls of caste, is all that can be conferred on anyone. In the social realm, as in the economic and the political realms, "equality of opportunity" is an accurate description of one desirable objective—provided it means what it says. When it is used in conjunction with "separation," in the separate-but-equal formula, it begins to mean something different. It then means the continuance of the compulsory inequalities of caste based on racial identity. The Jerusalem Council statement insists that there shall be no arbitrary inequalities, even in social relations, because of the racial identity of any individual. This insistence becomes doubly clear in the words:

In lands where different races live side by side full participation in social, cultural, and above all religious interracial fellowship, and the development of personal friendship which such intercourse engenders are the natural expression of our common Christianity, and are obviously to be welcomed as a step toward world-wide understanding.[8]

The Jerusalem Council declaration left no place for color caste.

As the Council elaborated the program that should implement its basic Christian impulses, it faced the knotty problem

[7] *Ibid.*, p. 195.
[8] *Ibid.*, p. 201.

of means and ends, and of the "practicable" over against the "visionary." It advocated no utopian irrelevancies; neither did it whittle away the demands of the Christian ethic for fear of appearing utopian. In reading the following quotation, much depends on whether the reader's mind emphasizes *utmost* or *practicable*; but the context of the Jerusalem discussions leaves no doubt that in the minds of the men and women who wrote and endorsed this statement the important word was *utmost*:

The difficulties which arise when two or more peoples, differing in color or race, live side by side in the same country would, this Council believes, be mitigated if steps were taken:

1. To establish the utmost practicable equality in such matters as the right to enter and follow all occupations and professions, the right to freedom of movement, and other rights before civil and criminal law, and the obtaining and exercising of the functions of citizenship, subject always to such general legislation as, *without discriminating between men on grounds of color and race*, may be necessary to maintain the social and economic standards of the community as a whole. . . .

3. To apply the Christian principle of brotherhood and equality in the eyes of God to matters of social relations and to the common life of the community.[9]

Not only in its statement of principles, but also in its program suggestions, the Jerusalem Council stood firmly and without equivocation for the equality of the races wherever Christianity is at work.

The program extended this notion of equality to the problems of immigration (in such nations as the United States and Australia, for example) when it said:

The Council recognizes that it is reasonable for the higher civilization to protect its standards, and to that end it may be expedient to restrict immigration into its territories. But such restriction, it believes, *should never make discrimination among intending immigrants upon grounds of color or race*, neither of which can, in the opinion of this Council, be held to be in itself a legitimate ground for exclusion.[10]

[9] *Ibid.*, p. 197. (Italics are mine. B.G.G.)
[10] *Ibid.*, p. 198. (Italics are mine. B.G.G.)

The final section of the statement on program is as explicit as words can make it:

... there are certain grave problems which still escape the salutary check of the international conscience. In particular:

1. The relations between peoples of a metropolitan State and those of its colonies, possessions, and other dependencies;

2. The virtual hegemony exercised by one people over another as a result of the establishment of financial and economic control;

3. The acquisition of special privileges, of which the leading example is the status of extra-territoriality;

The Council looks forward to the time when such relations, where they still exist, will be made amenable to the public opinion, not of any one nation or group of nations, but of a world, organized and equipped to judge them by the standards of universal justice.[11]

But the story of "too little and too late," which characterized the military struggle a dozen years later, is also the story of the implementing of this program. Extraterritoriality was finally abrogated, for China only, as a part of the prosecution of World War II. The Council spoke in 1928: that would have been the time for action. Nothing has yet been done by the United States about its immigration quotas based on the census of 1890, although the Chinese are not now totally excluded as they were when the Jerusalem Council met and demanded an end to immigration policies based on race.

We are aware that the tragedy of permitting moralizing to take the place of moral action has overtaken the Jerusalem Council's declarations. Considerable progress was made, however, particularly in the areas under the control of the agencies constituting the Council: especially is this true in the naturalization of the younger churches. Yet, despite inadequate action since 1928, the Mount of Olives was at that time the setting for an affirmation of the inclusiveness of Christianity.in all its uncompromising fullness. The Council concluded its statement on race with a six-point program of "immediate action necessary," indicating its own impelling convic-

[11] *Ibid.*, p. 199.

tion that moralizing is not enough. "All our work," they said—and they meant *all*, "must have as its conscious goal the fulfillment of the Lord's prayer, 'That they may all be one.'"

2. The Laymen's Inquiry

Following hard on the heels of the Jerusalem Meeting of the International Missionary Council, the Laymen's Inquiry conducted an exhaustive study of the whole of the missionary effort in the Orient. Its chairman, Dr. Hocking of Harvard, may be permitted to speak in interpretation of the conclusions of the study:

The preliminary stage of Protestant missions in the Orient is past: a new stage is opening. The many clear-sighted men in the field, and the clear-sighted guides in its official councils, fully realize this truth. They best serve the cause who announce this truth in unmistakable terms. It is not superfluous to add that the necessity for change is wholly consistent with the changelessness of the fundamental message of Christianity and of the fundamental need of the human soul. It is the element of changelessness in central religious truth which requires—I do not say permits, but *requires*—changes in method and policy as the world changes, and as our conceptions of Christianity develop.[12]

The report of the Laymen's Inquiry appeared in a summary volume (*Rethinking Missions*),[13] together with seven volumes of reports of the Commission on Appraisal. If it were necessary, we could use the next twenty pages quoting from these reports to verify the fact that they are a comprehensive and intensive application of the findings of the Jerusalem Council to the whole of the foreign missions enterprise in the Orient. What happened is that the inquiry conducted by a distinguished group of Christian laymen strengthened the resolve of missionaries and mission boards in their purpose to

[12] W. E. Hocking, Introduction to Vol. I, supplementary series, *Laymen's Foreign Missions Inquiry*, Orville A. Petty, editor, pp. xii-xiii. Harpers, 1933. (Author's own italics.)
[13] Harpers, 1932.

carry out the decisions of the Jerusalem Meeting. While the effects of Jerusalem and of the Laymen's Inquiry upon the churches at home and upon the responsible governments of the missionary nations was scarcely to cause a ripple in the bland surface of racial complacency, their effect on the foreign field and in the councils of missionary statesmen was electrifying. The missionary boomerang which has at long last completed its swing to smite the Christian conscience in the home churches was given double impetus by Jerusalem and the Inquiry.

3. MADRAS

Following the World Conference at Jerusalem, a Department of Social and Economic Research and Council was set up at Geneva in 1930 by the International Missionary Council. It was charged with the obligation of collecting and distributing information on the economic and social developments which challenge the gospel of Christ and limit the growth of His Kingdom among the younger churches. A steady stream of reports and findings, based on careful and comprehensive field surveys, has come from this agency, under the headship of J. Merle Davis. Thus, when the International Missionary Council called its meetings at Tambaram, Madras, at Christmas in 1938, much material had been accumulated in the decade since Jerusalem to give substance and meaning to the declarations of principle and program which the earlier Council had made. If the tragedy of World War II had not eclipsed the subsequent efforts of the Council, there is little doubt that Madras would have been looked back upon as the time when the ecumenical church gathered its resources for a great world-wide offensive upon the iniquities of color caste.

Madras did not achieve complete unanimity; but the dissenters serve to underline and to emphasize the agreement of the great body of the Church. The gathering clouds of Nazi aggression cast their shadow before them, and the German delegation at Tambaram presented a statement to the conference pointing out that it was in "theological" disagreement with certain principal trends of the findings of the conference with reference to the relationship of "the Church and the Changing Social and Economic Order." This disagreement

centered in their belief that for the present period of history the orders of sex, family, nation, *and race* are divinely established, and therefore the Christian Church is not allowed to dissolve them.[14]

This is, of course, a difference that is related to theological considerations; but it is fundamentally an ethical, not a theological difference. It is an instance of the use of theological prestidigitation to hide ethical issues. This contrast of the opinion of the dissenting churches italicizes the unanimity of the balance of the Council in support of one of the most clearly formulated and most nearly definitive statements of the social obligation and function of the church that have yet been produced by Christian thinkers.[15]

Jerusalem had left little room for improvement in the formulation of the ethical judgment on race; but Madras made significant additions at certain points, principally in the area of implementation:

A Christian incentive to combat social sin requires two elements in inseparable unity: (1) ethical sensitiveness and (2) knowledge of social fact. Sensitiveness without knowledge leads to sentimentality; knowledge without sensitiveness leads to shallow humanism which lacks moral incentive.[16]

Working with this double attack of ethical insight and social knowledge to perfect the processes of social engineering, the Christian Church, in the opinion of the Madras Council

... would look on every man as a man, without prejudice or discrimination on account of race, birth, color, class, or culture. The sacredness of human personality becomes a working fact. . . . In this new Kingdom

[14] *The Economic Basis of the Church*, Vol. V of the Madras Series, edited by J. Merle Davis, p. 553 n. International Missionary Council, 1939. (Italics are mine. B.G.G.)

[15] Cf. Chap. XXX of *op. cit.*

[16] *Op. cit.*, p. 559.

there cannot be Greek and Jew—racial discrimination; there cannot be
Barbarian or Scythian—cultural discrimination; neither can there be
bond or free—social discrimination; there cannot be male or female—
sex discrimination. We would therefore make the unit of cooperation
the human race. . . . Mankind is one. There are undeveloped races and
classes, but none permanently superior or inferior. . . .

We would therefore demand equality of opportunity for every man
for his complete development. All men have not the same abilities, but
they should have equal opportunities.[17]

And when this demand for equality of opportunity for every
man is translated into specifics of social action and applied to
the local church, the Council maintained that

it should include in its membership people of varied economic, social,
racial, and national background, living in the area ordinarily served by
the local fellowship.[18]

Or, applied to the problem of the impact of the church upon
society, this means that the church

must subject the institutions of government and of society and the practices of groups or nations to the strong light of Christ's spirit. It must
judge, condemn and fearlessly declare the implications of the Gospel
when the existing order is contrary to the Will of God for His children.[19]

This is the voice of resolute courage with which the church
must speak in the hour of fateful decision now upon us.

4. THE ECUMENICAL CONFERENCES

Paralleling the developments of the International Missionary Council, which has begun to give to the Protestant churches
of the world a common unity of program and purpose in
missionary endeavor, is the ecumenical movement which has
grown from modest beginnings in a "preliminary meeting"

[17] *Ibid.* pp. 559-560.
[18] *Ibid.* p. 563.
[19] *Ibid.*, p. 564.

in Geneva in 1920 to the climactic achievements of Oxford and Edinburgh seventeen years later, to lay the foundations of a World Council of Churches embracing the entire non-Roman Christian world. With the meetings at Oxford, Edinburgh, and Madras, the ecumenical movement acquired a solidity and massiveness equaled only by the incisiveness of its ethical insights, uniting three great world movements of Christianity—the "Faith and Order" movement, the "Life and Work" movement, and the World Mission of the Church.[20] Embracing practically every communion of Christendom, including the Eastern Orthodox and the Lesser Eastern Churches, and excepting only the churches which owe allegiance to Rome, this ecumenical movement attempts to discover the fundamental unities that underlie the surface diversities and to give to Christianity the hope of a common sharing in united endeavor by all branches and divisions of the church.

After nine earlier attempts had failed, the movement succeeded in bringing together at Stockholm in 1925 the first ecumenical conference in which the Eastern Orthodox, Anglican, and Protestant communions met as one conference. Stockholm marked the formal inauguration of the Life and Work effort, matters of Faith and Order not being on the agenda; but the exploration of the unities of purpose and program made possible the convening two years later of the Lausanne conference to deal with problems of theology and ecclesiastical organization. Both Stockholm and Lausanne contributed, by their impetus, to the success of the Jerusalem Council; but 1937 marked the first attempt of all three movements—Faith and Order, Life and Work, and World Mission—to unite in a single great effort of exploration and understanding. At Oxford, matters of life and work were considered, while a week later at Edinburgh, common con-

[20] Cf. *A Pilgrimage Toward Unity: Report of the Preliminary Meeting at Geneva, Switzerland, August 12-20, 1920*, published by the Continuation Committee (1920); and Henry Smith Leiper, *World Chaos or World Christianity* (Willett, Clark & Co., 1937).

cerns of faith and order not merely brought together the representatives of church bodies, but also engaged the active participation of the International Missionary Council, the World Alliance for Friendship Through the Churches, the World Alliance of the Y.M.C.A.'s and the Y.W.C.A.'s, and the World's Student Christian Federation. The assembling of officials and delegated representatives from all over the world gave to these meetings an authenticity and inclusiveness which no previous meetings had had. There were also friendly and cordial, if unofficial, written representations from Roman Catholicism.

Just as Jerusalem and Madras were preceded by much study, research, and preparation, so Oxford and Edinburgh were not detached incidents. They were part of a process which began long before the conferences gathered, and which has continued right on through the weary war years. Commissions in a number of fields had prepared studies and reports which together made a respectable five-foot shelf, testifying to the hard thought and labor which men and women of every part of the globe had put into the preparation for Oxford and Edinburgh. The provisional council of the World Council of Churches is a going concern, operating on a sizable budget, and giving real promise of making possible a more effective ministry of the churches to the needs of Christendom in the postwar period than the world has yet known. It combines the Faith and Order and the Life and Work movements (which will probably not again meet separately) and works closely with the International Missionary Council; and it is expected that the formal organization will be consummated as soon as the world situation permits.

Christians of sixty lands, speaking a hundred or more different languages, representing every shade of theological opinion and every conceivable form of ecclesiastical structure (with the single exception of the Roman Church) have begun to come together in a common spirit and for a common purpose. The 1937 situation in Germany prevented the attendance of the delegates from the Germany Evangelical Church, who had, nevertheless, participated in all the preliminary work and studies.

The direct connection between sharpened ethical insight and increased theological convincingness is born out by the experiences of Oxford and Edinburgh. Oxford met first, to consider Life and Work. Edinburgh followed, on Faith and Order. Before the conferences met, there were many who feared that one would eclipse the other, or that the second would appear anticlimactic.

No such thing happened. As one very wise observer said afterwards: "Instead of eclipsing Edinburgh, Oxford vitalized it . . . It became clear that the church could not assume a functional responsibility of the magnitude envisaged at Oxford while its faith and order were broken into sectarian compartments."[21]

The chronology of effort, in which progressive discovery of common concerns of Life and Work has always been the harbinger of progress toward common understanding in matters of Faith and Order, and in which the latter advance has in turn reinforced the former for the next forward move, establishes pragmatically one of the principal arguments supporting the effort to strike down the barriers of caste: if Christians can unite in attacking color caste, the heat which that struggle generates will enable God's hammer to beat out on the anvil of experience new patterns of inclusive Christian brotherhood.

It is Dr. Leiper's opinion that the statements dealing with such matters as race, education, war, economics, and the problems of church and state which were adopted unanimously at Oxford in 1937 "register new high levels for united Christian thinking." One reason for the solid achievements at Oxford is the fact that it called into service a great group of lay people, from the universities and colleges and from the non-academic world as well. The church is more than the clergy;

[21] Leiper, *op. cit.*, pp. 172-173.

and its full powers will be unleashed only as the laity are enlisted, and are given full power and a full share in the enterprise.

Too long has it been assumed that the making of the church of tomorrow is the task of the clergy alone. Now, once more, as in the days of the early church, it is clearly seen that unless and until lay responsibility is recognized and lay cooperation encouraged there can be no real progress in the renewing of the life of the church or—even more important—in the increase of its impact upon the hostile elements in the social and international orders.[22]

The strength of the Oxford statement on race is that it is rooted in the conception of Christian community. In our age, two great sins violate the integrity of the Christian community: nationalism, which enthrones the nation as deity, and racism, which perpetuates in vicious form the error to which the Psalmist referred—"They limited the Holy One of Israel" (Psalm 78:41b, marginal translation). Both these evils are made possible by a third grave error of the church in permitting a widening of the breach between itself and the common life of mankind, in word and especially in deed. These three problems of nationalism, racism, and the divorcing of religion from the secular life of the world formulate the general problem of church and community. To overcome these evils, there is a call from God today:

1. *To every local congregation, to realize at any cost in its own self that unity, transcending all differences and barriers of class, social status, race, and nation*, which we believe the Holy Spirit can and will create in those who are ready to be led by him.

2. To different churches in any district, to come together for a local ecumenical witness in worship and work.

3. To all Christians, to a more passionate and costly concern for the outcast, the underprivileged, the persecuted and the despised in the community and beyond the community. The recrudescence of pitiless cruelty, hatreds, and race discriminations (including anti-Semitism) in the

[22] *Ibid.*, p. 178.

modern world is one of the major signs of its social disintegration. *To these must be brought not the weak rebuke of words but the powerful rebuke of deeds.* Thus the unity of the church is advanced. The Church has been called into existence by God not for itself but for the world. Only by going out of itself in the work of Christ can it find unity in itself.[23]

The foregoing "practical suggestions" were based on three brief paragraphs which constitute the heart of the Oxford statement as far as racial matters are concerned, and which are now quoted in full. They deserve careful study. Having spoken of the inimical effects of nationalism, and having demanded that the deification of the state "be utterly repudiated and irreconcilably opposed by the Christian conscience in the name of God and for the sake of the nation it is called to serve," the report turns to

The Church and Race. Even deeper are distinctions of race. The existence of black races, white races, yellow races, is to be accepted gladly and reverently as full of possibilities under God's purpose for the enrichment of human life. And there is no room for any differentiation between the races as to their intrinsic value. All share alike in the concern of God, being created by him to bring their unique and distinctive contributions to his service in the world.

Here again, however, the gift can be and is abused. The sin of man asserts itself in racial pride, racial hatreds and persecutions and in the exploitation of other races. Against this attitude in all its forms the church is called by God to set its face implacably and to utter its word unequivocally both within and without its own borders.

Moreover, it is a first responsibility of the church to demonstrate within its own fellowship the reality of community as God intends it. It is commissioned to call all men into the church, into a divine society that transcends all national and racial limitations and divisions. In the services of worship, in its more informal fellowship, in its organization and in the hospitality of the Christian home, there can be no place for exclusion or segregation because of race or color. "There is neither Jew nor Greek, bond nor free, for ye are all one in Christ." To allow the

[23] *The Oxford Conference (Official Report),* edited by J. H. Oldham, pp. 61-62. Willett, Clark & Co., 1937. (Italics are mine. B. G. G.)

church's lines of action to be determined by racial discrimination denies
the gospel whose proclamation is its task and commission.[24]

The revolutionary import of these words is apparent even
to the casual first reader. He who rereads them slowly and
with care will see in them an unqualified affirmation of racial
equality which extends even to the inner recesses of the home,
and sweeps out of the church of God every last vestige of
pride in race or distinctions based upon it. The report says:
"The deification of one's own people is a sin against God."[25]

5. MALVERN AND DELAWARE

The Archbishop of York called together in January, 1941,
at Malvern a conference of Church of England clergy and
laymen which issued a manifesto with far-reaching implications. His Majesty's First Minister might serve notice that
he did not come to that position for the purpose of presiding
at the liquidation of the British Empire, but the words spoken
by the Malvern conference stand in stark opposition to Mr.
Churchill's sentiments. None of the Malvern Manifesto is
irrelevant to Christian thought and action; but only part of it
is directly concerned with the problem of empire, which is
(for Englishmen) the essence of their problem of race.

Prior to the Malvern conference, a statement had been
released over the signatures of the heads of the Anglican,
Roman, and Free churches of England. The Malvern Manifesto begins by endorsing the ten proposals of this earlier
statement—proposals made for the consideration of responsible statesmen who would have to determine the policies
of England at the conclusion of the war. While couched
in general terms, these ten proposals imply no retreat from

[24] *Ibid.*, pp. 60-61.
[25] *Ibid.*, p. 64. There is a sense in which the whole of this book is nothing but
an elaboration on these three paragraphs from the Oxford report. I claim no
originality in my argument. It rests squarely on the ethical insights of Christendom, so clearly and unequivocally delineated in the Oxford, Madras, and
Jerusalem statements. B.G.G.

the stand taken at Oxford, and they flatly challenge the continuance of white supremacy in its British form, imperialism. Here are the sections bearing on race:

2. Every child, regardless of race or class, should have equal opportunities for education suitable to its capacities.

5. Resources of the earth should be used as God's gift for the whole human race and used with due consideration for the needs of present and future generations.

6. The right to life and independence of all nations, large and small, strong or weak, must be safeguarded.

9. Real needs and just demands of nations and peoples should be benevolently examined.

10. A peace settlement must be dictated by a sense of acute responsibility which weighs human statutes according to the holy, unshakable rules of divine law.[26]

There is enough dynamite in the Malvern declaration to blow the whole of the white man's imperialism with its racial inequities off the face of the earth—if it is acted upon. Placed alongside the evasive oratory and equivocal generalities of political statesmen (reviewed above in Chap. IV), the words of Malvern look courageous and adventurously sane.

Fourteen months later, at Delaware, Ohio, a national study conference met under the call of the Federal Council's Commission to Study the Bases of a Just and Durable Peace. Having affirmed its belief that reciprocity of trade was not enough to assure world justice in economic matters, the Delaware conference went on to say:

7. We believe that that government which derives its just powers from the consent of the governed is the truest expression of the rights and dignity of man. This requires that we seek autonomy for all subject and colonial peoples. Until that shall be realized, the task of colonial government is no longer one of exclusive national concern. It must be recognized as a common responsibility of mankind, to be carried out in

[26] The *Findings* of the Archbishop of York's Conference at Malvern, obtainable from the Industrial Christian Fellowship, 1 Broadway, Westminster, S.W.1, England (1941).

the interests of the colonial peoples, by the most appropriate form of organization. This would in many cases make colonial government a task of international collaboration for the benefit of colonial peoples who would, themselves, have a voice in their government. As the agencies for the promotion of world-wide political and economic security become effective, the moral, social and material welfare of colonial populations can be more fully realized.

9. We believe that the right of all men to pursue work of their own choosing and to enjoy security from want and oppression is not limited by race, color or creed. The rights and liberties of racial and religious minorities in all lands should be recognized and safeguarded. Freedom of religious worship, of speech and assembly, of the press, and of scientific inquiry and teaching are fundamental to human development and in keeping with the moral order.

Then, in words that should weigh heavily upon the conscience of any American who has a conscience (not because Delaware declares them, but because they are true), the Delaware Declaration continues:

10. We believe that, in bringing international relations into conformity with the moral law, a very heavy responsibility devolves upon the United States. For at least a generation we have held preponderant economic power in the world, and with it the capacity to influence decisively the shaping of world events. It should be a matter of shame and humiliation to us that actually the influences shaping the world have largely been irresponsible forces. Our own positive influence has been impaired because of concentration on self and on our short-range material gains. Many of the major preconditions of a just and durable peace require changes of national policy on the part of the United States. Among such may be mentioned: equal access to natural resources, economic collaboration, *equitable treatment of racial minorities*, international control of tariffs, limitation of armaments, participation in world government. We must be ready to subordinate immediate and particular national interests to the welfare of all. If the future is to be other than a repetition of the past, the United States must accept the responsibility for constructive action commensurate with its power and opportunity.

As Malvern spoke to the statesmen of England, so Delaware addressed its words to the responsible men of government in the United States. And the statement goes on to call on the church to take steps as far-reaching and courageous as those which the nation is asked to consider.

11. We believe that a supreme responsibility rests with the church. The church, being a creation of God in Jesus Christ, is called to proclaim to all men everywhere the way of life. Moreover, the church which is now in reality a world community, may be used of God to develop his righteousness and love in every race and nation and thus to make possible a just and durable peace . . .

Further, recognizing the universal peril that resolutions, statements, findings, and declarations can be hypocritical substitutes for constructive action unless they are put into action, the statement continues:

12. We believe that, as Christian citizens, we must seek to translate our beliefs into practical realities and to create a public opinion which will insure that the United States shall play its full and essential part in the creation of a moral way of international living. We must strive within the life of our own nation for change which will result in the more adequate application here of the principles above enumerated as the basis for a just and durable world order.

Moving on from these guiding principles, the Delaware Declaration then becomes specific, pointing out *the responsibility of the church* for the creation of a durable peace:

1. We believe it is the purpose of God to create a world-wide community in Jesus Christ, transcending nation, race and class . . . In order that its witness may be effective, in the fullest measure, it is important that the church reflect in every phase of its own life—congregational, denominational, interdenominational, and ecumenical—the reality of the peace, unity and cooperation which it recommends in secular society.

The temper of Delaware—an impatience with words piled upon words, while action halts—is shown in its second charge to the American churches:

2. We are penitently conscious of the many weaknesses and shortcomings of the church itself in the face of the tremendous responsibilities

with which it is confronted. We have not sufficiently borne witness to, nor even adequately recognized for the church itself, that very unity of mankind, beyond race and nation, which again and again we have declared in principle. We call upon our churches, therefore, to enter seriously and immediately upon the task of breaking down the barriers that so easily divide us into opposing groups. We would say to them: If you believe in peace for the world, if you are working for cooperation between nations, governments, races and peoples under the Fatherhood of God, you must set the example for such reconciliation and cooperation. The Christian churches must come to realize as they now do not, that joining the Church of Christ in any of its branches means entering a fellowship world-wide in extent, beyond denomination and race, and should involve responsible participation in the task of making spiritually more real our mystical fellowship in community life and in the world.[27]

6. CLEVELAND

To this message, and to the affirmations of Delaware (and an intermediate meeting at Princeton), the Cleveland meetings in January, 1945, added their unqualified reaffirmation. The voice of American Protestantism is as uncompromisingly forthright and thoroughgoing as any statement ever produced by a responsible body of churchmen on the matter of race at any time in the history of Christianity. Under the heading of "Human Rights," Cleveland said:

We have recommended that, in connection with the world organization proposed at Dumbarton Oaks, there be established a special commission on human rights and fundamental freedoms. We believe that religious liberty is basic to all human rights and that it should be accompanied by *equal and unsegregated opportunity for all races.* The commission we have recommended should seek an international agreement on the rights and freedoms to be secured to all people; it should further formulate the procedures for their realization by action of the world organization and of the separate states.

[27] *A Message from the National Study Conference on the Churches and a Just and Durable Peace.* The Commission, 1942.

When it turned specifically to the future of colonial populations, Cleveland declared:

Long and intimate relationships with the dependent peoples of Africa, southeast Asia and other parts of the world place on the Christian churches a responsibility to champion their right to freedom and to develop their capacity for self-government.

We therefore call upon our government and others: (1) to proclaim self-government as the goal for all dependent peoples; (2) where dependent peoples are ready for self-government, to give it now; (3) otherwise, to initiate progressive steps suitable for each area for achieving that goal; and (4) in the interim to provide that all such areas shall be administered under the supervision of world organization.

We cannot in good conscience be a party to the dismantling of the Japanese colonial possessions without at the same time insisting that the imperialism of the white man shall be brought to the speediest possible end. We cannot have a sound or stable world community so long as there is enforced submission of one people to the will of another whether in Korea, in India, in the Congo, in Puerto Rico or anywhere else.

In addition to these basic principles and demands of the Christian conscience, the Cleveland Declaration becomes specific and inexorable in its recommendations for action in the field of race relations:

Race prejudice is a primary obstacle to world brotherhood. It is strongly urged upon churches and church members that they wage a continuing campaign against race prejudice in all its forms. The churches should not only support all efforts to wipe out discriminations against minority groups, but they should also deliberately arrange cooperative programs in which racial barriers are broken down. We recommend active support by the churches of legislation providing for a permanent Fair Employment Practices Commission; providing for the repeal of poll tax and other discriminatory laws; providing for housing projects without discriminatory practices and other measures designed to advance the well-being and constitutional rights of Negroes and other underprivileged groups.[28]

[28] "The Churches and World Order," a message adopted at the second national study conference held at Cleveland, Ohio, January 16-19, 1945, under the auspices of the Commission on a Just and Durable Peace of the Federal

In this book I have been dealing with controversial matters, and dealing with them without using kid gloves. Some
readers may have felt that I have at times overstated the
case for "equal and unsegregated opportunity for all races."
It is useful to rest the discussion on a foundation laid by
what is recognized not as the mind of one man but of "the
most distinguished body of Protestant leaders to gather on
this continent in the present generation."[29] The quoted matter in this chapter, from the series of great meetings from
Jerusalem to Cleveland, gives majestic expression to the inclusive mind of Christ at work in our generation.

No more resolutions are necessary; but action is imperative. Unless we can bring forth fruits of Christian living,
both in seeing and in doing the Will of God as it is so
clearly known by us, we convict ourselves of the sin of pride
and hypocrisy as we fight against the Heavenly Vision.

Council of Churches of Christ in America. Printed in full in the *Christian
Century*, February 7, 1945, pp. 174-191. (Italics are mine. B.G.G.)
[29] Editorial comment in the *Christian Century*, Vol. LXII, No. 6, February 7,
1945, p. 166.

CHAPTER XI

DEEDS

If we listen to the voice of reason and duty, and pursue this day the line of conduct which they prescribe, some of us may live to see the reverse of that picture from which we now turn our eyes with shame and regret.

—WILLIAM PITT, ADDRESSING PARLIAMENT ON WILBERFORCE'S MOTION TO ABOLISH THE SLAVE TRADE (1792).

THE intolerable tensions of conscience, the sense of "shame and regret" with which we contemplate our involvement in the caste of color, can find constructive release. We have no need permanently to be enslaved to caste. We can discard its tyrannies and base our lives on the Christian ethic. The fact that many individuals in all racial groups have already done so, and are doing so today, is proof positive that it can be done by the rest of us—if we wish. We have only ourselves to blame if we refuse.

If, then, we wish to work for "equal and unsegregated opportunity" to replace the hypocrisy of "separate but equal" evasion of conscience, where do we begin and what do we do? There are a multitude of things waiting to be done, of which the following are a representative sampling.

1. AT THE LOCAL LEVEL

The caste system depends for its continuance upon many millions of people voluntarily observing its canons. To break with color caste is first and foremost a matter of voluntarily discarding and disregarding the etiquette of caste. It costs nothing to use the terms of polite address (Mr., Mrs., and Miss) as simple means of designating the sex and marital status of adults. To withhold these terms from the members of minorities is to insist that these minorities are made up of persons who must always stay in the social status of children. If persons of color are addressed only by their first or last names, without the courtesy title, it is as though one were constantly saying, "Although you are an adult, I insist on treating you as a menial or a child." When the courtesy titles are used, as a matter of habit, it is as though one said, "I know that I am like you, and we hold each other in mutual respect." It costs so little and means so much to be courteous. Only the small of soul can afford to be discourteous.

And there is the eating taboo. Throughout the world, from primitive to sophisticated societies, the universal symbol of common fellowship is eating together. That is why some American cities have felt it necessary to pass ordinances prohibiting the races from eating together in public—lest their common fellowship should be openly recognized. Where these laws exist, they are an affront to the Christian conscience. Direct action is needed to get them repealed. Where there are no such laws, there is no reason why the eating taboo of color caste should be followed. Where civil rights bills have been enacted to protect the right of men to break bread together without reference to race, these laws need the support of an active and appreciative citizenry. As at Emmaeus, so today and everywhere, He is known to us "in the breaking of the bread."

Our homes can become, immediately and without delay, centers of open friendship. The few friends whom we may temporarily lose will be more than offset by the rich friendships we gain.

As ministers and as church members, we can make the churches in which we worship and work inclusive rather than exclusive. There is nothing but human inertia and a certain unreasoning fear of the unfamiliar to stand in the way of our making every congregation in this nation a cross section of the family of God. There is no single thing that would more profoundly revolutionize the American churches and more vitally recall them to their high calling than for (say) half of them to become inclusive by 1950. The other half can be tolerated only until they also "listen to the voice of reason and duty." Integration must, of course, include the clergy of minority groups (as it does now, in some cases, with the ministers of the former Japanese Christian churches whose parishioners are being integrated into churches with other racial groups in all parts of the nation). As long as it is possible for a pastorate in a particular church to be filled only by a Caucasian, then that congregation is a Caucasian church. This does not mean that every church, or any particular church, must have only non-Caucasian ministers. It means only a "high indifference" to the complexion of ministry as well as parishioners. A collegiate ministry, of two or more men representing various racial groups, is a useful and helpful departure in facilitating the integration process. In those churches which use the confession as a sacrament, as well as in the more Protestant churches where it is customary for the minister to make public confession for the congregation, it is useful to include in the catalogue of sins to be confessed the sin of race prejudice. It is a sin which can be replaced, *at least* within the churches, by the virtue of inclusiveness.

In these simple, direct, and immediate ways we can quietly get rid of segregation in our homes and churches and in our private lives, and bring the day of "equal and unsegregated opportunity" to realization in these areas at once. There are many more things to be done at the local level, depending upon the section of the country, the size of the city or town, the local temper of the population, and many other factors. Newspapers, for instance, can, in many cases, adopt a more affirmative attitude toward minorities. Encouragement of editors and reporters, letters for publication, conference with editors and publishers, may take a little time but will usually bring improvements. How about the courts, the police, and other municipal agencies? The lawlessness of the law is one of the major irritants of race relations in many cities in all parts of the nation. It can only be changed by citizens in action, demanding something better from their elected officials and their appointed agents.

In every community there is a wide variety of opportunities for constructive interracial action—a sufficiently wide selection to afford an opportunity for every talent and temperament. Each one of us can find the activity for which his experience best fits him, and get to work. Health, hospitalization, maternity care, recreation, library facilities, and other cultural opportunities; problems of juvenile delinquency and adult crime; intercultural education and acquaintanceship; public forums and civic and community organizations (not overlooking women's club and parent-teacher associations); municipal government; public education; and a dozen more matters of similar character are waiting in practically every city and town in the United States—waiting for Christian concern to act. In a good many cases, the "best people" do not know these needs in their own cities or in surrounding rural areas; but a few hours of quiet inquiry will uncover more things to be done than can be handled in a year of intensive work. And speaking of "Things to be Done," there is a reprint under this title of an article by Lillian Smith which appeared in *South Today* in the Winter 1942-43 number. Published at Clayton, Georgia, it is worth writing for, reading, and acting upon.

How long is it since the service clubs in your city had a first-line speaker from one of the minority groups? And why is it that the membership of your service club is closed to non-Caucasians? You say it isn't closed, and that it "just happens" that all the members are white. Quit deceiving yourself. There are things to do at the local level.

And most of these are things which can be done without waiting for other people. They are things which individuals

can get to work on at once. They do not require much imagination or initiative. They require a little courage and a willingness to do what one knows is right when others laugh
or talk behind one's back. That is easy—and it is worth it.

2. At the Regional Level

Let's stop talking about "the South" if we are Northerners;
and if we are Southerners, let's stop talking about "Dam-
yankees." As long as we permit sectionalism to function as
one of the major scapegoats for emotionalism, we shall not
be able to make a constructive attack upon a racial problem
that belongs to the whole nation. There are enough things
to do right in your own region—whether you live in Portland, Oregon; Portland, Maine; Cairo, Illinois, or Cairo,
Egypt—without wasting much breath castigating people in
other parts of the nation or other sections of the globe for
their failures. The Civil War is over. Why must it be fought
again every week?

Once we get to work on the problems of color caste as
we know them within our own regions (New England, South,
Middle West, Far West, Southwest—*every section has its
own variant of color caste*), then we cease to be jittery about
what may be said in some other section about us and our
racial problems. Nothing would more quickly take the wind
out of the sails of political demagogues whose principal stock
in trade is sectional jealousies than for people to laugh gently
when they begin to rant and tear the air about what goes
on in some other section of the nation. Why must the American people be suckers for political oratory? Can we not see
through the fulminations of the aspirant for office who gives
us nothing but sectional prejudices? Whether it is a Native
Son on the Pacific slope, or a Southerner whose ancestry is
right, or a New Englander conscious of his *Mayflower* ante-
cedents, or a Midwesterner proud of his pioneer stock, or
perhaps just a small-town dentist who does not like to see

the farmers go to the near-by city for their bridgework—
we cannot permit the jealousies of sectional loyalty to stand
in the way of a united, constructive attack on our common
problems.

This means that Southerners, instead of using sectionalism
to defend themselves against Yankee criticism, turn their eyes
homeward and begin to clean up the dirty mess of poll taxes,
disfranchisement, and Jim Crow. It means that residents of
the Southwest, instead of crying about political chicanery in
Washington, roll up their sleeves and do something constructive about the painfully distressing plight of Americans of
Mexican ancestry in their midst. It means that the Pacific
slope ceases to be the mecca for the glib-tongued promoter;
and the descendant of a prospector who made his fortune
in the hard-bitten days of the Gold Rush becomes more concerned with the welfare of a half-million persons of minority
status than with the perpetuation of his own private niche of
prestige and privilege. It means that the New Englander
ceases to wall himself in with complacency, and bestirs himself about the national and racial minorities which have lately
swarmed across the pleasant countryside to capture his cities
and to invade the sanctity of his villages and farmsides. It
means that the Midwesterner ceases to congratulate himself
on the fact that he has, as yet, been relatively free from the
problems of minority racial groups, and bestirs himself to
make the Midwest a fit place for newcomers to live in.[1]

There are some things which can be done best—if at all—
only by sectional or regional action. None of us like to have
an "outsider" tell us what ought to be done, especially when
the outsider speaks words we know to be true. The only

[1] I write these lines with a peculiar sense of "belonging" to each of these
sections. My boyhood was spent in the Dakotas, Montana, and Minnesota; my
graduate education and early ministry were in New York City and its environs;
the major part of my professional life has been spent in the heart of the Deep
South, in Alabama; and I am now at work on the Pacific Coast. From personal
experience, having lived in each of these sections, I know how easily all of us
get into a sectional rut, compensate for our own failures at home by criticizing
other regions, and build up regional loyalties as defense mechanisms.

answer, then, is to do it ourselves, in our own regions. In that sense, and only in that sense, do we have any right to take pride in our region as the place where we are making real progress on ethical problems.

3. AT THE RACIAL LEVEL

This is not a matter for only one race to work on. The "fault" does not lie with the white man alone, nor can it be placed on any particular minority. *The fault* (if we must talk that way) *lies with the caste structure itself, which no persons now living have created,* and for which none of us, either individually or as racial groups, are rightfully responsible. Let's stop blaming the "other group" and get to work on the eradication of color caste.

Of course, there are some things which only one race, or the members of one race, can do. Every one of the racial minorities has considerable progress to make in its own development—every one, including the Caucasian. None of us is now "fit" for all the opportunities and privileges of democracy—not even the Caucasian. Every one of us must, therefore, work hard within his own racial group to prepare for the larger opportunities we wish to open. The Caucasian has got to get ready for democratic sharing. That will take a lot of readying. Instead of criticizing the Negro for failing to get rid of a criminal element, the Caucasian can get busy on the snobs who live in his block (or the snob he sees in the mirror when he shaves). Instead of criticizing the white man for persecuting him, the Negro can get busy on the loud and the lewd within his own group, preparing them for the responsibilities of constructive citizenship instead of the irresponsibilities of the ghetto.

The Chinese need to encourage each other to come out of Chinatown, to lose the "Chinatown shuffle," and to get ready to take their places in American life as American citizens. The Japanese in America have an unparalleled opportunity as they resettle themselves on leaving the concentration camps. Will they once again segregate themselves into a score of Little Tokyos, or will they have the foresight and the ingenuity to integrate themselves into American life? And why must the American Indian stay on the reservation forever, a ward only half citizen?

Are the members of minority groups resting content in nursing their feelings of hurt pride over the way the white man has treated them? Or are they preparing for integration by cultivating the habits of inclusiveness and the outlook of American citizens? What racial group does not need to go to work on itself and its members, preparing them for democratic living?

If we can get even a small fraction of the energy and heat which is now devoted to mutual recrimination and to fighting between the races to be devoted to the constructive improvement of each racial group by its own membership, we shall be, at long last, finding the only justification for any recognition of racial lines. And it is justifiable because it is a means of destroying caste—a temporary racial effort, designed to make racial efforts unnecessary. The avowed purpose of every segregated institution, and of every person whose professional life or avocational interest is bound up with a segregated institution, should be to work itself (or himself) out of a job by making the segregated institutions instruments of integration.

4. At the National Level

Here, we look two ways: from the nation outward and from the nation inward. On the one hand are all the things which need to be done to guarantee a secure and just peace, secure and just because it rests upon the foundation rock of the equality of all men everywhere. The words of the Cleveland conference are waiting to be translated into deeds. The statesmen of American Christianity are here charged with a solemn obligation to furnish to the government both the support for Cleveland's proposal and the personnel to implement it when called upon. The councils of the State Department ought never for one moment be permitted to forget the clear demands for the Christian conscience.

On the internal side at the national level, much needs to be done to purge our national government of racial discrimination in its own performance. The armed forces, the civil services, and the whole machinery of government will benefit by a thorough examination, with a good house cleaning in those places where a house cleaning is needed and with encouragement at those points where performance warrants it.

In addition, there are some things which desperately need to be done by national legislation because there is no other means for doing them. No single thing that the federal government could do would have a more constructive and more far-reaching effect in altering the patterns of color caste than to achieve, either through Supreme Court ruling or through legislation, the outlawing of the residential restrictive covenant. The restrictive covenant cannot be abrogated at the local level, because no city or state or section of a city is ready to take a step which it fears will place it at a disadvantage in being unrestricted in the midst of a restricted area. The local people envisage a sudden in-migration of swarms of the darker races following the announcement that a covenant has been abrogated; and they are not ready to "sacrifice their property values" for democracy. But if national legislation or judicial decision could eliminate, once and for all, from the whole nation the iniquitous restrictive covenants which limit residential areas according to race, the major battle for "equal and unsegregated opportunities" would be won.

It could be done on a national level, because no section or state or city or suburban development would be placed at a differential disadvantage. When covenants become illegal, no community can inflate its property values with these restrictions. From which it follows that, since any house anywhere could be purchased or leased and occupied by any man who had the means to occupy it, regardless of race, there would then be neither inflation of values through the use of the covenant nor deflation of values due to the proximity of members of other racial groups.

Moreover, this national action to remove restrictive residential covenants is essential to the long-term success of the effort to get integrated churches. It we want integrated churches, the most effective way to get them is to draw the membership from integrated communities. It is an artificial thing to reach out across overlapping miles of parish jurisdictions to draw for each congregation a membership that is a genuine cross section of the human race. Every church has to invade each of the several segregated residential areas and draw its people from widely scattered sections of town. As long as there is residential segregation, there is no other way to do it. But once segregation in residential matters is eliminated, each church then normally serves all the people of its neighborhood, becoming inclusive because it is in a neighborhood that is no longer exclusive.

Until residential segregation is done away with, the inclusive church has to be built across the lines of residential segregation. It can be done. Such churches are springing up in different parts of the nation. They are not experiments. They are a prophecy. They will become the pattern for the church of the nation more readily if residential segregation is outlawed and it becomes the natural, normal, and expected thing for all races to attend the same churches because they all live in the same neighborhoods. The integrated church becomes the spiritual center of the integrated community, re placing the segregated church, which is the center of spiritual arrogance in a segregated community.

Much could also be done through federal action about such

things as common carriers, public facilities (including the national parks), and the holding of elective and appointive offices. Some advances have been made in some of the governmental agencies; but much remains to be done to implement the national policies of integration. It is not uncommon for a federal agency to have one policy in Washington and another in Atlanta or San Diego. It is not unknown for two federation agencies to have policies diametrically opposed to each other, the constructive work of one agency being cancelled by the negative and obstructionist tactics of its teammate.

To get these matters corrected will require direct political action, which concerns itself with the inner workings of every nomination and election for national office. It calls for a degree of political astuteness and moral courage which the churches have yet to furnish. But unless the churches are ready to undertake this kind of political action, they have no moral right to talk about race in the terms with which they have committed themselves.

5. The Job of the Churches

In this whole matter, there is a special responsibility for the churches—local churches, regional and state conferences, national bodies, the Federal Council of Churches of Christ in America, the home and foreign missionary bodies, the Home and Foreign Missions Councils, and the World Council of Churches.

We have done much bold speaking, resolving, and talking. From Jerusalem to Cleveland, the record clearly commits us to an unrelenting, unremitting, kindly but insistent and indefatigable struggle for "equal and unsegregated opportunity." We know what we ought to do. If we try to implement these affirmations, and fail, we shall at least have made the effort to do what we clearly know is the Will of God in our generation. If we fail to try, we are then exposed as the hypocrites we shall have become—permitting moralizing to take the place of moral action. If we try, and succeed, we bring the whole family of God within the circle of brotherhood. That is where we belong.

ACKNOWLEDGMENTS

The students, alumni, faculty, and trustees of Talladega College, who were my colleagues for a decade, taught me much that is in these pages. Numerous participants in conferences, forums, and debates have helped to sharpen issues and ask better questions.

The actual work of writing the book was encouraged by Will W. Alexander, with the concurrence of Charles S. Johnson and a friendly nod from Edwin R. Embree. Alain Locke criticized the first outline constructively. George Williams was of particular help in guiding me into the materials for the third chapter. Arthur Spingarn contributed one important section of Chapter VI. Galen Fisher read the entire manuscript and made guiding comments. Fred Brownlee has been in the cheering section all through these eighteen months of labor. Franklin Cogswell and Willis Lamont encouraged me when the going was difficult. And Ordway Tead of Harper and Brothers had the courage to read a manuscript which I brought back a second time after a first rejection—and a cutting from seventeen to eleven chapters.

I have tried to acknowledge, with footnotes, all conscious indebtedness to other writers. To several editors I speak a word of gratitude for permission to use materials which appeared in different form in *Christendom*, the *Journal of Religious Thought*, the seventh *Symposium of the Conference on Science, Philosophy, and Religion*, and in a forthcoming book written for the Missionary Education Movement.

My wife and daughters have endured long silences and periods of irritating distractedness with amazing equanimity and understanding.

INDEX

Abyssinia: church of, 47; invasion of, 7

Adeney, Walter F., cited, 49

Africa: ancient civilization of, 80; not included in Atlantic Charter, 66; and French imperialism, 70; progress of Islam in, 190-5; industrialization of, 129; as possible home for Negro Americans, 135-141

African Church, 46-54

Alexander, Will W., cited, 105n, 234

Alexandria, La., riots in, 27

Allen, James S., cited, 147n

Amalgamation: one form of race equality, 160; not an immediate "solution of racial problems, 161; primary importance of doctrine of, 161; degree of, 162-5; confusingly identifies race and caste, 163; social function of doctrine of, 165; anxiety complexes centered around purity of white caste by, 166; safeguards against, 166-8; biological advisability of, 168-71; sociological discouragements to, 171-2

America First Party, 133

American Colonization Society, 136

American Missionary Association, 2

Ancestry, unwarranted pride in, 20

Ancient civilization superior to their contemporary "white" civilizations, 79-82

Anderson, Marian, 27, 122, 157

Anglo-Catholicism, 181

Aptheker, Herbert, cited, 95n

Arianism, 48

Arius, 53

Armed forces, discrimination in, 74-5

Aryan "race": proposed as a spiritual entity by Nazis 91-4; *See also* Racism, White supremacy

Asia: industrialization of, 129

Assis, Machada da, 124

Athanasius, 53

Atlantic Charter: source of hope when announced, 66; emasculated, 66-68

Attitudes, racial: acquired from social patterns, 3; acquired by contact with attitudes, 4; tools of social control, 24-25

Augustine, 46, 51

Australia: and industrialization of non-white world, 129; "white Australia" policy, and imperialism, 189-90; stymies declaration of equality at Versailles, 64-65

Axioms of caste. *See* Caste

Babylonia, ancient civilization of, 80

Barthe, Richard, 122

Beaumont, Texas: race riots in, 98

Beliefs, racial, 4

Benedict, Ruth, cited, 88n, 90n

Bias, author's, xi

Biblical passages cited: Amos 9: 7, 41; Psalm 78: 41, 212; I Peter 2: 9, 41

Bilbo, Theodore G.: quoted, 40; contributes to racial antagonism, 77; advocates colonization, 135-37; source of shame to fellow supporters of caste, 141

Biracialism. *See* "Separate but equal"

Birdsall, Paul, cited, 64n

"Black baby" myth, 168

Black Nationalism, 147-9

Bland, James, 125

Bowen, Trevor, quoted, 39

Boxer Uprising, 98

Brice, Carol, 122

Brotherhood: a necessary complement of Fatherhood, 10-12; even though limited by rite, may not be limited by race, 11; not optional, 12

Brown, Sterling, 123

Browning, Robert, 124n

Brownlee, Fred, 234

235